Watermelons: The Green Movement's True Colors

Watermelons
The Green Movement's True Colors

JAMES DELINGPOLE

PUBLIUS BOOKS

ISBN 9-780-9833-4740-8

First published in 2011 by Publius Books

Publius Books
PO Box 1096
New York, NY 10163–1096
info@publiusbooks.com
212.495.9596

Typeset in Minion by MacGuru Ltd
info@macguru.org.uk

Printed by Hill Print Solutions
915 South Peak St.
Dallas, Texas 75223

Cover design by Birch Creek Designs
www.birchcreekdesigns.com

CONTENTS

ABBREVIATIONS

AGU   American Geophysical Union
AGW   Anthropogenic Global Warming
BBC   British Broadcasting Corporation
CO_2 carbon dioxide
CRU   Climatic Research Unit [at the University of East Anglia]
IPCC   Intergovernmental Panel on Climate Change
MWP   Medieval Warm Period
NASA   National Aeronautics and Space Administration
UEA   University of East Anglia
UN   United Nations
WWF   Worldwide Fund for Nature
WUWT   Watts Up With That (www.wattsupwiththat.com)

CHAPTER 1

IMAGINE

In searching for a new enemy to unite us, we came up with the idea that pollution, the threat of global warming, water shortages, famine and the like would fit the bill.....all these dangers are caused by human intervention...the real enemy, then, is humanity itself.

The Council of the Club of Rome, 1991

Imagine if everything you knew about the environment was wrong.

Imagine that global warming was something to be desired, not feared.

Imagine that organic food, sustainability, biofuels and the WWF were far more harmful to the world and its inhabitants than GM food, industry, oil and ExxonMobil.

Imagine if it didn't matter one jot how big your carbon footprint was and you could go out and buy as many Hummers as you liked or accumulate as many air miles as you wanted without the need to feel the slightest sliver of guilt about the environmental damage you were causing.

Imagine if carbon dioxide were our friend.

Imagine if the world's biggest mass murderer was a woman who campaigned against chemicals and pesticides, and the world's biggest savior was the man who saved hundreds of millions from hunger with mutant crops and modern agricultural technologies.

Imagine if for a fraction of the money we're spending to "combat climate change" we could ensure that no child went hungry or was malnourished, and that everyone in the world had access to clean drinking water.

Imagine that "overpopulation" was an illusory problem.

Imagine that fossil fuels were a miracle we should cherish—not a curse.

Imagine if we could stop worrying about "scarce resources."

Imagine if the polar bears, glaciers, coral reefs, rain forests, Pacific islands, and the polar ice caps were all doing just fine.

Imagine if economic growth, far from destroying the world, made it cleaner, healthier, happier—and with more open spaces. Imagine....

As I'm sure you've guessed by now, I'm about to tell you that you don't need to imagine these things because they are all already true. And already, in anticipation, some readers' hackles will have risen and their skepticism boosters will have gone into overdrive, the synapses in their brain will have triggered hundreds of warning signals and a great big thought bubble will have appeared above their heads, with enormous capital letters, probably written in neon red with flashing light bulbs in the middle:

"And why should we believe you?"

Don't worry, I'm used to it. It's just a reflection of how so many of us have been conditioned to think about people who don't believe in "peak oil" or catastrophic man-made global warming, or recycling, or "sustainability", or organic food, or carbon footprints—or any of the other core tenets of the environmental religion.

We don't say: "Ah. There's a person with an interestingly different point of view. I wonder why he thinks that, and what evidence he has to support it."

We say: "That person's evil. He's probably funded by Big Oil, like most deniers. He's only saying that stuff because it's what he wants to believe, because he's too selfish to change his lifestyle. And anyway, what the hell does he know about anything, anyway? It's not like he's a climate scientist..."

So, before I delve more deeply into climate change and the misanthropy of green ideology, I thought I would give some indication of why you can trust what I have to say.

This shouldn't be necessary. In a rational world, people's arguments would be judged on the merits of their case rather than, say, on how "nice" they appear to be, or a long string of qualifications, or the number of politically correct minority boxes they tick. Unfortunately, we do not live in a rational world. Rather, we live in a world which is culturally in thrall to the politics of "identity"—where who you are and where you're coming often seems to count for more than what you actually have to say.

How many times—on a TV political debate program, a radio phone-in or a letter to the editor—have you heard someone qualify their statement: "As a black woman…", "as a gay man…", as "someone who has been disabled for fifteen years…"? When the person's identity is directly relevant to the point being made, that is of course fine. But often this modern preoccupation with identity corrupts the quality of the debate, rather than enhances it.

Consider the case of Lee Bidgood Jr., a Florida war veteran with whom I had a run-in over a letter he wrote to *Newsweek*, which said:

> Propaganda by global-warming skeptics and deniers reminds me of 1944, when as an Army officer I saw living skeletons in striped pajamas. Horror stories about Nazi concentration camps suddenly rang true. I wondered how intelligent people could commit such atrocities. History records the effectiveness of Joseph Goebbels's propaganda. I hope Al Gore and others can prevail over today's anti-science propaganda.

Or, as he might just as well have abbreviated it: "Global warming is real because I witnessed the Holocaust; climate-change deniers are as bad as Nazis." When I first read the letter I assumed it was a fake. I know many World War II veterans—all humble fellows who would never dream of trying to parlay their experiences (of which they speak only reluctantly) into such a tendentious political point.

But how many of the people who read that letter in *Newsweek* shared my skepticism? My suspicion is that those few who did were far outnumbered by the ones who subconsciously thought: "Dear old chap. He has served his country and witnessed the 20th Century's greatest crime. Clearly we must take his views on climate change seriously…"

An even bigger problem with this identity-centric approach to political debate is that it implies that people who do not belong to the correct privileged group—whether a cultural minority or an "expert" in their field—can safely be excluded from an argument simply by dint of who they are and what they represent.

This technique was used in an attempt to silence the critics who debunked Michael Mann's "Hockey Stick". The reason this matters was because the Hockey Stick was—and to some extent still is—the central pillar on which the case for catastrophic and unprecedented man-made global warming relied. You'll have seen a version of the Hockey Stick in Al Gore's "An Inconvenient Truth". It's the graph which shows how global temperatures have changed in the last millennium.

From the year 1000 AD until the late 20th Century, the trend is pretty much flat. But suddenly, at the end, there's a dramatic upward tick—like the blade of an ice-hockey stick. Taken at face value, the graph says: "Never in modern human history has there been a period of global warming so intense and sudden. We should all be very afraid and act now for this is almost certainly the result of manmade carbon emissions."

That, at least, is how the IPCC's Third Assessment Report (TAR) chose to interpret it. Mann's Hockey Stick was given star billing in the "Summary for Policymakers" (otherwise known as the bit everyone reads)—it was repeated no fewer than five times within the actual report, and the media launch featured a gigantic blown-up image as the backdrop. Likewise, environmental lobby groups gave it a heavy rotation. It was widely cited at the UN's 1997 Kyoto climate meeting (where the infamous carbon reduction treaty originated), and every household in Canada received a leaflet which claimed that the earth was experiencing historically unprecedented warming (i.e. the conclusion of the Hockey Stick graph).

All of that is fine and dandy—except the Hockey Stick was flawed to the point of uselessness. The chart was based on tree ring data, but the scary upward bit at the end was the result of an overemphasis on data from one tree, bristlecone pine, which is widely acknowledged to be an unreliable indicator of 20th Century climate change. The shape was derived from the combination of this dodgy data with a statistical sausage machine that would turn it into a hockey stick every time. As Andrew Montford, author of *The Hockey Stick Illusion*, explains:

> This meant that it didn't matter what data you put into Mann's algorithm, if there was one series within it that had a hockey-stick shape, there is a strong chance that, depending on the number of other series, a hockey-stick graph would emerge as the result. The algorithm was heavily weighted in favour of hockey sticks. It effectively disregarded any data that conflicted with, or contradicted, the hockey-stick finding.

Two Canadians, Steve McIntyre and Ross McKitrick—neither of whom is a professional climate scientist—exposed this chicanery. Note Mann's witheringly contemptuous posting at RealClimate, a website established by his friends and colleagues ("The Hockey Team", as they fashion themselves) to discredit critics of the Hockey Stick:

> False claims of the existence of errors in the Mann et al (1998) reconstruction can also be traced to spurious allegations made by two individuals, McIntyre and McKitrick (McIntyre works in the mining industry, while McKitrick is an economist). The false claims

were first made in an article....published in a non-scientific (social science) journal 'Energy and Environment'.

Mann uses the same technique in a letter to a Dutch science journalist, Marcel Crok:

> I hope you are not fooled by any of the 'myths' about the hockey stick that are perpetrated by contrarians, right-wing think tanks and fossil fuel industry disinformation....I must begin by emphasizing that McIntyre and McKitrick are not taken seriously in the scientific community. Neither are scientists....

The brandishing of the word "scientists" as a totem of unquestionable and absolute authority, the paranoid invocation of "right-wing think tanks" and "fossil fuel industry disinformation", and the belittling and rejection of scientific journals which don't fit in with the alarmist consensus, are ruses that crop up again and again over the next few pages. It's worth getting used to them, because they are vital to understanding both the nature of the corruption and malfeasance revealed in the Climategate emails and also the flaws in the case for anthropogenic global warming (AGW). Just ask yourself: if scientists like Michael Mann possess such solid, incontrovertible evidence to support their theory, why don't they fight their critics' supposed errors with factual arguments? Why, instead, must they resort to smears and "arguments from authority"? Why do they make it all so personal?

Now I'm acutely aware that one or two of you reading this may be sincere believers in man-made Global Warming. The last thing I want to do right now is insult you by suggesting that you're gullible and thick. I think you've been brainwashed, that's all—and even the cleverest people can be brainwashed or back the wrong team now and again. Look at Bernie Madoff's poor victims (or at least, much poorer now).

So, you might ask, why have I been brainwashed?

If I were not on my side, it's a question I'd ask too. After all, I'm not a meteorologist or a climatologist or a geologist or an astrophysicist or indeed a scientist of any description. As arch-Warmist blogger Jo Abbess is fond of pointing out on her blog, the only qualification I have to my name is a modest MA in English language and literature from Oxford University. Yet I, a mere arts graduate, have the temerity to question the expertise of the thousands, if not millions, of Ph.D.'s all around the world who know for absolute certain that AGW is real and if we don't do something soon it's going to kill us all.

There are lots of good answers to this, one of which comprises just two words.

No, not that one.

I mean:

"Only Connect."

Those words come from a novel by EM Forster called *Howards End*. I'm personally not a great fan of Forster but I do like that quote. Not only is it easy to remember, but it's true. Years before James Cameron invented that touchy-feely, healing, shiny tree thing in "Avatar", years even before James Lovelock invented Gaia theory, Forster understood that the more closely and carefully you look at the world, the more you appreciate the extraordinary degree to which everything is interconnected.

The interconnectedness I explore in this book is that between AGW and the ideology of the liberal-left generally—ranging from the green policy of the Nazis through to the cultural Marxism of Antonio Gramsci to the environmental legislation of Barack Obama to the propagandizing of Greenpeace. And you really don't need a science degree to understand that kind of thing. All you need is to look at the world around you. And be able to read.

Indeed, quite often I've asked myself how I would fare were I to go out for a coffee one rainy morning, only to find that my entire office had been wiped out by mysterious assassins with silenced machine pistols. And the answer, I've decided, is that I'd fare pretty well. Why? For the same reason one of the CIA operatives gives in "Three Days of the Condor" when asked how the Robert Redford character—despite having had no special agent training—has nevertheless learned his clever evasive moves:

"He reads."

At the beginning of each term, my English professor Mr. Conrad would hand us a sheaf of paper listing all the term's lectures. "I'm supposed to give you these," he'd say, contemptuously. "But why bother going to lectures when you can read the critics? And why read the critics when you can read the texts?"

When you're 19 or 20 years old, this is probably the second most exciting thing anyone could say after "Fancy coming back to my room for coffee?" Here is your professor—the man whose wisdom and intellect you revere above all others, an actual proper Oxford don no less—telling you, a lowly undergraduate, that it's quite OK not to bother with lectures. Nor even to wade through all those tedious critical textbooks (which you know from your friends that they're forced read at other universities).

All he wants is for you to read the books you're studying that term and form a judgment. Your own judgment. And that's the key. What he wants is independent thought, considered analysis and personal insight. That is quite a tall order when your entire education up to that point has been based on spoon-feeding and regurgitation. Even in our very best universities, the teaching method I describe barely survives today, the result of a combination of underfunding, over-subscription and the dismal trend towards anti-elitism and dumbing down. It's been anatomized in books like Allan Bloom's *The Closing of the American Mind*. And what this means, unfortunately, is that even our supposed "intellectual elite" no longer necessarily think with the nimbleness and independence of mind that were once the natural product of a sound education.

Not only do people not know enough; but too easily they take for granted the opinions of supposed experts who pretend to have the answer to everything.

We can see this sorry decline even in institutions like the Royal Society (founded 1660). Its proud motto is *Nullius In Verba*—"Take no man's word for it"—and it hardly squares with the way the organization jumped so wholeheartedly on the AGW bandwagon, with barely a thought as to whether the underlying science supports it.

More broadly we can see it in the way a theory as manifestly flawed as the Great Climate Change Peril still has managed to penetrate so deeply into our culture, all but unchallenged even by clever people with science degrees like Jo Abbess. It's an odd thing in this age of anti-elitism—when almost nobody defers to anyone over anything but the AGW meme would never have spread so far or fast if not for the supine willingness of the many to surrender to the received ideas of the amazingly few.

Really, I'd like to deflate the popular greenie notion that the sort of people who don't believe in "climate change" or "man-made global warming" are buttoned-up, "right wing" nature-haters who are so addicted to their expensive, metropolitan lifestyles and their carbon-belching death machines that they simply refuse (as a matter of selfishness and lifestyle choice) to listen to all reason. That caricature bears little resemblance to any of the Climate realists I've met, most of whom are in this game because they love nature too much, not too little. What drives them above all—as it certainly does me—is their absolute horror at what is being done to our world by the green movement in the name of "saving" it. The rainforests are being devastated and people are starving as a result of biofuels policies. Wildlife is destroyed and the countryside is blighted by wind farms. We must feel guilty about the natural world, instead of enjoying it.

I believe that people are never happier than when they are free, and that there is no problem in the world that cannot be made worse by statists trying to make things "better" with their good intentions.

It began with the advent of former British Prime Minister Tony Blair. Large swathes of the UK, even parts which had traditionally voted Tory, were in ecstasies about Blair's new regime. It seemed, through some magical new formula known as the "Third Way", to have created a perfect synthesis between the economic freedoms favored by the right and the social justice favored by the left. What was there possibly not to like?

Britain was groovy again. No less an authority than *Vanity Fair* told us so in its "Cool Britannia" edition. Pop stars came to Downing Street to pay court to Blair. Everyone in the country could now afford an iPod, a state-of-the-art mobile phone, a 50-inch flat screen TV, and at least three or four holidays a year in places they'd never heard of before like Riga, Ljubljana and Plovdiv—now magically cheap, thanks to wonderful new no-frills flights on EasyJet and Ryan Air.

Well, almost everyone. As one of the unlucky few who wasn't employed in London's financial sector or a lawyer or in the lavish pay of some government-funded bureaucracy, it was with growing bewilderment that I surveyed Blair's new "young country". The weekend newspapers were filled with articles claiming that we'd never had it so good. In fact, we'd now reached a point of such absurd overabundance that, really, the time had come for us all to start re-examining our lifestyles: to exchange the material for the spiritual, to downsize to riverside cottages. We'd then live on organically grown vegetables and bacon, made from pigs we'd personally reared and lovingly slaughtered, while our beautiful blond children like models from the Boden catalogue frolicked in the mud (just as they used to, before antibiotics and the industrial age ruined this healthy, natural lifestyle).

And I'd read these articles thinking: "Yep. I'm all up for that. Just as soon as I've actually acquired a lifestyle comfortable enough to re-examine, I too will be down-sizing and re-spiritualizing and pig-breeding. Until then, though, I've got a mortgage to pay and kids to feed and a job to slave away at for next to no money. Soon as the overabundance kicks in I'll let you know...."

More than feeling poor, though, I was starting to feel uneasy. I could sense that beneath this apparent abundance something stank.

But what?

Not the economy, clearly. That was so strong it was obviously going to last forever. But something about Britain was definitely changing. And so quickly, that the country I'd known under Margaret Thatcher had now all but vanished. Instead of the culture, tradition, reserve, hierarchy, reason, and stoicism which had won us the Second World War—and the Falklands War too—we seemed to have turned into a nation of emotionally incontinent, bleeding-heart whiners, with a highly refined sense of what our government could do for us but very limited concepts of what we might offer our country in return.

With Blair, we had entered a new age of "political correctness gone mad". Civic gardeners were banned by Cheltenham council from planting pansies under trees, lest they sprain their wrists in the root-filled soil. The BBC issued staff with "Revolving Security Door User Instructions" after a woman caught her foot in the door at BBC Birmingham. Paper napkins in Tewkesbury, Gloucestershire, were withdrawn by the council from the meals-on-wheels service for fear that pensioners and disabled people might choke on them. Simultaneously—like those skeletons in Jason and the Argonauts, only considerably uglier and much harder to slay—an army of bureaucrats and petty officials sprang up unbidden from the soil, ready to police and micromanage every last detail of our private lives. They wanted to control how much we drank, the kinds of food we could eat, the kinds of jokes it was acceptable for us to tell, when (and when not) it was appropriate to fly a Union flag from our home, and the size of our carbon footprint. To make it easier for the authorities to snoop on us and fine us for any of a growing number of minor infractions, there were spy cameras in our streets, speed cameras on every road, even microchips in our rubbish bins—all paid for by us, of course.

In its thirteen years in power, the New Labour government managed to create over 3,000 new offenses. Nearly half of these could land you in jail, including: not having a license for a church concert, smoking in a public place, selling a grey squirrel, trans-shipping unlicensed fish, or disobeying a health and safety inspector.

What the hell was going on? And perhaps, more to the point, how on earth were the bastards getting away with it? What kind of crazed, topsy-turvy world did we inhabit where mean-spirited, controlling, pessimistic left-wingers were seen as the "good guys", whereas those of us who believed in greater freedom for everyone were viewed as the Devil Incarnate?

It was in seeking to answer these questions that I first heard about an Italian Marxist named Antonio Gramsci. He was the man—round glasses, weird sticky-up hair—whose writings in the 1920s and 30s led to the idea of a "culture war". Gramsci argued that in the great ideological battle between left and right, it didn't much matter what happened in the arena of pure politics. Presidents, prime ministers and political parties may come and go, but if you can capture the hearts and minds of an entire society, then you've won the war for all eternity. So it was that the left-wing disciples of Gramsci began their "long march through the institutions". They occupied schools, universities, the media, the arts—anywhere where they could exert their power to shape the way the broader culture (that's you and me) thinks about the world.

Consider how many university departments around the world are still held mental hostage by French philosophers like Foucault and Derrida, whose rejection of authority, hierarchy and empiricism seeks to undermine and destroy almost everything of value in the Western intellectual tradition. (As we'll see in a later chapter, not even scientific rationalism was immune from this dismal trend.) Consider how remarkably few books, plays, films, newspapers or TV documentaries do anything other than endorse a view of the world in which capitalism is bad, businessmen are greedy, America is a bully, the West must learn to be more like the East, terrorism is kind of our fault, mankind is a blot on the landscape, and, yes, right-wing people are way nastier than left-wing people.

We live in a culture whose values are defined almost entirely in terms set by the liberal-left. Yet because those values have become so commonplace—affecting everything from the language we use to the way we think—we don't even notice them.

Who controls the language controls the culture. Who controls the culture wins the political argument. George Orwell realized this years ago. In his appendix to *1984*, he explained that one of the most effective ways of suppressing heretical thought was to eliminate undesirable words or strip them of their meaning. The example he gave was "free". The word continued to exist in Newspeak, but only in the sense of "This field is free from weeds" or "The dog is free from lice"—not in the old sense of "politically free" or "intellectually free."

This is exactly what happened in Blair's Britain. Freedom, formerly a state of liberty, now came to mean "an entitlement to services administered by the state"—as in "freedom to use the National Health Service", "freedom from discrimination." And there was plenty more where that came from. As observed by Dan Hannan, a journalist and Member of the European Parliament, once-neutral words like "discrimination", "diversity", "community", "profit", "public", "elite" and "competition" became so tainted by association with the value system of the liberal left that their original meanings almost vanished.

Orwell wrote, "Newspeak was designed not to extend but to diminish the range of thought…"

All this is a very long and roundabout way of saying that the reason I came to distrust AGW theory is because I recognized it as part of a familiar socio-political pattern: the advance of government through stealth. Sometimes, as we've seen above, this was achieved by subtle shifts in the language. Sometimes it was achieved by exploiting popular hysteria, for example in the AIDS scare of the early 80s, the "Killer egg" salmonella scare of the late 80s, the Mad Cow/BSE scare and the Millennium bug scare. As Christopher Booker and Richard North note in their excellent book *Scared to Death*, all of these scare stories followed an almost identical trajectory. In each case, a potential hazard was identified by scientists, hyped up by the media—in collusion with the scientists who weren't at all averse to the extra publicity and the possible funding implications—and then "dealt with", incompetently and pointlessly at vast expense by a government keen to show that it was responding to its electorate's fears. Then—the part that was often not so well reported by the media—it would gradually be recognized that the threat wasn't as great as previously thought, that in fact it had probably been a most spectacular waste of money. But none of the scientists or politicians would ever admit this publicly, preferring to maintain that whatever the rights and wrongs of the affair, their action had been justified on the grounds of "the precautionary principle".

Ah, but how do I know that global warming—or climate change if you prefer—is not the exception that proves the rule? After all, just because the scientists and politicians were wrong about AIDS and salmonella and Mad Cow disease and the Millennium Bug and, more recently, the great SARS, bird flu and Swine flu non-epidemics, doesn't necessarily mean they're wrong this time, does it?

No it doesn't. It's possible that the climate alarmists are right: that the planet really is on the verge of frying, that it's all man's fault and that skeptics like me will one day be proved to have been foolishly complacent. But then it's also possible that David Icke is right and that if you pull hard enough on the hair of the Queen, her human mask will slip off to reveal the hideous green reptilian head that marks her as a member of the sinister master race they call the Babylonian Brother. And it's possible that the movie "Independence Day" is right, and that Doctor Who is right, and that the universe is chock full of evil alien races hell bent on colonizing Planet Earth. And it's possible that this book you think you're reading is a figment of your imagination and that actually you're a very intelligent duck who just thinks he is human because of the special Distorto Mirrors and Mind Warpo Rays employed by the Cockroach People who grew you in a pod just for the hell of it last week.

And that is the problem with this whole debate on catastrophic anthropogenic global warming. We have been gulled by politicians and activist scientists and propagandists into thinking that the key question is—"Is it impossible?" (to which the answer is "no")—when in fact the far more germane one is "Is it likely?"

This is why it really doesn't matter who I am, how much science I know, whether I'm in it for the money or because I'm a contrarian show-off or because I'm genuinely committed and sincere. That's because the onus on me is not to prove whether or not "climate change" is a man-made-disaster about to happen. I never will because it's impossible to prove a negative.

What I can do—and am indeed about to do—is prove to you the only things that need to be proven in this sorry tale of foolishness and mindless waste as great as any in human history. The people who tell you that AGW is a near-certainty are a bunch of liars, cheats and frauds. Your taxes will be raised, your liberties curtailed, and your money squandered to deal with a "crisis" so exceedingly unlikely and so poorly supported by real world data or objective science that it might just as well not exist.

CHAPTER TWO

CLIMATEGATE: HOW IT HAPPENED

> By the late tenth to twelfth centuries most of the world for which we
> have evidence seems to have been enjoying a renewal of warmth,
> which at times during those centuries may have approached the level
> of the warmest millennia of post-glacial times.
>
> Professor H. H. Lamb, *Climate, History and the Modern World*, 1982

It was another dreary November morning in 2009 and I was sitting
at my desk, wondering what to write next for my *Telegraph* blog,
which I'd been writing for the previous seven or eight months. Into
my lap dropped the story—Climategate—which would not only
change my life forever, but quite possibly help save Western Civilization from the greatest threat it has ever known.

It went like this (reproduced here with its original errors, noted in
the reference section at the back of this book):

If you own any shares in alternative energy companies I should start dumping
them NOW. The conspiracy behind the Anthropogenic Global Warming myth (aka
AGW; aka ManBearPig) has been suddenly, brutally and quite deliciously exposed
after a hacker broke into the computers at the University of East Anglia's Climate
Research Unit (aka CRU) and released 61 megabytes of confidential files onto the
internet. (Hat tip: Watts Up With That)

When you read some of those files—including 1079 emails and 72 documents—you realize just why the boffins at CRU might have preferred to keep them confidential. As Andrew Bolt puts it, this scandal could well be "the greatest in modern science". These alleged emails—supposedly exchanged by some of the most prominent scientists pushing AGW theory—suggest:

> Conspiracy, collusion in exaggerating warming data, possibly illegal destruction of embarrassing information, organised resistance to disclosure, manipulation of data, private admissions of flaws in their public claims and much more.

One of the alleged emails has a gentle gloat over the death in 2004 of John L. Daly (one of the first climate change skeptics, founder of the Still Waiting For Greenhouse site), commenting:

> "In an odd way this is cheering news."

But perhaps the most damaging revelations—the scientific equivalent of the *Telegraph*'s MPs' expenses scandal– are those concerning the way Warmist scientists may variously have manipulated or suppressed evidence in order to support their cause.

Here are a few tasters.

Manipulation of evidence:
> I've just completed Mike's Nature trick of adding in the real temps to each series for the last 20 years (i.e. from 1981 onwards) and from 1961 for Keith's to hide the decline.

Private doubts about whether the world really is heating up:
> The fact is that we can't account for the lack of warming at the moment and it is a travesty that we can't. The CERES data published in the August BAMS 09 supplement on 2008 shows there should be even more warming: but the data are surely wrong. Our observing system is inadequate.

Suppression of evidence:

Can you delete any emails you may have had with Keith re AR4?
Keith will do likewise. He's not in at the moment—minor family crisis.
Can you also email Gene and get him to do the same? I don't have his
new email address.
We will be getting Caspar to do likewise.

Fantasies of violence against prominent Climate Skeptic scientists:

Next time I see Pat Michaels at a scientific meeting, I'll be tempted to beat
the crap out of him. Very tempted.

**Attempts to disguise the inconvenient truth of the Medieval Warm Period
(MWP):**

......Phil and I have recently submitted a paper using about a dozen NH
records that fit this category, and many of which are available nearly 2K
back–I think that trying to adopt a timeframe of 2K, rather than the usual 1K,
addresses a good earlier point that Peck made w/ regard to the memo, that it
would be nice to try to "contain" the putative "MWP", even if we don't yet have
a hemispheric mean reconstruction available that far back....

And, perhaps most reprehensibly, a long series of communications discussing **how
best to squeeze dissenting scientists out of the peer review process**. How, in
other words, to create a scientific climate in which anyone who disagrees with
AGW can be written off as a crank, whose views do not have a scrap of authority.

"This was the danger of always criticising the skeptics for not publishing
in the "peer-reviewed literature". Obviously, they found a solution to that–
take over a journal! So what do we do about this? I think we have to stop
considering "Climate Research" as a legitimate peer-reviewed journal.
Perhaps we should encourage our colleagues in the climate research
community to no longer submit to, or cite papers in, this journal. We would
also need to consider what we tell or request of our more reasonable
colleagues who currently sit on the editorial board...What do others think?"

"I will be emailing the journal to tell them I'm having nothing more to do with it until they rid themselves of this troublesome editor." "It results from this journal having a number of editors. The responsible one for this is a well-known skeptic in NZ. He has let a few papers through by Michaels and Gray in the past. I've had words with Hans von Storch about this, but got nowhere. Another thing to discuss in Nice !"

Hadley CRU has form in this regard. In September—I wrote the story up here as "How the global warming industry is based on a massive lie"—CRU's researchers were exposed as having "cherry-picked" data in order to support their untrue claim that global temperatures had risen higher at the end of the 20th century than at any time in the last millennium. CRU was also the organization which—in contravention of all acceptable behavior in the international scientific community—spent years withholding data from researchers it deemed unhelpful to its cause. This matters because CRU, established in 1990 by the Met Office [sic] is a government-funded body which is supposed to be a model of rectitude. Its HadCRUT record is one of the four official sources of global temperature data used by the IPCC.

I asked in my title whether this will be the final nail in the coffin of Anthropogenic Global Warming. This was wishful thinking, of course. In the run up to Copenhagen, we will see more and more hysterical (and grotesquely exaggerated) stories such as this in the Mainstream Media. And we will see ever-more-virulent campaigns conducted by eco-fascist activists, such as this risible new advertising campaign by Plane Stupid showing CGI polar bears falling from the sky and exploding because kind of, like, man, that's sort of what happens whenever you take another trip on an airplane.

The world is currently cooling; electorates are increasingly reluctant to support eco-policies leading to more oppressive regulation, higher taxes and higher utility bills; the tide is turning against Al Gore's Anthropogenic Global Warming theory. The so-called "skeptical" view is now also, thank heaven, the majority view.

Unfortunately, we've a long, long way to go before the public mood (and scientific truth) is reflected by our policy makers. There are too many vested interests in AGW, with far too much to lose either in terms of reputation or money, for this to end without a bitter fight.

But to judge by the way—despite the best efforts of the MSM not to report on it—the CRU scandal is spreading like wildfire across the internet, this shabby story represents a blow to the AGW lobby's credibility from which it is never likely to recover.

I first read the story at Anthony Watts' website—Watts Up With That? (WUWT). The story is headlined "Breaking news story Hadley CRU has apparently been hacked—hundreds of files released." Revisiting the original story gives you a sense of the mix of excitement, astonishment, caution and trepidation it generated among skeptics that day. "WOW! That's all I can say right now!" is one of the first comments. "Be careful here. It is not unusual for files released by hackers to contain all kinds of nasty stuff, from viruses and worms to simple worthless junk," says the next.

One or two immediately spot the significance of the soon-to-be infamous "Mike's Nature trick" and "hide the decline" email. "Holy crap, if that's what it sounds like there [sic] a smoking gun," says one. "Smoking gun? More like a blazing armoury!" says another.

A few more comments down, someone has asked rather flatteringly:

Imagine what Delingpole will make of it.

Imagine no more. Delingpole is, of course, wetting his pants with excitement. But he's also a bit nervous. If it turns out this stuff is a hoax, might it not have legal implications—like libel? (British libel laws are much more stringent than U.S. ones.) On the other hand, this is clearly a story that needs to be reported quickly. Blogging, even more than print journalism, is very time-sensitive. The last thing you want is your copy sitting with your in-house lawyers for a couple of hours, while your competitors steal a march on you. You don't get linked on Drudge if you get to the story second.... What

I decided in the end, as you'll see from my original blog above, was a classic journalist's fudge. I took out all the names so that nobody could claim that they had been personally libeled, I stuck in "allegedly" a few times, colored it with a bit of informed background, views from other sources, and personal animus. *Et voilà.* Up went—though I didn't yet know this—the biggest and most important story of my entire career.

Though I was the first *journalist* to christen the story "Climategate", by the way, I want to stress in all modesty that I was not the first *person.* That honor went to a commenter on WUWT called Bulldust, who wrote: "Hmm how long before this is dubbed ClimateGate." All I did was to pick up his ball and run with it. Looking back, Mark Steyn's "Warmergate" was infinitely more clever but it arrived just a little too late in the day to gain the traction it deserved. That's because within a few hours, my story got picked up by Matt Drudge. And when a story gets "Drudged" there's no stopping it. Climategate was about to go viral.

Going viral is something every blogger dreams of doing. I'd seen it happen to Daniel Hannan, a fellow Telegraph blogger, a few months before. For those of you who aren't among the more than two million people who saw the 2009 YouTube video in which Hannan eviscerates then Prime Minister Gordon Brown to his face in the European Parliament, you might know him for his frequent guest appearances on Fox News during the Obamacare debate, explaining the perils of government-run healthcare systems such as Britain's National Health Service.

Now something similar happened to me. My hit rates climbed and climbed so that within a few days, my blog had 1.5 million visitors—more than the combined total of all my other blogs, all my other print articles possibly, in my entire career.

Climategate, meanwhile, had entered the global vocabulary. By the end of the week, it had 30 million Google entries, making it almost certainly the most popularly sought-after news story of the week.

But to listen to some people, you'd think Climategate didn't matter at all.

Here's Elizabeth May, head of Canada's Green Party, just a few days after the story broke:

How dare the world's media fall into the trap set by contrarian propagandists without reading the whole set [of emails]?

Here's Professor Myles Allen of Oxford University:

Take, for example, the "trick" of combining instrumental data and tree-ring evidence in a single graph to "hide the decline" in temperatures over recent decades that would be suggested by a naive interpretation of the tree-ring record. The journalists repeating this phrase as an example of "scientists accused of manipulating their data" know perfectly well that the decline in question is a spurious artefact of the tree-ring data that has been documented in the literature for years, and that "trick" does not mean "deceit".

Here's Professor Kerry Emanuel of MIT:

What we have here [are] thousands of emails collectively showing scientists hard at work, trying to figure out the meaning of evidence that confronts them. Among a few messages, there are a few lines showing the human failings of a few scientists…Scientifically, it means nothing.

Here's a RealClimate regular, Steve Easterbrook:

What looks to the outsider like a bunch of scientists trying to subvert some gold standard of scientific truth is really just scientists trying to goad one another into doing a better job in what we all know is a messy, noisy process.

Here is Fred Pearce, a British environmental journalist, writing in the *Guardian*:

> Many of the most widely publicized claims from skeptics about what is in the emails are demonstrably unfounded. There is no conspiracy to "hide the decline" in temperatures. Nor that a lack of warming in the data is a "travesty"—still less of attempts to fix the data.

And Pearce continues, in an article titled "How the 'Climategate' scandal is bogus and based on climate skeptics' lies" and subtitled "Claims based on email soundbites are demonstrably false—there is manifestly no evidence of clandestine data manipulation":

> Almost all the media and political discussion about the hacked climate emails has been based on brief soundbites publicized by professional skeptics and their blogs. In many cases, these have been taken out of context and twisted to mean something they were never intended to......If those journalists had read even a few words beyond the soundbites, they would have realized that they were often being fed lies.

In other words, "Move along. Nothing to see here."

So let's do that, shall we? Let's take the Warmists, and their amen corner in the mainstream media, at their word. After all, some of us don't even have PhDs. How are we to know that when a scientist uses a word like "trick" he doesn't in fact mean a "cheat" but "a widely respected practice, employed throughout the global scientific community to, um, enhance data in such as a way as to make it—uh, yes, that's it—*even more impeccably accurate* than ever before?" Or that when a scientist says "Hide the decline" he doesn't mean, so much, "hide" in the sense of "conceal" or "fudge" but in the sense of "hyd se deoclina", an Anglo-Saxon druidical phrase still colloquially employed in the top echelons of science research to mean "aggregate the filter analysis in an entirely correct way but one which non-scientists could not hope to understand in a million years, the ignorant fools."

Or...

Nah. Just kidding. This is "dog ate my homework" level excuse-making.

Let me show you why.

The first thing you need to realize is that the scientists implicated in these Climategate emails aren't junior lab assistants at some minor-league research establishment in the back end of the beyond.

The Climatic Research Unit (CRU) at the University of East Anglia (UEA), whence those emails were leaked, is probably the single most important climate research establishment in the world. And the scientists implicated in those emails are at the very heart of the process informing the IPCC. Not only were they personally responsible for some of the more alarmist predictions in the IPCC's four assessment reports, but they were also in control of the scientific data used to make those predictions. Given that the IPCC's reports are supposed to represent—in Barack Obama's phrase—the gold standard of scientific thinking on AGW, this makes the Climategate scientists very significant figures indeed.

Which is why, of course, Climategate was such a momentous scandal. In scientific terms, it's the equivalent of police acting on a routine tip off and stumbling upon Fu Manchu, Jack the Ripper, the Boston Strangler, and Charles Manson gathered around a table—complete with incriminating notes—and talking about all their past and future crimes. It's not that the police hadn't suspected before that these guys were up to no good. What they had lacked until now was the smoking gun...

The two names that dominate the emails are those of two leading climate scientists, one American and one British: Michael Mann and Phil Jones. Professor Phil Jones, not widely known outside his scientific circle until Climategate broke, was and is head of the CRU. Professor Michael Mann of Penn State University was already a legend in his own lunchtime thanks to his world-renowned invention of the marvellous, extraordinary and dramatic Hockey Stick chart. Besides the two male leads, the character stalwarts in this drama include Keith Briffa, a researcher into some soon-to-be-deeply-controversial tree ring samples; Dr. Tom Wigley, one of Al Gore's scientific advisors; and Ben Santer, a young hothead with an already proven track record of pushing AGW alarmism rather further than most responsible scientists would have considered decent.

Sadly Al Gore doesn't appear, nor does Rajendra Pachauri, head of the IPCC, while Dr. James Hansen does so only fleetingly. But those omissions apart, you'd be hard pressed to find a more representative selection of the scientists at the heart of the AGW industry. That's because they're a tightly knit group of people, and are more than happy to play the system in order to help each other clamber up the greasy pole of the climate science hierarchy.

This "you scratch my back, I'll scratch yours" approach is most deliciously exemplified in an email exchange between the two main protagonists, beginning on December 4th, 2007, when Mann offers to nominate Jones for an award from the American Geophysical Union and asks which one he'd fancy. Jones tells him, gets one, then Mann asks Jones whether he might return the favour.

Mann to Jones, December 4, 2007: By the way, still looking into nominating you for an AGU award, I've been told that the Ewing medal wouldn't be the right one. Let me know if you have any particular options you'd like me to investigate…

Jones to Mann, same date: As for AGU—just getting one of their Fellowships would be fine.

Mann to Jones, same date: Will look into the AGU fellowship situation ASAP .

Mann to Jones, June 2, 2008: Hi Phil, This is coming along nicely. I've got 5 very strong supporting letter writers lined up to support your AGU Fellowship nomination (confidentially: Ben Santer, Tom Karl, Jean Jouzel, and Lonnie Thompson have all agreed, waiting to hear back from one more individual, maximum is six letters including mine as nominator).

Sure enough, in January 2009, Jones hears the wonderful news that he—surprise!—has won an AGU fellowship. Four months later, Mann decides that a sufficiently decent interval has elapsed to ask Jones oh-so-parenthetically:

Mann to Jones, May 16, 2009: On a completely unrelated note, I was wondering if you, perhaps in tandem w/ some of the other usual suspects, might be interested in returning the favor this year;) I've looked over the current list of AGU fellows, and it seems to me that there are quite a few who have gotten in (e.g. Kurt Cuffey, Amy Clement, and many others) who aren't as far along as me in their careers, so I think I ought to be a strong candidate. anyway, I don't want to pressure you in any way, but if you think you'd be willing to help organize, I would naturally be much obliged. Perhaps you could convince Ray or Malcolm to take the lead? The deadline looks as if it is again July 1 this year.

All this is very entertaining, to be sure, but making too much of it would play right into the enemy's hands. After all, as their subsequent defenses have shown (see quotes above), there is nothing that the Climategate scientists would like more than to be seen as fundamentally normal, decent guys: the kind of regular Joes who enjoy a bit of edgy banter, sail close to the wind occasionally, and aren't averse to helping out a mate by bending the rules. Their only real crime, we are invited to believe, was to have their venial slips exposed by the publication of emails that ought to have stayed private. It's no coincidence that whenever alarmists refer to Climategate they talk about "hacked" or "stolen" emails, rather than "leaked" ones. The implication is that the exposed scientists aren't so much crime perpetrators as crime victims. For this same reason, there's no point dwelling on emails like the one where Phil Jones has a sly gloat over the sudden death of one of his arch-enemies, Australian climate skeptic John Daly ("In an odd way this is cheering news!"). Or the one from October 9, 2009, where Ben Santer writes to Phil Jones about a well-known skeptic:

> I'm really sorry that you have to go through all this stuff, Phil. Next time I see Pat Michaels at a scientific meeting, I'll be tempted to beat the crap out of him. Very tempted.

It's fun to quote these passages, obviously, which is why I've done so. But let's not kid ourselves that they have any connection with the real scandal revealed by Climategate, which has much more to do with the corruption of the scientific process by privileged and enormously powerful scientists whose salaries and expenses we fund, and whose abuses threaten to have a serious, deleterious impact on all our lives.

Climategate is really about the systematic abuse of the "scientific method". Naturally, the apologists for Climategate scientists—such as Steve Easterbrook—have worked very hard to put us off the scent. Their tactic is to make out that science is a realm so rarefied and remote from ordinary life that mere mortals cannot hope to comprehend the subtle, mysterious ways of the chosen white-coated ones with their peer-reviewed papers and their wondrous computer models. "Don't worry your pretty little heads about these complicated matters," their message runs. "It might look dodgy, but that's only because you don't understand how science works."

This is utter hogwash. There are accepted standards of behavior which have applied for years throughout the scientific community, based on principles which are very easily understood by the layman. They include rigor (sticking to what your experiments show, rather than what you might like them to show); openness (sharing your research with other scientists, so that they can evaluate your work and then build upon it) and honesty (telling the truth, not making stuff up, not deleting awkward emails or data when subject to a Freedom of Information request—that kind of thing). At the heart of this scientific method is something called "peer review". This is the benchmark by which most new scientific research tends to be judged. If that research is to be taken seriously by the scientific community then it must be accepted for publication by an academic journal such as *Nature* or *Science*.

Peer-review is not a perfect system. In the golden era of early 20th Century science, it wasn't even thought necessary: neither Watson and Crick nor Einstein were peer-reviewed. But in today's abstruse, fragmented world where the various branches of science have grown increasingly recondite and specialized, peer-review has become widely accepted as the least worst method by which quality science can be sifted from junk science.

And nowhere more so than within the climate science community. In the run-up to Climategate, one of the main weapons used by those within "the consensus" against dissenting scientists was that their various papers picking holes in AGW theory had not been "peer-reviewed" and were therefore invalid. As Phil Jones puts it in one of his emails:

The peer review system is the safeguard science has adopted to stop bad science being published.

Besides "peer review", the other concept that's worth explaining before we delve into the Climategate emails more closely is something called the Medieval Warm Period (MWP). It features quite heavily in the correspondence between the Warmist scientists.

Why so? Because of all the climate-change-related evidence from recorded history, the MWP is the one piece of evidence that does most to undermine the cause of AGW. The MWP (given very short shrift at Wikipedia, incidentally, for reasons not unconnected with the Warmist bias of those involved in editing relevant Wikipedia entries) was that era of bounteous warmth and fruitfulness which existed throughout the world between roughly 900 AD and 1280 AD.

This was the era when the now-all-but-uninhabitable Greenland actually lived up to its name (at least in some parts)—enabling Vikings to settle, grow barley and raise sheep and cattle. It was, records the *Domesday Book*, a time when grapes were grown in parts of England where they could ill-survive today. But it wasn't just Northern Europe that benefited from this period of balmy fruitfulness. There is good evidence that it spread as far as China and Japan, Africa, South and North America. And to the extent that it is possible to assess any temperature in an era without temperature records, it seems plausible at least—based on what we know of the vegetation and human habits of the day—that global average temperatures were significantly warmer than they are today. And that was what eminent climate scientists such as Prof. H. H. Lamb, the first director of the CRU, argued in his seminal book, *Climate, History and the Modern World*.

Now just imagine how annoying this would be if you were a committed believer in man-made global warming. For one thing, it would horribly contradict your scary, attention-grabbing claim that late 20th Century temperature highs were dramatic and unprecedented. For another, it would seriously hamper your line about CO_2 emissions being a significant driver of climate change. After all, there were no CO_2-belching coal-fired power stations, no factories, no airplanes or cars in the 11th century. So how do you possibly explain that average temperatures then were even higher than they are now? Mightn't this suggest, to the neutral observer, that perhaps climate is capable of changing quite independently of human activity? And if this was true 1,000 years ago, why is it suddenly not true today? Moreover, if people were able to thrive in a warmer world, why should we be worried about a little AGW?

OK. Now we're ready to examine those emails more closely. I am indebted here to the brilliant, detailed analysis done by Dr. John Costella, an Australian scientist. Costella believes that what is essentially going on here is a breach of trust. He writes:

[In science] scientists assume that the rules of the scientific method have been followed, at least in any discipline that publishes its results for public consumption. It is that trust in the process that allows me, for example, to believe that the human genome has been mapped—despite my knowing nothing about that field of science at all. That same trust has allowed scientists at large to similarly believe in the results of climate science. Until now.

Costella compares it to a bent trial:

Everyone knows what happens if police obtain evidence by illegal means: the evidence is ruled inadmissible; and, if a case rests on that tainted evidence, it is thrown out of court.

(The big difference, Costella might have added, being that if this particular court case leads to the wrong verdict, it's not just going to be the innocent defendant who ends up in the slammer, but the entire world.)

Let us turn, then to exhibit A. The one everyone has heard of, not least because it was turned into a catchy viral hit on YouTube by Minnesotans for Global Warming—complete with Michael Mann dancing amid reindeer, Christmas trees and guitar-strumming cats:

Makin' up data the old hard way
Fudgin' the numbers day by day

Ignoring the snow and the cold and a downward line.
Hide the decline (hide the decline).

Here's the relevant passage—in an email from Phil Jones to Ray Bradley, Mike Mann, Malcolm Hughes, Keith Briffa and Tim Osborn, regarding a diagram for a World Meteorological Organization Statement—dated November 16, 1999.

I've just completed Mike's Nature trick of adding in the real temps to each series for the last 20 years (i.e. from 1981 onwards) [and] from 1961 for Keith's to hide the decline.

No, it doesn't mean "hide the decline" in temperature—excitingly damning though that might be—but something rather more subtly incriminating. It has to do with our friend Keith Briffa and his increasing concerns that his tortured, mangled, brutalized evidence is still stubbornly refusing to scream.

Just so it's not taken out of context, here is Briffa outlining the problem in an earlier email from September 22, 1999. This email finds him worrying that his colleagues might be about to overegg the doom'n'disaster pudding in the next IPCC assessment:

I know there is pressure to present a nice tidy story as regards 'apparent unprecedented warming in a thousand years or more in the proxy data' but in reality the situation is not quite so simple. We don't have a lot of proxies that come right up to date and those that do (at least a significant number of tree proxies). [There are] some unexpected changes in response that do not match the recent warming. I do not think it wise that this issue be ignored in the chapter.

By proxy, Briffa means a temperature substitute. Because hardly any thermometers existed prior to 1850, paleo-climatologists like Briffa must find other ways to calculate past temperatures. One method is to look at the variations in width and density on the rings of trees which grew hundreds, or better still, thousands of years ago. But Briffa is having a problem with his tree samples: at the very point in the late 20th Century when the real world thermometers show temperatures are going up, his pesky trees are telling him that temperatures are going down. He has encountered what is known as a "divergence" problem.

Which is more likely to be accurate: spiffy modern weather stations with state of the art thermometers, or the relative width of rings on the stump of an old tree?

Actually that's a trick question: weather stations for a number of reasons can be quite inaccurate too, to the point where some scientists doubt whether even the records showing late 20th Century warming can be taken seriously. But yes, by and large you're right. When it comes to judging how high or low average global temperatures might have been 20 years ago, let alone a thousand, tree ring samples are barely a twig away from utter uselessness. Consider, for a moment, the variables that might affect a tree's growth in a particular year: the amount of sunlight that falls on its leaves; how hot or cold it is; how much it rains; the soil conditions; the amount of CO_2 it breathes. Already that makes four unknowns besides temperature, and we haven't even factored in further complexities such as competition (i.e. suppose for a period of years the sample tree was overshadowed by a much bigger tree which later died and disappeared) or insect infestation. So there are lots of things those tree rings might show other than temperature—hence the need to treat them with great caution.

Now suppose you're Keith Briffa. Using your proxy data, you've constructed this fabulous chart which proves pretty much everything the rest of your gang would like to see proved, namely: that the MWP and the Little Ice Age (LIA) which followed were relatively insignificant when compared to the massive, ice-hockey-blade shaped temperature spike which occurred at the end of the 20th Century. Your big, scary bully of a gang leader Mike Mann is pleased with you (for once) and is keen for your chart to be included in the next IPCC assessment report. But then—despite all the peer pressure you remain a reasonably honest fellow—you do a bit of due diligence and realize (oh the horror!) that the entire basis of your graph may be a crock.

That bad? Yes. Really that bad. You see, while there's no easy way to check the accuracy of tree ring proxies from a thousand years ago, there's a perfectly simple way to check the most recent ones.

You—duh!—compare them with actual thermometer readings. And if they don't coincide, you have one hell of a problem, for it means your tree ring proxies aren't accurate. Not for the last 40 years, certainly; and therefore, most likely, not ever.

Poor Keith, you can see now why his emails convey such an anguished tone. His last few years of research look as if they have been entirely wasted. Damn it, he can't even bring himself to agree with the rest of the gang's assessment that the MWP is insignificant. He says, later in the email: "I believe that the recent warmth was probably matched about 1,000 years ago." Yet his gang leaders are planning on co-opting his research in their efforts to prove otherwise. What is he to do?

Luckily, his gang leader Mike Mann has a cunning plan. Is it— most honorable option—to publish the data, warts and all, so that fellow scientists and other interested parties can decide for themselves how viable it is? Nope. Is it, then, to cut it out of the IPCC assessment altogether? Nope. Mann has found what Tony Blair would no doubt call a Third Way, but which you and I would more likely call a devious fudge.

Here he outlines his scheme:

I am perfectly amenable to keeping Keith's series in the plot, and can ask Ian Macadam (Chris?) to add it to the plot he has been preparing (nobody liked my own color/plotting conventions so I've given up doing this myself). The key thing is making sure the series are vertically aligned in a reasonable way. I had been using the entire 20th century, but in the case of Keith's, we need to align the first half of the 20th century w/ the corresponding mean values of the other series, due to the late 20th century decline.

This email marks the genesis of Mann's infamous "green graph"— the green tree-ring line in the graph on the IPCC report that mysteriously passes behind the other lines in the year 1961, but never comes out the other side.

"Mike's Nature trick" is something slightly different. It refers to a cheat, presumably invented by Mann but enthusiastically adopted by Jones, whereby at the point where the tree ring data start giving out the wrong message (i.e. post-1960) they are spliced with thermometer temperature data instead. This is deeply unscientific: like pretending that apples are the same as oranges. But as Jones rightly suggests, it's really rather useful when there's a "decline" you want to "hide".

At some point, Phil Jones wonders how best to conceal data that he has been asked to disclose under a Freedom of Information request. "The two Ms have been after the CRU station data for years," he writes, meaning his nemeses McIntyre and McKitrick. "If they ever hear there is a freedom of information act now in the UK, I think I'll delete the file rather than send it to anyone." Deleting data subject to an FOI request is a criminal offence.

Such is the nature of the Climategate emails: the worst devilry often lies in the obscure and frankly rather tedious detail. If you were hoping for emails saying things like: "Teehee! Wonder how much longer we're going to get away with this ridiculous 'Anthropogenic Global Warming' scam" or "Hey, I know. Let's add another 10 degrees to the 1980s summer temperature dataset", you will be disappointed. There is little evidence to suggest that the Climategate scientists don't believe in AGW. On the contrary: most of the email evidence suggests that they believe in it all too fervently. So fervently, in fact, that they see almost nothing wrong with distorting the evidence in order to give a greater impression of scientific certainty and "consensus" on AGW than actually exists. Therein lies the real scandal of Climategate: it's a case of scientists breaking the rules of science and behaving instead like political activists.

We see them "cherry-picking" data that supports their theories and burying data that doesn't. We see them drawing conclusions based on gut-feeling rather than evidence. We see them ganging up to bully editors, journalists and fellow scientists who disagree with them. We see them orchestrating smear campaigns. We see them subverting and debasing the peer-review process. We see them insert bogus graphs and misleading information into official reports which are supposed to represent the "gold standard" of international scientific knowledge. We see them not only fail to keep proper records but actually losing the vital, irreplaceable raw data which they are paid by governments to collect and maintain. We see them obstructing, in every possible way, requests for data under the Freedom of Information Act.

You don't need to be a scientist to know that this is not how proper scientists should behave. And if you're in any doubt, read what the U.S. National Academy of Sciences has to say on the subject in its book *On Being a Scientist*:

> Researchers who manipulate their data in ways that deceive others, even if the manipulation seems insignificant at the time, are violating both the basic values and widely accepted professional standards of science. Researchers draw conclusions based on their observations of nature. If data are altered to present a case that is stronger than the data warrant, researchers fail to fulfill all three of the obligations described at the beginning of this guide. They mislead their colleagues and potentially impede progress in their field or research. They undermine their own authority and trustworthiness as researchers. And they introduce information into the scientific record that could cause harm to the broader society, as when the dangers of a medical treatment are understated.

What makes it worse is that the Climategate scientists wield such extraordinary power. The men you see in the emails—bickering like schoolgirls, jetting to junkets from Trieste to Hawaii to Venice to Finland to Tanzania, ganging up on their enemies—they may not sound like people you'd ever like to be seated next to at a dinner party, but you cannot ignore them. That's because grasped within their sweaty palms and being squeezed ever tighter are some extremely sensitive and tender parts of your anatomy.

Perhaps you take the indulgent view that this is simply a case of boys being boys, and that if your private emails or my private emails were exposed to public scrutiny, none of us would be shown in any more flattering a light than those poor, put-upon, much-misunderstood Climategate scientists.

Personally, I'm not at all convinced by this "everyone's a crook at heart" defense. This isn't a formal invitation for you to hack my emails. But if you did, I think you'd be disappointed. You'd find nothing there so embarrassing or untoward that I'd feel my reputation had been damaged, especially not regarding my role as a card carrying global warming denier. No secret payments from Big Oil (what a pity). No cozy exchanges with Marc Morano or Christopher Booker or Pat Michaels, discussing how best to trick the data so it makes it look like AGW isn't really happening. It's just not how we skeptics operate.

Why not? Because we don't need to. We're not trying to hide anything, and we're certainly not on a mission to disseminate lies. Quite the opposite. All we care about is that the truth be published. If that truth takes the form of conclusive evidence that anthropogenic CO_2 emissions are a significant, unprecedented and dangerous driver of climate, then fine: we'll lay aside our skepticism and start discussing how to address the problem. Until that happens, what we'd like is an open and honest debate in which the known facts are made available and in which the best-supported case is allowed to prevail until such time as it's replaced by an even better one.

This is what differentiates us from our opponents and it's a fact that emerges very clearly from those Climategate emails. The very last thing those scientists want is openness and honesty. At the merest whiff of dissent, instead of responding with the superior force of their argument, they crush it with bullying, blackmail and ad hominem assaults.

Consider their response when two Harvard astronomers—Willie Soon and Sallie Baliunas—had the temerity to publish a paper suggesting that the MWP was significant and widespread. The "Hockey Team" sees this not as a valuable contribution to the state of scientific understanding, but as a personal threat. Here, for example, is Tom Wigley's suggestion of how to deal with them:

> Might be interesting to see how frequently Soon and Baliunas, individually, are cited (as astronomers). Are they any good in their own fields? Perhaps we could start referring to them as astrologers (excusable as … 'oops, just a typo').

Wigley does love a smear. Earlier, he can be seen discussing how best to blacken the name of the peer-reviewed journal *Climate Research* (CR), whose editor Hans von Storch published the offending Soon and Baliunas paper.

> PS Re CR, I do not know the best way to handle the specifics of the editing [sic]. Hans von Storch is partly to blame—he encourages the publication of crap science 'in order to stimulate debate'. One approach is to go direct to the publishers and point out the fact that their journal is perceived as being a medium for disseminating misinformation under the guise of refereed work. I use the word 'perceived' here, since whether it is true or not is not what the publishers care about—it is how the journal is seen by the community that counts.

Michael Mann has another idea:

Much like a server which has been compromised as a launching point for computer viruses, I fear that "Climate Research" has become a hopelessly compromised vehicle in the skeptics' (can we find a better word?) disinformation campaign, and some of the discussion that I've seen (e.g. a potential threat of mass resignation among the legitimate members of the CR editorial board) seems, in my opinion, to have some potential merit.

Peer-review, as far as Mann and his Hockey Team are concerned, is clearly a one-way street. A vital badge of distinction if attached to papers supporting his cause; utterly worthless if those peer-reviewed papers happen to disagree with him. He states this quite explicitly here, as he dismisses another peer-reviewed journal, *Energy and Environment*.

I don't read E&E, gives me indigestion—I don't even consider it peer-reviewed science, and in my view we should treat it that way. i.e., don't cite, and if journalists ask us about a paper, simply explain its [sic] not peer-reviewed science, and Sonja B-C, the editor, has even admitted to an anti-Kyoto agenda!

Perhaps the most sympathetic complexion one can put on this approach is that the Climategate scientists genuinely believed they were men on a mission to save the world, and that by suppressing any dissent they were doing us all a favor. If so, this was essentially a political decision, not a scientific one. I'll discuss the dangers of scientists behaving like political activists in another chapter. What I want to do, by way of conclusion to this one, is to ask a simple question. Suppose for a moment that there really is a strong consensus in favor of AGW; and suppose that the scientific evidence for AGW theory is—as Mann, Jones et al. seem to think—so compellingly rock solid that it brooks no opposition. Then why is that, throughout the Climategate emails, the scientists pushing AGW emerge as being so utterly terrified of having their research, opinions and credibility exposed to the crucible of open public debate? What exactly are they trying to hide?

CHAPTER 3

IT'S NOT ABOUT "THE SCIENCE"

For generations, we have assumed that the efforts of mankind would leave the fundamental equilibrium of the world's systems and atmosphere stable. But it is possible that with all these enormous changes (population, agricultural, use of fossil fuels) concentrated into such a short period of time, we have unwittingly begun a massive experiment with the system of this planet itself.

Margaret Thatcher, Speech to the Royal Society, Fishmongers' Hall, City of London, Sept. 27, 1988

So you see, yet again, it was all Margaret Thatcher's fault. As so many left-liberal commentators tell us, she was responsible for everything from the decline of Britain's industrial base, the Falklands war, and the death of Britain's mining and shipbuilding communities, to the rise of greed and selfishness and the Big Bang in the City of London which of course led to the current economic crisis. So why not add AGW alarmism to the charge sheet, too?

And if you think that first quote is damning, wait until you read what she said next:

Recently three changes in atmospheric chemistry have become familiar subjects of concern. The first is the increase in the greenhouse gases—carbon dioxide, methane, and chlorofluorocarbons—which has led some to fear that we are creating a global heat trap which could lead to climatic instability. We are told that a warming effect of 1°C per decade would greatly exceed the capacity of our natural habitat to cope. Such warming could cause accelerated melting of glacial ice and a consequent increase in the sea level of several feet over the next century. This was brought home to me at the Commonwealth Conference in Vancouver last year when the President of the Maldive Islands reminded us that the highest part of the Maldives is only six feet above sea level. The population is 177,000. It is noteworthy that the five warmest years in a century of records have all been in the 1980s—though we may not have seen much evidence in Britain!

Shocking, eh? Some of us cherish the Iron Lady as the shining exemplar of rigorous empiricism, robust common sense, and achingly sound Conservative values. But here she comes across like some eco-freak with a dog on a rope, a battered VW bus and an outdoor compost toilet. And this was long before the 21st Century, when the "Save the Sinking Maldives" meme was spreading faster than Spanish flu. In fact, it was long before anyone had heard of Rajendra Pachauri or the IPCC or the Hockey Stick or "An Inconvenient Truth".

Indeed it has been suggested that "probably the most important fact in the entire global warming issue" is this: "Margaret Thatcher had a B.Sc. degree in chemistry."

Can this be true?

Up to a point, yes.

It was at Margaret Thatcher's personal instigation that the UK Met Office set up its Hadley Centre for Climate Prediction and Research, which—in one of her final acts as Prime Minister—she opened in 1990. The Hadley Centre, in turn, helped to produce the primary data set which was used by the newly founded IPCC to "assess observed global warming". Under the leadership of committed Warmist Sir John Houghton, Hadley was also responsible for selecting the lead authors for the IPCC's scientific working group (Working Group I)—authors who, it need hardly be said, would reliably push the IPCC's reports in the "correct" alarmist direction.

Was she stupid? Crazy? Ill-advised? What?

One of the more cynical theories is that Mrs. Thatcher's early adoption of the "climate change" issue was rooted in *realpolitik*. After the challenge to her power posed by the 1984 Miners' strike, she wanted to ensure that never again could Britain be held hostage by the National Union of Mineworkers. By posing it as a global environmental issue quite beyond the realm of party politics, she could cunningly reduce Britain's reliance on coal without provoking further confrontation with the miners.

What's more, she could use CO_2 reduction—just as Swedish Prime Minister Olaf Palme did in the mid-70s—as an excuse to justify a push for otherwise unpopular nuclear energy. Two years after the Chernobyl disaster, a nuclear-plant-building program would hardly have been a great vote-winner, but the Conservative government needed nuclear processing facilities in order to upgrade its nuclear deterrent with the Trident missile system.

The more prosaic explanation is that Mrs. Thatcher was influenced by one of her senior advisors, career diplomat and British ambassador to the United Nations, Sir Crispin Tickell. Though no one who worked with Margaret Thatcher has ever accused her of being the suggestible type, it may be that the smoothie ambassador managed to, ahem, "tickell" her pride in her Oxford Natural Sciences degree and her former job as an industrial research chemist. Certainly it was at Tickell's suggestion that Thatcher made her influential speech to the Royal Society.

Tickell had long been a keen amateur student of "climate change". In the 70s, he took a sabbatical from his job as a civil servant to study climate science at Harvard, which in turn inspired him in 1977 to publish a book on the imminent doom facing mankind: *Climatic Change and World Affairs*. Mysteriously, his website and CV fail to mention that the form of doom he was predicting at the time was global cooling.

Eleven years later, in the revised 1988 edition of the book, Tickell was hedging his bets: "Why then does the climate change? And what is its time scale? There is no short, complete or even adequate answer to either question, and most of the ideas which have been put forward remain controversial." Despite this admitted uncertainty, however, Tickell was quite sure of one thing: something needed to be done—and quickly.

Perhaps unsurprisingly given his job, Tickell's proposed solution to this apparently urgent crisis (the precise nature of which he did not yet understand) was the creation of a new supranational environmental body to be run under the auspices of the United Nations to act as "international custodian of the world's climate". As Tickell writes in his book, its job would be to shame and bully the countries of the world into ecological correctness:

> In the last resort the policing of agreements on climate as on other aspects of the environment would depend on the translation of a consensus of opinion into means of mobilising, persuading, and if necessary, shaming governments into co-operation and compliance.

Among the carrots and sticks it might use were "taxes on the use of fossil fuels to promote wider use of energy resources" and punitive import tariffs. All this, remember, to deal with a problem whose precise nature and cause Tickell admitted he couldn't identify.

Within a few years, Tickell's wishes came true. In November that very same year, the Intergovernmental Panel on Climate Change was formed, set up under two UN umbrella bodies: the World Meteorological Organization (WMO) and the United Nations Environment Program (UNEP).

Do you find this kind of detail deathly dull? I do too. But unfortunately, it's very much grist to the mill of the kind of good-intentioned technocrats and diplomats such as Tickell who are compelled to work for organizations such as the United Nations and the European Union. They wear outsiders down with the tedium of their arguments and the smallness of their fine print. By the time anyone else notices what they're up to, the damage has been done and it's too late to do anything about it.

In the European Union, this process of enlargement of powers by stealth is known as "engrenage"—which means "gearing"—i.e. "ratcheting up little by little." As the EU's founders—notably the wily cognac salesman Jean Monnet—understood all too well, no electorate would allow its nation's sovereignty to be abandoned for the sake of some pie-in-the-sky, Socialist Euro project. The only way to get around this, they realized, was always to pretend what was happening wasn't really happening.

The Times incisively analyzed this process:

> It is at first denied that any radical new plan exists; it is then conceded that it exists but ministers swear blind that it is not even on the political agenda; it is then noted that it might well be on the agenda but is not a serious proposition; it is later conceded that it is a serious proposition but that it will never be implemented; after that it is acknowledged that it will be implemented but in such a diluted form that it will make no difference to the lives of ordinary people; at some point it is finally recognised that it has made such a difference, but it was always known that it would and voters were told so from the outset.

Follow the history of the various UN bodies concerned with global warming and you'll notice the same process. The obscure obsessions of a handful of activists mutate into mainstream thought, then almost holy writ. Tiny, obscure, feeble, toothless committees blossom into mighty institutions employing thousands and costing tens of millions. Bodies which were initially established purely in an advisory capacity gradually accumulate the authority, influence and regulatory powers of government. *Engrenage.*

In the 1970s, global warming—climate change generally—was little more than a minor cult followed by a few tousled eccentrics. By the late 80s it had become an important policy issue for all the world's serious nations. By the mid-90s, it was one of the greatest crises ever to face mankind. And by the 21st Century it was the world's most powerful religion—its guilt-laden mantras taught in every classroom, its pontiffs, mullahs and vicars-general enriched, almighty and triumphant, its tenets rigorously applied in almost every last detail of daily life from waste disposal, to household illumination, to food and fuel prices to air travel. How?

Engrenage.

Yeah, all right, but just because I keep saying "engrenage" in that knowing way doesn't necessarily make it so, does it? Surely the more likely explanation for the way AGW gained the world spotlight is because scientists found more and more evidence to show it was happening and that it posed a real threat. Surely politicians took note, and legislation was passed accordingly?

A reasonable supposition, I would agree. But as we've already seen elsewhere in the book, one of the truly astonishing things about AGW theory is how little solid, reliable evidence there actually is to support it. If there were, all that skullduggery we saw in the Climategate emails would have been entirely unnecessary. The facts would have spoken for themselves.

What you'll see in this chapter is that far from being a scientific process, the AGW industry is essentially a political one. Sure a bit of science comes into it—scientists behaving like politicians, politicians à la Margaret Thatcher behaving like failed scientists—but the science on each occasion is little more than a handy excuse. Climate change, as we shall see, is far less important as a scientific reality than as a Rahm Emanuel-style crisis: real or imagined, it doesn't much matter, as far its high priests are concerned. It's a pretext for action by a handful of dedicated individuals determined to impose their peculiar views of how things should be done, and how we should live our lives, not just on their own families, or even their own nation states, but on the entire world.

If you shared these people's motives, you'd no doubt consider them heroes. One of your heroes, definitely, would be Professor Bert Bolin, the mild-mannered, self-effacing Swedish meteorologist (1925–2007) who had talked up the carbon terror since as early as 1959, when he travelled to Washington to warn the National Academy of Sciences of the potential threat posed by increased CO_2 emissions. It was Bolin who came up with the notion (now commonplace among policymakers) that if atmospheric CO_2 concentration goes beyond a certain tipping point (450ppm was the figure he came up with), then we are all doomed. He was also author of the 500-page, keynote paper which set the alarmist tone for an influential UN-sponsored conference on man-made global warming in Villach, Austria, in 1985. This in turn paved the way three years later for the creation of the IPCC, with Bolin himself as its first chairman. As Al Gore said on collecting his Nobel Peace Prize (given jointly to him and the IPCC for their work in supposedly combating global warming): "Bert, without you we would not have come to where we are today."

Bolin's theories were based on one first formulated by a fellow Swede—a chemist named Svante Arrhenius. In 1896 Arrhenius tried to calculate what might happen if, as a result of man's burning of fossil fuels, the natural quantity of CO_2 in the atmosphere were to double. It would, he decided, increase the earth's average temperature by a hefty 5°C.

Arrhenius's calculations were in turn based on those of two earlier scientists, Josephe Fourier and John Tyndall. Fourier was a French mathematician and engineer who discovered the "greenhouse effect" (in which the earth's atmosphere traps heat radiated by the sun, delaying its escape into space, and thus keeping our planet habitable). Tyndall, an Irish physicist, discovered that only certain gases have this property—not nitrogen and oxygen, which constitute about 99 percent of the atmosphere, but mainly water vapor—which contributes 95 per cent of the greenhouse effect—followed by carbon dioxide (3.62 per cent), nitrous oxide (0.95 per cent); methane (0.36 per cent) and others, including CFCs or chlorofluorocarbons (0.07 per cent).

Many Warmists revere these scientists as the high priests of their faith. Twice, when debating British journalist George Monbiot, I have been treated to a little homily on the lines that anyone who denies AGW must also either be in denial or ignorance of the basic physics of Fourier, Tyndall and Arrhenius. At this point, our George likes to cock his head, a triumphant smile on his lips, as if to say: "Hah! You've no answer to that!"

But I do. Science advances all the time. Just because Fourier theorized something in 1824 or Tyndall in 1860 or Arrhenius in 1896 does not make it an Immutable Law of Irrefutable Truth. It would be like me trying to pooh-pooh your theory that oxygen is a vital part of combustion, on the grounds that in the 17th century it was entirely disproved by the discovery of phlogiston by the great Johann Joachim Becher.

The other key figure in the genesis of the great AGW scare—albeit unwittingly—was Dr. Roger Revelle. Today, thanks to "An Inconvenient Truth", Revelle is best remembered as the Harvard professor who first alerted the young Al Gore to the threat of man-made climate change. This is a bit like Orson Welles being best remembered as the man who provided the off-camera voice of Robin Masters in Magnum PI—deeply unfair, but also entirely typical of the reverse Midas effect Gore has on everything from presidential aspirations to distinguished former professors.

Before Gore dragged him into his web, Revelle was a well-respected oceanographer whose team at California's Scripps Institution of Oceanography had speculated (in 1957) that the amount of CO_2 being pumped into the atmosphere by the burning of fossil fuels might be too great to be absorbed completely by the oceans. According to science historian Spencer Weart in *The Discovery of Global Warming*, they never considered it more than a "side issue…a detour from their main professional work to which they soon returned." Nevertheless, to test their theory they dispatched Dr. Charles Keeling, a young geochemist, to a weather station atop the Hawaiian volcano Mauna Loa to try to establish a baseline snapshot of atmospheric CO_2 levels.

Sure enough, Keeling and the Scripps team discovered that levels were increasing. In 1956, the amount of CO_2 in the atmosphere was 316 parts per million (ppm); by 1980, this figure had risen to nearly 340 ppm. (Cue massive panic among those who wished to see this as a cause for panic.) CO_2—or *carbon* as greens increasingly took to calling it, because carbon sounds all black and evil and scary whereas CO_2 just sounds like the boring, harmless, plant-feeding gas you learned about in biology—was the hideous new menace that was going to kill us all!

Now those of you with a rudimentary scientific background may have noticed an ozone-over-the-Antarctic-sized hole in this argument. "All right," you may say. "Atmospheric CO_2 levels are rising. I accept that. But how can we be so sure that this will lead to dangerously increasing temperatures? What if Arrhenius got his calculations wrong? What if, maybe, global climate is controlled by something a bit more complicated than the atmospheric concentration of a trace gas?"

And if this what you're saying, you may be absolutely right. The key phrase to remember here is: "correlation is not causation." Yes, it's perfectly true that from the mid 1970s to the late 1990s global mean temperatures increased. It's also true that in that same period, man-made CO_2 emissions rose and the concentration of CO_2 in the atmosphere increased. But then, so too in that same period did the price of oil. And the number of actors who have played Doctor Who. And the value of Microsoft's shares. And the total amount of flatus produced by my bottom. Are we really saying then that global warming has in fact been caused by a weird combination of CO_2

emissions, the Middle East, Bill Gates, Jon Pertwee, Tom Baker, Peter Davison, Colin Baker, Sylvester McCoy, Paul McGann—and all of flatulent humanity?

Well no, clearly not; that would be absurd. But in scientific terms, it is no more absurd than to conclude that because CO_2 levels have increased and temperatures have risen is, therefore, proof of cause and effect. That is only correlation, not an explanation of causation.

Indeed, if you were to glean just one single fact from this book, I'd suggest it should be this: **no one in the entire history of climate science has ever managed to prove that there is a connection between man-made carbon emissions and *dangerous* climate change**. Not one scientist. Ever.

That isn't to suggest that the greenhouse effect doesn't exist. Nor is it to say that industrial civilization and agriculture have no effect on global climate—of course they do. The methane emitted by beef and dairy cattle undoubtedly contributes to the heating of the atmosphere. At the same time, cities create localized warming (known as the Urban Heat Island Effect, which explains why, for example, as a Londoner I don't bother digging up my dahlia tubers before each winter, because I know the frost is never likely to be severe enough to kill them).

I'm not even suggesting that there might not be a dangerous causative link, and that sometime in the future this connection will be discovered, forcing Evil Climate Change Deniers like me to blush for shame. Possibly we'd end up being tried by kangaroo courts staged by hardcore greenies, and sentenced to death for culpability in having encouraged such toxic complacency about the very real threat to Gaia in the days when there was still time to do something about it.

But I do say that the jury on AGW is still out. This is a fact which proponents of AGW theory have tried very hard to suppress, by using techniques more traditionally associated with fascist politics—lies, bullying, black propaganda—than with the dignified neutrality of real science.

Ethical scientists have long understood this, among them the afore-mentioned Roger Revelle. Revelle's skepticism proved most incon-venient for Al Gore. While campaigning in the 1992 Presidential election on a fashionable eco-warrior ticket, Gore published a book called *Earth in the Balance*. It praised Professor Revelle's influence in alerting him to the "global environmental threat" posed by CO_2.

Revelle's position, however, was rather different from his student protégé's. In July 1988, he had written to Senator Tim Wirth of Colo-rado, chairman of a Senate committee investigation into the green-house effect and climate change, urging caution. "We should be careful not to arouse too much alarm until the rate and amount of warming becomes clearer," he said.

Later, Revelle made his skepticism even more explicit in a paper written in collaboration with his old friend Dr. Fred Singer, profes-sor of environmental science at the University of Virginia, and with an energy expert, Dr. Chauncey Starr. Published in the small-circu-lation journal *Cosmos*, the authors stated: "Drastic, precipitous and especially unilateral steps to delay the putative greenhouse impacts can cost jobs and prosperity and increase the human costs of global poverty without being effective." It concluded: "The scientific base for a greenhouse warming is too uncertain to justify drastic action at this time."

Al Gore's response? To mount a campaign of disinformation and character assassination. He persuaded a friend to circulate the story that the elderly Revelle (who died shortly after the *Cosmos* article appeared) was coerced into putting his name to the article while sick and not in his right mind. (Singer later successfully sued his accuser for libel.) Gore also rang the ABC news presenter Ted Koppel, urging him to expose the alleged fact that Singer and his fellow skeptics were being funded by the fossil fuel industry.

Koppel's principled on-air response could scarcely have summed up the truth of the matter more perfectly. Koppel noted that there was:

...some irony in the fact that Vice-President Gore—one of the most scientifically literate men to sit in the White House in this century—(is) resorting to political means to achieve what should ultimately be resolved on a purely scientific basis. The measure of good science is neither the politics of the scientists nor the people with whom the scientist associates. It is the immersion of the hypothesis into the acid of truth. That's the hard way to do it, but it's the only way that works.

I'm as shocked as Koppel was, though some readers may find this naïve: "Ach, politicians. They're all as rotten as each other." But it's one thing to know that politicians are capable of corruption and to doubt their ability to make things better. It's quite another, I would suggest, to be so thoroughly cynical that one no longer either expects them to behave honorably, or feels able to condemn them when they behave dishonorably. That way anarchy lies.

What kind of behavior do we expect of our politicians—and scientists? This issue has a vital bearing on one of the key questions of this whole debate: how did a theory as loony as AGW manage to gain such widespread traction to become one of the defining political ideas of our age?

One answer, I believe, lies in the instinctive faith we have in our public representatives, be they politicians, diplomats, experts, technocrats or scientists doing vital work at state-financed institutions. (Yeah, all right, I hear all you conspiracy theorists in the peanut gallery—you've known better all along. I'm thinking more of the voting public in general.) I'd suggest that when our public representatives tell us something is true, most of us still rather sweetly believe that it's because they've done their due diligence and they're presenting us with the facts as they know them. Especially when that something is of such all pervasive, life-changing, economy-shifting, geopolitical importance as AGW.

Yet as we've seen with Al Gore, this simply hasn't been the case. Nor has it been so with Dr. James Hansen, director of NASA's Goddard Institute for Space Studies (GISS). Nor with Dr. Phil Jones, the head of the Climatic Research Unit at the University of East Anglia. Nor with Rajendra Pachauri of the IPCC. Nor Ben Santer of the Lawrence Livermore National Laboratory.

Ben who? Well quite. Unless his name rings a bell as the guy from the Climategate emails who wanted to "beat the crap out of" climate skeptic Pat Michaels, you almost certainly won't have heard of him. Yet in the mid-90s, this climate modeling nonentity was somehow placed in the extraordinary position of being able to dictate world opinion on global warming at the stroke of a pen.

He achieved this in his role as lead author of Chapter 8 of the scientific working group report on the IPCC's Second Assessment Report in 1995. Nothing to write home about there, you might think, except that Santer was personally responsible for the most widely reported sentence in the entire report, originating in the "Summary for Policymakers". The sentence in question claimed that "the balance of evidence suggests that there is a discernible human influence on global climate."

But was this line actually true? Was this really a fair summary—the kind of summary the IPCC purports to rigorously and definitively provide—of the general state of scientific understanding at that particular moment? Well, not according to some of the scientists who contributed to that chapter of the report.

The original version of the chapter—as agreed on and signed off by all 28 contributing authors—expressed considerably more doubt about AGW than was indicated in Santer's summary. It included these passages:

None of the studies cited above has shown clear evidence that we can attribute the observed changes to the specific cause of increases in greenhouse gases.

No study to date has positively attributed all or part (of the climate change observed) to (man-made) causes.

Any claims of positive detection and attribution of significant climate change are likely to remain controversial until uncertainties in the total natural variability of the climate system are reduced.

When will an anthropogenic climate be identified? It is not surprising that the best answer to the question is "We do not know."

Strangely, none of these passages made it to the final draft. They were among 15 deleted by Santer, who also inserted a phrase entirely of his own to the effect that "the body of statistical evidence" now "points to a discernible human influence on climate." In other words, the chapter did not represent the "consensus" position reached by 28 scientists. What it in fact represented was the scientifically unsupported opinion of one man: Benjamin D. Santer.

Among the old school scientists disgusted by this behavior was Prof. Frederick Seitz, formerly president of the National Academy of Sciences. In a *Wall Street Journal* article titled "A Major Deception on Global Warming", he wrote: "I have never witnessed a more disturbing corruption of the peer-review process than the events which led up to this IPCC report."

He concluded:

IPCC reports are often called the "consensus" view. If they lead to carbon taxes and restraints on economic growth, they will have a major and almost certainly destructive impact on the economies of the world. Whatever the intent was of those who made these significant changes, their effect is to deceive policy makers and the public into believing that the scientific evidence shows human activities are causing global warming.

In this he was entirely correct. Subsequently it emerged that orders had come from a letter issued by the U.S. State Department to Sir John Houghton, then head of the IPCC. The letter stated that "chapter authors should be prevailed upon to modify their text in an appropriate manner". In all likelihood, the letter was issued at the behest of one of Vice-President Al Gore's closest political allies, former Colorado Senator Tim Wirth, who was employed in the Clinton Administration as Under Secretary for Global Affairs.

"Appropriate" of course meant "more alarmist". With the UN's Kyoto conference on the horizon (to be held in late 1997), Gore, Wirth and fellow believers in the "True Faith" of AGW were naturally anxious that the U.S. should show itself to be a more willing combatant in the "War on Climate Change". So far, the U.S. had only committed to "non-binding agreements."

Sure enough, the certainty expressed in that one line penned by Santer had the desired effect. At the next international climate meeting—a pre-Kyoto discussion held in Geneva—the U.S. finally declared itself willing to accept a "realistic but binding target" on carbon emissions. The reason for this change in attitude, Senator Wirth admitted, was that "the science is convincing, concern about global warming is real".

Finally, let me tell you a story that shows perhaps better than any other that the entire global warming industry is built not on solid science but on smoke, mirrors and lies. It concerns a day in the summer of 1988 when global warming became a household phrase, thanks to a memorable, widely reported White House committee meeting into the "greenhouse effect and global climate-change" chaired by our old friend Senator Tim Wirth, and attended by his Senate colleague Al Gore.

This was the occasion on which Dr. James Hansen, of NASA's Goddard Institute, memorably and dramatically testified that "the earth is warmer in 1988 than at any time in the history of instrumental measurements." The four hottest years ever recorded all had been in the 1980s, rising to a peak in 1987—and this massive warming could "with a high degree of confidence" be ascribed to the "greenhouse effect", said Hansen at the meeting.

What made this speech so memorable and dramatic was that first, no leading scientist had ever discussed dangerous, man-made global warming with such certainty, and second, as Hansen spoke, he was filmed with sweat visibly pouring from his brow. No wonder *Time* magazine was inspired to write a big story titled "Is the Earth Warming Up?" and the *New York Times* reported: "Global warming has begun, expert tells Senate." No wonder a senior *New York Times* journalist subsequently described the moment as a "major breakthrough".

The true reasons for this didn't emerge until much later, by which time the damage to public debate was irreversible. It turned out that the whole event was elaborate stagecraft, arranged by Wirth and his collaborators to gain maximum public attention. Having found their tame NASA scientist with his out-there message of doom, they rang up the Weather Bureau to inquire which day of the year was likely to be the hottest—and scheduled his testimony for that day.

Then, as Wirth proudly confessed to a U.S. Public Broadcasting System (PBS) documentary in 2007, they rigged the temperature of the room where the hearing took place:

> What we did is that we went in the night before and opened all the windows inside the room...so that the air conditioning wasn't working...so when the hearing occurred there wasn't only bliss which is television cameras in double figures, but it was really hot.

So Al Gore lied. So Tim Wirth rigged a congressional hearing. So James Hansen exaggerated. So Ben Santer rewrote the report. So Sir Crispin Tickell flattered and cajoled Prime Minister Margaret Thatcher into taking a highly influential public line on "climate change" which she would subsequently regret. So an obscure Swedish scientist called Bert Bolin suddenly became renowned when his hitherto disregarded theory came to suit the mood of the times. So what?

So what, indeed. Not a single example I've given in this chapter in any way proves that AGW isn't happening or that it's not a serious problem worthy of our urgent attention. But what these examples do show quite clearly, I hope, is how grievously we have been deceived.

For over twenty years now, scientists, politicians and environmentalists have been telling us, with ever increasing shrillness and urgency, that the science of global warming is settled, the time for inaction is over, and that catastrophe can be averted only by making radical shifts to our lifestyles and economy. Yet what we've seen throughout this chapter is that both the degree of scientific certainty and the unanimity of opinion are almost fictitious.

In this, our trust has been exploited and betrayed. Like the majority of citizens in free democracies we hold—despite the occasional profession of cynicism—a reasonable measure of faith in our public officials. We expect that when they warn us of a major new threat, they have done their research and they are speaking the truth. We don't expect them to make major policy decisions based on the corrupt word of a handful of biased activists. Nor do we expect them to abuse the apparatus of the state to try to quell our entirely justified doubts with a deluge of disinformation and propaganda.

I'm thinking, for example, of the British government's 2009 "Bedtime Stories" advertising campaign, organized by the Department of Energy and Climate Change. This propaganda exercise squandered £6 million of taxpayers' money to scare kids and misinform grown-ups with a pack of lies about "climate change". After nearly a thousand complaints from members of the public, the Advertising Standards Authority (ASA) ruled that at least two of the posters had breached its "legal, decent, honest, truthful" guidelines.

One poster said: "Jack and Jill went up the hill to fetch a pail of water. There was none as extreme weather due to climate change had caused a drought." Beneath was written: "Extreme weather conditions such as flooding, heat waves and storms will become more frequent and intense."

The other said: "Rub a dub dub, three men in a tub — a necessary course of action due to flash flooding caused by climate change." It was captioned: "Climate change is happening. Temperature and sea levels are rising. Extreme weather events such as storms, floods and heat waves will become more frequent and intense. If we carry on at this rate, life in 25 years could be very different."

If the ASA had been better informed and more robust, it also would have censured the most offensive advertisement of the lot—a TV ad campaign in which a father is shown reading a bedtime story to his sweet little girl:

> ....Scientists said it was being caused by too much CO_2 which went into the sky when the grown-ups used energy. They said it was getting dangerous. Its effects were happening faster than they had thought. Some places could even disappear under the sea. And it was the children of the land who'd have to live with the horrible consequences....

The little girl frowns as she looks at the illustrations in the picture book: a scary black-fanged carbon monster ravaging the drowning land; a cartoon cat floating on an upturned table, reaching out in vain to stop a cartoon dog—or is it a rabbit?—from disappearing beneath the grim, grey floodwater.

Beyond the high production values, it's the kind of ad you can imagine generating a warm glow of recognition in, say, Nazi Germany or Czechoslovakia during the Soviet occupation, or Kim Jong Il's North Korea. But in a supposedly liberal Western democracy like Britain, it's surely odd that in the depths of a recession, a government with a massive structural deficit should yet consider it proper to spend £6 million to peddle blatant lies. Of course, it was justified as a way to butter up the public for yet more green taxes and regulations, which an increasing proportion of that public suspects to be unnecessary.

This is the stage we have now reached in the public debate on "climate change." The more skeptical and better informed we ordinary punters become about "Climate Change", the more our governments strive to push, bully, brainwash, coax, seduce and bribe us in the opposite direction. It's as if we're living in parallel universes—the real world you and I inhabit, and the fantasy world occupied by the political class where apparently Climategate never happened, the scientists are still trustworthy, and the consensus is as strong as ever.

Consider, for example, this statement made in Britain's House of Lords in July 2010 by Lord Marland, the Energy and Climate Change Under-Secretary for the Coalition government:

> We must have two million heat pumps by 2020. We must have bioenergy, which will create 100,000 jobs at a value of £116 million. Wind alone should create 130,000 jobs at a value of £36 billion. At a time when the country needs investment, these are heartening numbers.

Heartening, perhaps, to the blissfully ignorant public—but not to anyone familiar with the disastrous experience in Spain, where for every such "green job" created by government subsidy, another 2.2 jobs were lost in the real economy. Heartening, maybe, to those unaware of the shortage of specialist engineers and British-based wind farm manufacturing plants (which means the majority of those jobs and economic activity will be created in countries like China). Heartening to anyone still clueless enough to imagine that "alternative energy" is anything other than an alternative to energy, that wind farms aren't a costly, grotesquely inefficient eco-blight, and that any of the government's draconian reductions in carbon emissions will make the slightest bit of difference to global climate anyway.

Increasingly when you read what is said and done by our

governments in the name of "combating climate change", you have to pinch yourself in disbelief. In school history classes, we are taught to look back with a mixture of pity and superior scorn at the outrageous and destructive self-denial of Stalin's Soviet Union or Mao's China. Yet if one substitutes "carbon emissions reductions" and "green jobs" for "tractor production targets" and "five-year plans", you realize that exactly the same brand of wishful thinking and economically suicidal lunacy has managed to worm its way into 21st Century representative democracy.

Among the many wise individuals who have seen through this political madness is the author of a 2003 book called *Statecraft*. In a passage entitled "Hot Air and Global Warming", the author pours scorn on the "doomsters" who exaggerate sea level rises, demonize CO_2, and ignore the lessons of the Medieval Warm Period that global warming is more a blessing than a curse. She goes on to argue that these distortions in the science are being used to advance an anti-capitalist, left-wing political agenda which threatens the progress and prosperity of mankind.

And this clear-sighted woman's name?

Baroness Thatcher—perhaps better known under her old name Margaret Thatcher: ex-industrial chemist, ex-Prime Minister…and very, very much ex-believer in that frightful gibberish she was gulled into spouting on that regrettable evening at Fishmongers' Hall in the City of London on September 27th, 1988.

CHAPTER 4

IN THE PAY OF BIG KOCH

Carter Roberts, President and CEO, World Wildlife Fund Inc.,
  Total Compensation (2009): $455,147
Frances Beinecke, President, Natural Resources Defense Council,
  Total Compensation (2009): $432,742
Fred Krupp, President, Environmental Defense Fund,
  Total Compensation (2009): $423,359
James Delingpole, Blogger, *Daily Telegraph*,
  Total Compensation (2010): less than $24,000

One of my favorite late afternoon pastimes—before the witching hour of 6pm and the moment arrives for my customary *foie gras* on toasted Poilane bread served with Chateau d'Yquem and poached gull's or leatherback turtle's eggs (depending on the season)—is to lie face down on my bespoke Philippe Starck massage table, while my Crimean masseuse Ivana pours hot oil onto my back and gives me a really good pummeling, to the soothing sounds of my personal string quartet in the billiard room of my private wing of the modest £50 million Regency townhouse I own on the edge of Regent's Park. It's a tough life but such are the sacrifices a fellow has to make when he is funded by Big Oil.

I wish.

The more prosaic truth about Climategate is that it has been the biggest financial disaster of my career. Instead of being able to write on any number of different subjects for diverse newspapers, as I used to in my money-earning days, I now spend huge chunks of my time trawling round the internet, boning up on science papers, keeping up with the latest climate research and finding new material for my *Telegraph* blog.

Yes it's nice having a popular blog, I suppose. But unfortunately blogs don't pay. Ask Jo Nova, ask Richard North, ask Bishop Hill, ask Steve McIntyre, ask Anthony Watts, ask Donna Laframboise. Most of them can barely raise enough money to pay for their running costs, let alone make a modest living out of it. There may be all sorts of reasons why we're involved in climate skepticism—love, duty, fun, the challenge, masochism—but the money most definitely isn't one of them.

If you want to make a living, then you should definitely choose to be a Warmist rather than a skeptic. In Warmism, there are grants, salaries and jobs galore. In skepticism, even now that the tide of opinion is beginning to turn, there is little but the modest satisfaction of knowing you are right.

Before Climategate I wrote articles about cooking, men's fashion, books, TV, rock music, drugs, politics, cars, motorbikes, popular culture. I did film reviews, interviews and restaurant criticism. I went down coal mines, I dived with great white sharks, I got to hang with Jimmy Page and Robert Plant at the Sunset Marquee in Hollywood. I travelled to Tirana, to the Skeleton Coast, from the souks of Essaouira to the brothels of Accra. I wrote darkly funny autobiographical books like *Thinly Disguised Autobiography* and darkly funny political books like *How to Be Right* and darkly funny war books like *Coward On the Beach*. I was nobody's bitch. I was free. I wrote about whatever I wanted to write about because that was the kind of writer I was. Mister Generalist. Mister Surprising. Mister Hey-I-Wonder-What-He's-Going-To-Turn-His-Hand-To-This-Week?

Not any more though. Today, tomorrow, next week, next month and—oh God I hope not but quite possibly—next year, I am, and will be, Mister Climate Change Skeptic. If you're a skeptic yourself, I'm one of those bloggers you rely on to give you the latest skeptic news. And if you're not a skeptic, I'm one of those bloggers you love to hate. Either way, and there's no getting out of it, Global Warming is my schtick.

Normally in journalism acquiring a specialty is helpful and financially rewarding. If you're a movie buff, you get to go to all the advance screenings, and you land the reviews, the interviews, the on-location reports and the Hollywood junkets; in everything from theatre and music to fashion and sport, much the same rules apply. Once you've established yourself as an expert, your knowledge base and contacts book and reputation earn you a string of lucrative commissions.

With climate skepticism, unfortunately, these rules don't apply. You can be as fluent in sunspots and negative feedbacks and isostatic rebounds as a motoring specialist is on torque, handling and pistons, but it will make sod-all difference to your ability to get paid commissions.

The reason is that in Britain—and the same rules apply from Australia to the U.S.—almost all the coverage given to AGW in the mainstream media (MSM) is written from a Warmist perspective. This is true even of my own blog-hosting newspaper, the *Daily Telegraph*. It employs an Environment Editor and an Environment Correspondent, both of whom (unlike me) are on full salaries; both of whom are committed Warmists; both of whom get to publish stories on the subject in print (as opposed to a mere blog) six days a week.

Even if I had a really juicy climate story, there are very few publications that would pay me for it. They are limited to the *Daily Mail* and the *Mail On Sunday*, though they don't run skeptical stuff that often and competition when they do is stiff, the *Express* and the *Sunday Express*, and the *Spectator*. On top of that, you might be able to earn £75 a throw here and there, by appearing on the odd BBC TV or radio show as their token evil climate "denier". And on top of that, if you're really lucky you might get invited to speak at the Heartland Institute's Climate Skeptics conference. None of this will turn you into the next Bill Gates.

Can you see now, from a journalist's perspective, why climate change skepticism would be the last route you'd want to take if you really were in it for the money? The ratio of time-spent-on-research to number-of-paid-articles-published is about as lousy as it gets. It's a journalist's nightmare. It's a journalist's bank manager's nightmare. Above all—just ask my wife—it's a journalist's spouse's nightmare.

Mind you, there's always Big Oil, isn't there? Big Oil, which according to environmental activist George Monbiot is largely responsible for funding the lies and disinformation fomented by the foolish media. In one of his *Guardian* articles, he sought to prove his point with four "shocking" examples:

1. In 1991 a group of fossil fuel companies set up a group called Information Company for the Environment (ICE) which spent $510,000 on a campaign designed to sow doubt in the minds of the vulnerable about AGW. Its target groups were "Older, less educated males" and "younger, lower income women." (!)
2. Climate skeptic Dr. Pat Michaels, of the Cato Institute, was once paid $100,000 by the Intermountain Rural Electric Association. (!!)
3. The Heartland Institute—which received grants from ExxonMobil totaling $676,000 over a period of more than a decade—once published a list of "500 Scientists Whose Research Contradicts Man-Made Global Warming Scares". And 45 of them got upset that they'd been included on the list. (!!!)
4. The Competitive Enterprise Institute, which received a little more than $2,000,000 from ExxonMobil between 1998–2005, was shown (in a memo leaked in 2004 to *Harpers* magazine) to have collaborated with the Bush administration to discredit a report on climate change by the Environmental Protection Agency. (!!!!)

Those "!!!!" I inserted were ironic, by the way. This wouldn't be the first time I've been struck by the Grand-Canyon-sized gulf between the momentousness of Monbiot's apparent "scandal" and the ho-hum banality of what he actually reveals. For its bizarre mix of absurdity and hypocrisy, that particular column really is one of the Great Moonbat's more collectable pieces of lunacy. It's the eco equivalent of Mahmoud Ahmadinejad lecturing the West on human rights abuses, moments after he's had another 13-year old schoolgirl hanged from a crane for "adultery".

Why? Well, apart from the fairly obvious point that, of course, big industry is going to fund right-wing think tanks to push an agenda that favors industry over left-leaning, anti-competitive, regulatory bodies like the Environmental Protection Agency, let us do the math.

Let's add up all those shocking figures: They come to a grand total of $3,286,000.

Now let's give Monbiot the benefit of the doubt and assume these aren't the only occasions when the fossil fuel industry/Big Oil/sinister vested interests have bankrolled the cause of skepticism. If we are to believe the UK campaigning organization Campaign Against Climate Change (Honorary president: one G. Monbiot), the figure may well be at least twenty times higher.

"An insight into how sceptics work—follow the funding", it urges on its website. It says: "It has recently been revealed that Koch Industries, a little-known, privately owned U.S. oil company, paid nearly US$50 million to climate denial groups and individuals between 1997 and 2008. In a similar period ExxonMobil paid out around $17 to $23 million."

Actually when you examine this a bit more closely—the figures come from Greenpeace—you notice that the sums went towards funding conservative think tanks generally (Mercatus Center; Americans for Prosperity Foundation; the Heritage Foundation; Cato Institute) rather than the cause of Evil Climate Change Denialism™ specifically. But let's be generous and let that detail pass. In fact, let's be uber-generous, and more than double that $73 million total. Let's say that's since 1997, Big Oil, Big Koch, Big Coal and their Satanic Industrial Confreres have splurged a total of $200 million to

IN THE PAY OF BIG KOCH

fund Evil Climate Change Denialism™. Does that sound sufficiently scary? It jolly well should do. Not even Michael Mann's friends at RealClimate have managed to drum up a figure that high.

So how are we Skeptics going to answer it, this damning charge that is leveled against us with such wearisome frequency by our Warmist critics that they evidently imagine it's an argument-clincher? Well, I suppose the first line of defense would be to point out that they are guilty of what philosopher Jamie Whyte calls the "Motive Fallacy". This is the demonstrably false notion that if you have some particular interest (financial or otherwise) in holding an opinion this must automatically render it untrue.

Whyte offers a simple example in his book *Bad Thoughts: A Guide to Clear Thinking*: "A man may stand to gain a great deal of peace and quiet from telling his wife that he loves her. But he may really love her nevertheless." Equally, the fact that I am heavily in the pay of Big Koch—I'm not really: this is just a fantasy of mine, and I like saying "Big Koch" even though the joke isn't as funny as it could be because the Koch brothers' surname is in fact pronounced "Coke"— does not necessarily mean my argument is corrupt.

What we see being employed here, in fact, is a classic technique beloved by left-liberals, greenies and greenie liberal-lefties alike. It's known as "Closing down the argument." Rather than engage their opponents in a debate they probably cannot win, they instead duck the issue by impugning their opponent's motives. The technique says: "This right-wing person in the pay of Big Oil is so unspeakably vile that his despicable views cannot be taken seriously".

You find it in most of areas of political debate. Worried about immigration? You're a racist. Want your kids to get a good education? You're an elitist. Suspect all the fuss about AGW might be a little overdone? You're just the kind of scummy Nazi-sympathizing revisionist who thinks Hitler didn't murder six million Jews...

The term "denier", it goes without saying, was designed explicitly to provoke comparisons with Holocaust Denial. Shortly after

Climategate, I took part in a debate with George Monbiot. When I put this point to him he—funnily enough—*denied* he was making any such connection. So I gently reminded him of a *Guardian* article he'd written in 2006: "Almost everywhere, climate change denial now looks as stupid and unacceptable as Holocaust denial."

Now this might seem to be a get-at-George-Monbiot chapter, which was never my intention. He only figures so prominently here because, as one of the green movement's favorite authors, columnists and spokesmen, he has become its perfect synecdoche. As Monbiot thinks, speaks and opines, so do greenies across the universe. This view of the AGW debate—as being essentially a battle in which self-less, honest, caring, science-respecting greenies are pitted against a network of corrupt, irresponsible skeptics in the pay of the Carbon Industry—is not some maverick theory dreamt up by Monbiot on a particularly crazy day to get more hits for his blog. It's how most greens really do see it: a terrible THEM vs. US conspiracy by Big Business to hide the truth and destroy the world.

Here, for example, is Al Gore pushing this line in *An Inconvenient Truth*:

> The misconception that there is a serious disagreement among scientists about global warming is actually an illusion that has been deliberately fostered by a relatively small but extremely well-funded cadre of special interests, including ExxonMobil and a few other oil, coal, and utilities companies. These companies want to prevent any new policies that would interfere with their current business plans...
>
> One of the internal memos prepared by this group to guide the employees they hired to run their disinformation campaign was discovered by the Pulitzer Prize-winning reporter Ross Gelbspan. Here was the group's stated objective: to "reposition global warming as theory, rather than fact".

You see this same strain of paranoia—and I will show you why it *is* paranoia—running through the Climategate emails. Here is one (October 2003) from our friend Michael Mann to Robert Matthews, science correspondent of the UK *Sunday Telegraph*. Matthews has politely written to ask Mann whether he has any response to the critics who have questioned his methodology on a paper about the Medieval Warm Period. Mann replies:

> These comments have not been made by scientists in the peer-reviewed literature, but rather, on a website that, according to published accounts, is run by individuals sponsored by Exxon Mobile [sic] corporation, hardly an objective source of information.

It's as if somehow this very fact absolves him of all responsibility to defend his claims.

You might suppose that this is just a convenient ruse, intended only for public consumption. But no, even when the Warmists are writing to one another rather than to journalists, it seems they view themselves as maverick outsiders engaged in a thankless and heroic struggle against a vastly more powerful, better-funded political and industrial Establishment.

Or, as Michael Mann hilariously put it in February 2010 when complaining about the "very well-honed, well-funded organized machine" he was up against:

"It's literally like a marine in battle against a cub scout when it comes to the scientists defending themselves...." (What? Really *literally*, Mike?) "We're not PR experts like they are, we're not lawyers and lobbyists like they are. We're scientists, trained to do science."

To understand the absurdity of such "poor little me" laments, let us continue doing that math. We've already established a generous ballpark figure for the amount of money Big Carbon has spent encouraging AGW skepticism: call it $20 million a year over a ten-year period. Sounds like a lot, doesn't it? At least it does until you realize how much money goes to the other side of the debate.

Consider, for example, this job advertisement from April 2010 from the charity Oxfam:

Senior Press Officer—Climate Change
Date posted: 15/04/10
Closing date: 25/04/10
Employer: Oxfam
Salary: £33,700-£41,710
Location: Oxford
Campaigning for action on climate change is Oxfam's key priority. It is already happening and it is the world's poorest that are already feeling its effects, even though they are often the least responsible. By joining our press office you will lead the media work in publicising actions to cut emissions, plus the need for money to help people adapt to the impact of climate change.

Note that as far as this particular employer is concerned, the debate on AGW is over. The candidate's job, as the ad makes quite explicit, will be to fight in the propaganda war demanding greater political action on climate change.

That's just *one* AGW-promoting job (among many, I think we can safely assume, given that Oxfam is a large organization and that "campaigning for action on climate change" is its stated "key priority") at just one UK-based organization. Now think of all the thousands of similar organizations out there throughout the world promoting a similar message, each with its own paid-up team of activists, policy wonks, directors, press officers and PR managers singing from the same AGW hymn sheet. When you realize that of these, the World Wide Fund for Nature had an annual income of more than $640 million in 2010—not a penny of which, we can be fairly sure, goes on encouraging climate change skepticism—you'll begin to appreciate that "Big Eco" is a rather more significant player in the AGW propaganda game than anything Big Carbon can muster.

Here are a few more examples of the vast network of financial support backing the AGW industry:

* £1.1 million—spent by British Council on "Challenge Europe", a three-year project which "aspires to make a definite and lasting impact on the climate change debate, and is ambitious in its aim to accelerate change to a low carbon future".
* £2.5 million—spent by British Council on International Climate Champions program which "engages young people around the world as communicators who will help to influence and educate their peers and the general public on the urgency of climate change".
* £6 million—spent by British government on "hard-hitting" Bedtime Stories ad to target climate skeptics, which claims unequivocally that Man is causing global warming and endangering life on earth (October 2009).
* £13.7 million—received in grants since 1990 by Phil Jones, director of the Climatic Research Unit at University of East Anglia.
* A$ 13.9 million—spent by Australian government on its 2009 "Think Climate Think Change" ad campaign.
* US$70 million—pledged by Rockefeller Foundation for five-year Initiative on Climate Change Resilience to help cities and towns prepare for potentially damaging effects of global climate change (August 2007).
* $100 million—donated by ExxonMobil (yes *that* ExxonMobil) to Stanford University's Global Climate and Energy Project.
* £243 million—paid by UK government since 1990 to fund Met Office's "climate prediction" program.
* £650 million—paid by European Union for "Specific programme of research and technological development in the field of environment and climate" (1994–1998).
* $4 billion—allocated in 2011 U.S. Federal budget for climate research.

* $126 billion—World Bank estimate of carbon trading industry turnover in 2008.

And so on.

So vast and labyrinthine is the funding mechanism behind the AGW industry, we shall probably never know exactly how much has been squandered on it. British government spending, for example, is allocated among a number of different departments, including its Department for Environment, Food and Rural Affairs and its Department of Energy and Climate Change, as well as to agencies and quangos (quasi-NGOs) such as the Carbon Trust.

The best estimate so far comes from Australian blogger Jo Nova, who in March 2010 calculated that U.S. government spending on climate research and technology since 1989 had amounted to $79 billion. Sure, she conceded, some of this funding paid for things like "satellites and studies." But as she noted, it also bought "a band-wagon of support, a repetitive rain of press releases, and includes PR departments of institutions like NOAA, NASA, the Climate Change Science Program and the Climate Change Technology Program." It is, she observed, about 3,500 times as much as anything offered to skeptics. And she's just talking about U.S. government funding. Her figures don't include spending by other western governments and private industry, and are not adjusted for inflation—so the total spending is likely to be considerably higher.

At the EU Referendum blog, Dr. Richard North did some of his own calculations. He calculated the amount spent on climate funding since 1989 by the European Union at well over $100 billion. In terms of equivalent spending, he says, this means that AGW has proved five times more costly than the most expensive project in history—the Manhattan Project to build the atomic bomb. But at the end of the Manhattan Project, having spent all those bucks, they did at least get a couple of bangs.

So what conclusions are we to draw from all this?

For me, almost as shocking as the outrageous sums of money (much of it extorted from you and me via the tax system) being hosed down the drain in the name of AGW is the Warmists' sheer effrontery. Talk about spotting the speck in your brother's eye but not the beam in your own! Surely, you would have thought, after this embarrassing discrepancy was revealed publicly, they would have had the decency to blush, study their footwear, change the subject and never mention it again.

But no. Even now, the "funded by Big Oil" accusation remains one of the key weapons in the Warmists' armory, shamelessly trotted out on every conceivable occasion to "prove" the rightness of their cause. Are they dim-witted? Desperate? Too dumb to notice the difference between a few million and several billion?

Or could it perhaps be that the policy is entirely deliberate—that they know exactly what they're doing and that they have made a ruthless and cynical calculation?

Before I answer, let me ask you a question: How stupid do you think you are?

I would hope you feel quite affronted by my impertinence. You're clever and inquisitive enough to have read this far in the book, for goodness' sake, and it's not always an easy read—not with all these indigestible facts and figures the author keeps chucking in, and words like "synecdoche", not to mention all the digressions and random asides he seems to find so amusing. How clever do I want you to be? Einstein?

OK: so we've established you're not stupid. Now let me ask you to imagine yourself brainstorming two concepts: the first is the WWF. And the second is ExxonMobil. What kind of images come to mind?

Don't worry, it's not a trick question. I don't expect you to conjure up a giant vampire bat with WWF written on its wings, sucking the blood from the neck of a small child labeled "Global Prosperity." Nor do I expect you to sum up ExxonMobil with lush, rolling pastures abundant with spring flowers, leaping lambs and flopsy bunnies.

No, the sort of thing I expect you to imagine is the same thing I would. With the WWF, it would be the panda motif, which has been part of my consciousness since early childhood. Maybe images of stranded lemurs being rescued from flooded rainforests, or the world viewed from outer space. With ExxonMobil, on the other hand, the images would be mostly bad. Even that double "X" in the middle of the name has something evil about it. And you, like me, might conjure up images of seabirds and sea otters coated in thick, gunky oil, splurged in Prince William Sound in the Exxon Valdez disaster. And heartless executives touring derricks in hard hats and surveying the devastated landscape and cackling "Mwah ha hahaha!"

My point here is that however independent-minded and politically acute we may think we are, we're all prey to certain cultural attitudes so deeply ingrained that we're probably not even aware of them. One of these is the popular notion that funding from Big Business (Big Oil, Big Carbon, Big Koch…) is tainted, compromised and almost inevitably corrupting, while funding from a nature charity, or even from a government agency with a nice-sounding concept like "Environmental Protection" in its title must be well over 3,500 times nicer.

Why? Well because charities are nice—aren't they? They're run by volunteers. They care. Their motives are pure. *Yeah right.* Let's have a look at one of them more closely. How about Greenpeace, whose name bespeaks verdancy and tranquility and caring environmentalism? Surely its stirring propaganda videos of plucky young men and women being hosed down by evil, blood-stained Japanese whale fishermen cannot fail to awaken the Gaia-worshipper within us all?

Well, almost all. I have to say, those videos leave me cold. I've seen a fair few of them because quite often between sets on the main stage at Glastonbury Festival, Britain's annual answer to Woodstock. They are broadcast on a loop on the big screens either side of the speakers. You can almost hear the people in the crowd either side of you, mentally urging the protestors on: "Way to go, Greenpeace!

Stick it to those whalers! Block those sewage outlet pipes into the sea! Rappel down that chimney and show those polluting power stations just how horrid they are!" That's what happens when you're young and you're stoned and direct action in the name of the environment seems a desirable, sexy thing.

But not me. I'm the one grinding his teeth, and hissing to his wife: "That white stuff coming out of that cooling tower isn't pollution, for God's sake. It's steam! It's bloody water vapor! So why are they pretending it's pollution!" and "What? They expect us to be grateful, do they? They think, what, it's a good thing that the operation of the power station was shut for a day, making our electricity even more bloody expensive than it was before they started adding on all those carbon taxes?" And my wife's the one hissing back: "Shh! Someone might hear you."

Look, I'm not saying that everything Greenpeace does is evil. (I too have a soft spot for whales.) What I am saying is that it most definitely isn't the force for unmitigated good you might infer from its public image and its "holier than thou" press releases. Morally speaking, I'd put Greenpeace on a rough par with ExxonMobil. Economically speaking, way below it. Certainly, in terms of the way it operates and the way it behaves, there's scarcely a cigarette paper's difference between the sanctimonious prigs of "Big Eco" and the card-carrying Satan-worshippers at "Big Oil".

In fact, their aims are much the same. A charity, like big business, depends on growth for its success. How does it achieve this? By boosting its public donations. How does it get more donations? By raising its profile. How does it raise its profile? By what Tony Blair used to call "eye-catching initiatives"—publicity stunts—which help generate in its target audience a constant, and preferably ever-heightening, sense of imminent crisis.

Clearly, this sense of imminent crisis is key for a charity like Greenpeace. You're not going to give a dime to Greenpeace's Project Thin Ice to save the polar bear if you think the species is good for

WATERMELONS: THE GREEN MOVEMENT'S TRUE COLORS

another 10,000 years. You'll only hand over the cash if Greenpeace takes a more persuasive approach, along the lines of: "This is worse than we thought. It seems our very latest models are telling us that polar bears are going to be entirely wiped out by next summer at the latest. Unless you hand over that buck—in which case they'll all be okay, especially the cute baby ones that slide down that snow bank like on BBC's Planet Earth. Up to you, mate."

So that's what Greenpeace does—and so do all its rival green pressure groups. Part of their job is saying what their customers want to hear. Kind of like the sales assistant in the expensive boutique who is asked by the woman trying on a new pair of jeans "Does my bum look big in these?", they are required by the needs of their business to be somewhat economical with the truth.

Greenpeace has plenty of form in this regard. In 1995, for example, it launched a noisy, highly successful campaign against Shell's plans to dispose of a disused oil rig—Brent Spar—by sinking it in the mid-Atlantic. As the UK's Natural Environmental Research Council subsequently confirmed, this was by far the most eco-friendly option and, as shipwrecks do, would have provided a fine habitat for all manner of marine life.

Unfortunately "Environmental group applauds oil company's commonsense eco-solution" doesn't make a very good headline. Europe-wide boycotts of all Shell petrol stations, on the other hand, do—so that's what Greenpeace did. It subsequently apologized for the inaccuracy of some of its claims but by then, the damage was done. Greenpeace got its publicity, but at the expense not only of Shell's blameless shareholders but also of the environment Greenpeace is supposedly committed to saving.

You and I might call this bare-faced lying. But Greenpeace is a master of PR tactics, employing a more nuanced explanation on this as on other occasions. In July 2009, it was caught out on a press release claiming that ice was going to vanish from the Arctic as early as 2030. When BBC interviewer Stephen Sackur (against all standard

BBC conventions that Warmists are to be given an easy ride) accused then-director Gerd Leipold of talking nonsense, Leipold defended his position thus: "We as a pressure group have to emotionalise issues and we're not ashamed of emotionalising issues."

(Brilliant. Must try that one at home some time. "No darling, I wasn't *lying* when I told you the only reason I made mad passionate love to that blonde 20-year old fan at the literary festival was because she had a gun and said that if I didn't do exactly as she told me she would kill a puppy. I was just *emotionalizing the issue*.")

But it wasn't always this way. At least not if we're to believe Patrick Moore, the Canadian environmentalist who co-founded Greenpeace in 1971—but quit 15 years later, in disgust at the aggressively politicized direction taken by his beloved organization.

He described his decision in *The Wall Street Journal*:

> At first, many of the causes we championed, such as opposition to nuclear testing and protection of whales, stemmed from our scientific knowledge of nuclear physics and marine biology. But after six years as one of five directors of Greenpeace International, I observed that none of my fellow directors had any formal science education. They were either political activists or environmental entrepreneurs. Ultimately, a trend toward abandoning scientific objectivity in favor of political agendas forced me to leave Greenpeace in 1986.

The clincher was when his colleagues decided that Greenpeace's policy would be to ban chlorine. "How can you ban a naturally occurring element?" Moore wanted to know. An element, he added, which when added to water systems in tiny quantities was responsible for the biggest advance in the history of public health, virtually eradicating cholera.

What Moore witnessed was the beginning of a process which would accelerate in 1989 after the fall of the Berlin Wall: the supplanting in the Green movement of the old guard of ageing hippies with a new breed of zealots less interested in saving Planet Earth than in destroying the capitalist system. These are the "Watermelons" of this book's title—green on the outside, red on the inside. You can detect their handiwork in campaign leaflets like the one sitting on my desk from Friends of the Earth.

On the front it says: "Profit before planet. Who is making deals with your government?" Inside, it says:

> Oil companies. Supermarkets. Petro-chemical firms. Airlines.
>
> Globally they spend millions of pounds undermining environmental policy.
>
> Big businesses spend serious money on advertising and PR telling us that they are doing their bit for the environment. But away from the public eye they're spending many millions holding back environmental progress.
>
> Airlines are spending millions to persuade governments to expand airports. Petro-chemical companies are blocking environmentally friendly measures because of the cost to them. Oil companies are funding "independent think tanks", designed to undermine serious climate change research. And they are all doing it for one thing. Profit.

The reason I keep this leaflet on my desk is because it does my work for me. If I'd tried writing some spoof advertising copy myself to show just how brazenly, unapologetically left-wing the green movement now is, I'm sure I couldn't have produced anything better. I love the way it brandishes words like "oil companies" and "airlines" in the way a hellfire preacher might invoke "Beelzebub" and "Anti-Christ". I love the danger quotes around "independent think tanks", like some massive nudge in the ribs designed to indicate "But *we* the enlightened ones know they're *anything but independent*, don't we, readers?" I love its insistence, against all evidence, that in the eco-propaganda wars green organizations like Friends of the Earth are plucky little Davids, doing their best against the Goliaths of Big

Business. I love the way that final word "Profit" is deployed at the end, as if it were the *ne plus ultra* of unmitigated evil.

What I love above all, though, is the way the leaflet doesn't even *try* to pretend that it's about anything so fluffy and vague and nice as "Saving the planet." The enemy, it makes palpably clear, is capitalism. And it assumes that the target audience thinks in exactly the same way. Why else would it say such things on a leaflet designed to enlist donations, if it wasn't what their "people" wanted to hear?

Now the temptation here is to say: "Yeah? And?" "Environmental group turns out to be unrepentantly left-wing" is an intuition right up there with "Pope found worshipping regularly at St. Peter's Basilica". I understand this temptation. These groups, by their very nature, will tend to appeal especially to the young, sensitive and idealistic. These individuals are likely to be at a stage of their lives where, before they've had to deal with children, mortgages or significant tax bills, they still imagine that capitalism is the problem, not the solution.

And perhaps this wouldn't matter so much if these green groups were still the humble, small-scale, grassroots organizations they were in their early days. The problem is that in the intervening years, these cute, well-meaning, panda-hugging, three-men-and-a-dog outfits have mutated into global corporate behemoths, with budgets the size of multinational companies. They now wield the kind of power and influence you'd normally associate with medium-to-large nation states.

Probably the most ambitious is the WWF which, in early 2010, was exposed by Christopher Booker and Richard North as being part of an extraordinary scam whereby it planned to snaffle the lion's share of $60 *billion* worth of carbon credits. Already, with an annual funding of at least £640 million, the WWF is one of the world's richest green groups. This scheme—and it still may yet come off—would earn more money for the WWF than the annual GDP of half of the world's countries. Booker explains:

In 2002, after lengthy negotiations with WWF and other NGOs, the Brazilian government set up its Amazon Region Protected Areas (ARPA) project, supported by nearly $80 million of funding. Of this, $18 million was given to the WWF by the U.S.'s Gordon and Betty Moore Foundation, $18 million to its Brazilian NGO partner by the Brazilian government, plus $30 million from the World Bank...

The aim was that the NGOs, led by the WWF, should administer chunks of the Brazilian rainforest to ensure either that they were left alone or managed "sustainably". Added to them, as the largest area of all, was 31,000 square miles on Brazil's all but inaccessible northern frontier; half designated as the Tumucumaque National Park, the world's largest nature reserve, the other half to be left largely untouched but allowing for sustainable development. This is remote from any part of the Amazonian forest likely to be damaged by loggers, mining or agriculture...

In 2008, funded by $7 million from the Moore Foundation and working in partnership with the WWF on the Tumucumaque project, Woods Hole [Research Center] came up with the formula required: a way of valuing all that carbon stored in Brazil's protected rainforests, so that it could be traded under the [UN's Clean Development Mechanism]. The CO_2 to be "saved" by the ARPA programme, it calculated, amounted to 5.1 billion tons. Based on the [UN Framework Convention on Climate Change] valuation of CO_2 at $12.50 per ton, this valued the trees in Brazil's protected areas at over $60 billion...

Unfortunately (for the WWF), the scheme foundered. Partly this was a result of the chaos at the 2009 Copenhagen climate summit. Partly it was as a result of President Obama's failure—thank goodness—to force through the "Cap and Trade" scheme, which would have helped to establish a global market in CO_2. The fact that the WWF even attempted this scheme gives you some idea of the scale on which ostensibly innocuous NGOs are now capable of operating.

Of course, if you sympathize with the political objectives of these

NGOs, you might consider this kind of clandestine attempted power grab no bad thing. But if you don't, then you'll surely agree that this is a worrying case of power without responsibility and, indirectly, taxation without representation. You didn't vote for Greenpeace, or the WWF, or Friends of the Earth, or the Sierra Club or the Australian Conservation Club. They never consulted you about how the world should be run or how your money should be spent or how much freedom you should be allowed to have. Yet they are making these decisions for you all the same.

You see this cropping up in the Climategate files, in a July 1999 email from the WWF's Adam Markham to the University of East Anglia climate scientist Mike Hulme, regarding a paper that Hulme had written about climate change in Australasia:

> Hi Mike,
> I'm sure you will get some comments direct from Mike Rae in WWF Australia, but I wanted to pass on the gist of what they've said to me so far. They are worried that this may present a slightly more conservative approach to the risks than they are hearing from [Hulme's counterparts in Australia]. In particular, they would like to see the section on variability and extreme events beefed up if possible....

This gives you an idea of how presumptuous a modern environmental campaigner can be. Here is a political activist from the WWF behaving as if he is entirely comfortable with the notion of telling a research scientist at a government-funded climate research laboratory how to do his job, as if scientific data were the stuff of advertising.

More egregious still is the influence green NGOs have been allowed over the supposedly authoritative, "neutral" IPCC. Canadian blogger Donna Laframboise—of No Frakking Consensus—subjected the IPCC's Fourth Assessment Report to a crowd-sourcing audit. She found that of the 18,531 sources cited, at least 5,587 (30 percent) were not peer-reviewed. Of these non-peer-reviewed references, dozens came not from scientists but from "grey literature"—eco-propaganda, essentially—produced by the activists at Greenpeace, WWF, et al. For example, the sole source for the IPCC's claim that climate change is linked to coral reef degradation turned out to be a Greenpeace report entitled "Pacific in Peril".

Nor were the 2,500 "expert reviewers" boasted by the IPCC quite as neutral as they might have been. Among those who had an input to just one portion—Working Group III of the Fourth Assessment Report—were "three Greenpeace employees, two Friends of the Earth representatives, two Climate Action Network reps, and a person each from activist organizations WWF International, Environmental Defense and the David Suzuki Foundation."

Can anyone spot the contradiction here? We live in a world where the mainstream media takes its environmental stories directly from the press releases of green organizations. The UN and the EU conduct their environment programs in close association with those green organizations. Governments live in terror of offending environmental groups and tailor their policies accordingly. The IPCC report, which supposedly represents the gold standard of scientific knowledge on climate change, is in fact heavily in debt to the political spin of those groups. Yet at the same time, we are daily asked to swallow the line that these massively powerful eco-thugs represent some kind of lovable, tragically malnourished underdog, whose sweet and good intentions are continuously thwarted by the wicked, Big-Oil-funded bullies of the heartless establishment.

This is exactly the kind of large-scale popular delusion that the French psychologist Gustave Le Bon analysed so brilliantly in his landmark book *The Crowd*. It was published as early as 1895, though you'd never guess it, for its insights feel so modern and relevant. That's probably because it has gone on to influence everyone from Freud, Hitler and Mussolini using methods still employed by politicians and spin-doctors to this day. One is to keep your message simple: crowds, argues Le Bon, are only as clever as the thickest person within them. Another—for much the same reason—is to repeat that message over and over again. By these means do demagogues create the "contagion" which occurs when an unstoppable idea holds a culture in its grip and when it takes a brave man indeed to try fighting against the current. Le Bon wrote:

> When an affirmation has been sufficiently repeated and there is unanimity in this repetition … what is called a current of opinion is formed and the powerful mechanism of contagion intervenes. Ideas, sentiments, emotions, and beliefs possess in crowds a contagious power as intense of that of microbes.

Every idea has its day. In the 1930s, it was the fascistic impulse that swept the world from Hitler's brownshirts, Mussolini's and Oswald Mosley's black shirts and—as Jonah Goldberg has convincingly argued—travelled even as far as FDR's United States. In the 1780s it was the Revolutionary fervour of the Sans Culottes. In pre-Millennial Europe it was the imminent advent of the End Times. In the 1950s and 1960s it was nuclear annihilation. In the 1970s, it was the coming Ice Age. Today, it's the widespread notion that Anthropogenic Global Warming is the greatest threat mankind has ever faced and that unless we act NOW we're all going to fry.

If you wanted to, you could allow yourself to get very, very depressed by these outbreaks of mass stupidity—and about the foolishness, credulousness and suggestibility apparently hardwired into a worryingly high percentage of our species. Personally, I don't. This isn't because I'm a terribly "up" guy—in fact I am as prone to melancholia and despair as the next miserable depressive sod—but since entering the lists in the cause of climate realism, I've been struck by something rather uplifting and deeply encouraging: the truth always wins in the end.

Let me cite, by way of illustration, the work of a man from Phoenix,

Arizona, named Russell Cook, who describes himself as "a complete nobody". One day Cook set himself the task of tracing the "funded by Big Oil" story to its source—and he discovered some interesting facts. One was that Ross Gelbspan, "Pulitzer prize-winning reporter" (as he was described by Al Gore and several others) has never won a Pulitzer Prize. Another was that the blanket smear about the alleged corruption of science under the direction of the fossil fuel industry can be traced to just one line of one memo, produced as part of a public relations campaign by the coal industry in the early 1990s with the aim of showing—not unreasonably, you might think—that the debate on AGW was anything but settled.

On this wafer-thin foundation, the environmental movement has managed to construct almost its entire propaganda edifice.

What does this tale prove? On its own, very little. Cook—a graphic artist, not a scientist or a reporter—is just another ordinary citizen who has harnessed the powers of the internet to find information which, a decade or two ago, might well have remained buried. The "funded by Big Oil" meme would have spread through endless repetition. And no one would have been in a position to question it.

But now they can. Anyone can. Out there right now are hundreds if not thousands of Russell Cooks tapping away on their keyboards, following hunches, satisfying their idle curiosity, not taking "no" for an answer, and generally living up to the motto of the (now sadly discredited: see next chapter) Royal Society "*Nullius in Verba.*" Take no one's word for it.

And by taking no one's word for it, they are making some extraordinary breakthroughs. With the internet, the cause of openness and liberty has made its greatest technological leap since Gutenberg invented the printing press. For similar reasons, too. Before printing made books cheaper and more widespread, information could be controlled and guarded by a self-serving, self-perpetuating power elite. Before the internet made it possible for any quantity of data to be disseminated across the world at almost zero expense, it would have been all too easy for the compromised scientists at the UEA and Penn State to keep their skullduggery concealed behind the walls of academia. Without the internet, Climategate could never have happened.

Thanks to the World Wide Web, the citadels of arbitrary and unearned authority are crumbling. No longer is a PhD or a history that goes back 350 years or a Nobel Prize sufficient proof, on its own, against the questing probes of the world's seekers of truth. If James Hansen or the Royal Society or the IPCC or, for that matter, the BBC or CNBC want their claims to be believed, it isn't enough for them to hide behind the tired old bluster of "Don't you know who I am?" From now on, they must convince with hard evidence and show their workings.

This is how ultimately, I believe, the climate wars will be won. Not suddenly and dramatically—Climategate was a rare exception—but slowly through the relentless drip, drip, drip of honest, diligent, liberty-loving citizens doing their bit for the greater cause of openness and truth.

I hope that doesn't sound too sanctimonious. There was a time, I admit, when it might have struck me as such. When Tony Blair followed America's example and in 2000 introduced Britain's first Freedom of Information Act, I remember thinking that it would only lead to more taxpayer expense as government time was wasted dealing with frivolous queries by professional troublemakers. I just couldn't see the point.

But that was when I still retained a vestige of faith in what—for want of a better word, I suppose—I must call "the Establishment". By this I mean not just the various agencies of government, but also institutions like the BBC, the universities, the learned bodies such as the Royal Society and the National Academy of Sciences, and so on. Of course, even then I recognized that these institutions had their flaws. But I was prepared to give them the benefit of the doubt in that casually trusting way most of us do with authority figures and authority bodies. We believe in them because they are The Authorities.

Climategate killed all that. And almost worse than the revelations in those emails were the official lies and cover-ups that followed Climategate. Everyone was at it—from the IPCC's Rajendra Pachauri, to the governing bodies of the University of East Anglia and Penn State University in the U.S., to the Gordon Brown Labour administration and the David Cameron Coalition administration, from the United Nations to the European Union, from Obama's USA to the CSIRO in Kevin Rudd's and Julia Gillard's low-carbon-suicide Australia. Climategate exposed one of the greatest scientific scandals in the history of the world, on which billions of dollars of taxpayers' money was being squandered.

And what was the almost unanimous reaction of the Establishment across the world? Why, to use all the considerable power and resources and authority at its disposal to deny the problems revealed by Climategate.

Ten, twenty, thirty years ago, they would probably have gotten away with it too. Today, it simply isn't possible. From the patient, painstaking demolition of the Hockey Stick by McIntyre and McKitrick, to blogger Richard North's forensic deconstruction of a false, non-peer-reviewed claim made in the IPCC's Fourth Assessment Report about the effects of climate change in the Amazon, from Donna Laframboise's crowd-sourcing audits to David Holland's and Andrew Montford's cussedly determined Freedom of Information requests, the lying liars of the great green eco-fraud are being subjected to scrutiny so relentless and merciless you almost feel sorry for them.

Almost.

CHAPTER 5

THE SCIENCE IS UNSETTLED

Let's be clear: the work of science has nothing whatever to do with consensus. Consensus is the business of politics. Science, on the contrary, requires only one investigator who happens to be right, which means that he or she has results that are verifiable by reference to the real world. In science consensus is irrelevant. What is relevant is reproducible results. The greatest scientists in history are great precisely because they broke with the consensus.

There is no such thing as consensus science. If it's consensus, it isn't science. If it's science, it isn't consensus. Period.

Michael Crichton, The Caltech Michelin Lecture, January 17, 2003

Do you remember those science experiments you used to do at school?

In my day you got to dissect frogs and mice; and chuck sodium into water and watch it hiss, jump and burn blinding white, prompting the thrilling, shuddery thought that if it were to land on your hand, it would burn right through just like napalm.

But that was before the first one got banned by the animal rights lobby and the second one by the health and safety brigade. Still, even if you're too young to have experienced the joy of slicing up amphibians or nearly burning your hand off, you'll probably have grown a copper sulphate crystal. They haven't banned that one yet, I hope.

Okay, so if you remember growing copper sulphate crystals, you'll also remember how annoying it was when your classmates' crystals grew bigger than yours. Or, worse, when your crystal didn't grow at all because your copper sulphate solution wasn't saturated or the seed crystal wasn't dangling properly in the water—or some other basic error you'd made.

Afterwards you had to write up the experiment and if you're anything like me, you wanted to write up the experiment as it ought to have worked—just like it said in the textbook—rather than in the way it actually worked for you, which was rather crappy and embarrassing.

Your science teacher, though, would have insisted. "Use your own measurements, not the ones in the textbook," he would have said (or she, in my case: Miss Jones her name was. I still remember how prettily she blushed when she took us for *that* human biology class).

And your teacher was quite right, of course. He was attempting to instill in you the principles of scientific method. Never mind what *ought* to be happening in this experiment you're carrying out. Concentrate on what *actually* happened when you did it. To do otherwise isn't science. It's cheating.

Not only that, but it's the enemy of scientific progress. Think, say, of the German physicist Wilhelm Roentgen in his lab in Wurzburg in November 1895. He's trying to repeat a fairly routine experiment with cathode rays when suddenly he notices that something bizarre has happened. A barium platinocyanide screen some distance from his shielded apparatus keeps glowing whenever the cathode ray discharge is in process.

Does Roentgen at this point say "Yeah, yeah. Whatever"—or "Ja. Ja. Was auch immer," presumably—and move that inconvenient barium platinocyanide screen out of the way, since it has no relevance to the experiment he's trying to conduct?

Why, no, of course he doesn't. Being a good scientist, he's immediately intrigued by this anomaly and sets out to investigate further. Over the next few weeks—eating and sleeping in his lab—he prepares a series of further experiments which lead him to discover what are sometimes called Roentgen Rays but which he himself terms X-rays (X being the mathematical designation for something unknown). The name catches on. First subject for an X-ray photograph is the hand of his wife Anna Bertha, ring and all. Seeing the skeletal shape she declares cheerily: "I have seen my death."

Many of the world's greatest scientific discoveries have happened in this way: with a scientist setting out to replicate a routine and familiar experiment and instead, quite by chance, stumbling on something marvelous. When this happens, rival scientists are inclined to mutter jealously under their breaths: "You jammy bugger!", and sometimes, to pour scorn on the new discovery and try to undermine it. When the physicist Lord Kelvin first heard about X-rays, his immediate reaction was to declare them an elaborate hoax.

Australian scientists Robin Warren and Barry Marshall were greeted with similar skepticism in 1982 when they came up with the novel hypothesis that, contrary to the accepted belief that stomach ulcers were caused by stress, they were in fact created by the *Helicobacter pylori* bacterium. No one believed them until Marshall drank a Petri dish of the stuff and went on to win (with Warren) the Nobel Prize for Medicine.

What those two Aussies had instigated was an unusually rapid and dramatic version of what Thomas Kuhn, in his seminal 1962 work *The Structure of Scientific Revolutions*, called a "paradigm shift". That's the book where I found the story about Roentgen's discovery of X-rays.

In the 90s, "paradigm shift" turned into one of those buzzy phrases used by marketing men to describe any apparently dramatic move in popular cultural thinking. But what Kuhn meant by "paradigm" was the current, more-or-less universally-accepted worldview held by the scientific community.

A paradigm shift, Kuhn says, takes place when a growing number of dissenting scientists niggle away at "anomalies"—inconsistencies in the paradigm—leading to a period of uncertainty and foment ("crisis"), which in turn leads to the creation of a new paradigm. This is how science advances. It's why we no longer think that the world is flat, or that the sun revolves round the earth, or that the human body is governed by four competing humors. Someone, somewhere, came up with a more plausible theory of how the world really works, and this theory was gradually, universally accepted.

Science is never settled. That's not how it works. "The science" is neither more nor less than a series of hypotheses, none of which lasts any longer than it takes some impertinent, iconoclastic upstart to come along, prove it wrong, and replace it with some fancy new improved hypothesis of his own. As the philosopher Karl Popper first argued in the 1930s, in order to be properly scientific, a theory (or hypothesis) must be "falsifiable": that is, it must be capable of being proven false either through observation or experiment. In other words, a useful theory holds the key to its own destruction.

Let's pick a theory, any scientific theory, and see how this works in action, shall we? Hey. I've just thought of a good one. How about the theory—widely promulgated by leading members of the scientific community since the mid-80s—that the world is becoming inexorably, dangerously, unprecedentedly warmer and that the main driver of this increase is manmade CO_2 emissions? You may have encountered this theory before. It's quite topical.

Right, so if this theory is correct then clearly we should all be very afraid. It would mean, essentially, that Industrial Civilization is destroying our planet. Our only hope of survival is to halt economic growth and slash our CO_2 emissions to near zero, since CO_2 is an unavoidable by-product of almost every conventional industrial process. It means we need to bomb ourselves back to the agrarian age, restore the barter system, live in mud huts and subsist contentedly on mung beans, Brussels sprouts, and lentils, among pungent clouds of flatus, smugness and self-righteousness, secure in the knowledge that we have saved Mother Gaia for "the children"...

Some people actually believe this stuff. Well they would, what with "the science" being "settled" and "all the world's top scientists" having reached a "consensus" that global warming is real and it's man-made and it's very dangerous and it's unprecedented and it's happening *now*. Who are we—we puny, ignorant non-scientists—to dispute the considered judgment of so many wise and revered and authoritative experts in their field?

You get a lot of this at parties. For Warmists, it's the first line of defense. "What?" they say to me. "If it's a choice between the opinion of James Delingpole—novelist and journalist—and the opinion of the 2,500 scientists who contributed to the IPCC's Fourth Assessment Report, the president of the Royal Society (and former Astronomer Royal) Lord Rees, top NASA scientist Dr. James Hansen, and the British government's former chief scientific advisor Professor Sir David King, well I'm sorry, but I know which side I'm backing."

And I totally see where they're coming from, of course. I mean, I'm not altogether sure that even I (love him though I do) trust James Delingpole's scientific opinion because I know, perhaps better than any man alive, just how woefully inadequate his science background actually is.

That stuff at the beginning of this chapter about growing copper sulphate crystals? That was, pretty much, the extent of my scientific expertise. OK, so I did get a grade B at my Physics O-level exam. But everything I ever learned about the subject I've completely forgotten, because I only studied it on sufferance. I really wanted to study Biology, but I'd read somewhere that to be an RAF fighter pilot you needed Physics, so I thought I'd better do it just in case I decided to diverge from my primary career plan of being an SAS troop commander who'd win a Victoria Cross (Britain's highest military honor, comparable to the U.S. Medal of Honor) in the upcoming war against the Soviets.

Now let's be even more harsh. Let us compare and contrast the scientific expertise of James Delingpole with that of the Royal Society.

James Delingpole Motto: *Illegitimi non carborundum*— "don't let the bastards grind you down"	The Royal Society Motto: *Nullius in verba*—"take nobody's word for it"

Born 1965
Major Scientific achievements:
  successfully grew conker (horse
  chestnut) in jar on bed of water and
  cotton wool (1970)
achieved similar success with broad bean
  (1971)
turned litmus paper blue by dipping in
  alkali (1973)
noted presence of gall insects in oak tree
  (1974)
dissected rat (1979)
began fumbling experiments with
  human biology (early 1980s)
finally got result (1985)
helped create male human specimen
  (1998) and female specimen (2000)
now engaged in costly, demanding,
  ongoing experiment studying
  divergent behavior patterns of male
  and female species (1998 -)
	Founded 1660 as "a Colledge for the
	  Promoting of Physico-Mathematicall
	  Experimentall Learning"
	Members and Presidents: Sir
	  Christopher Wren, Samuel Pepys,
	  Robert Boyle, Robert Hooke, Sir
	  Joseph Banks, Sir Isaac Newton,
	  Sir Hans Sloane, Thomas Huxley,
	  Joseph Hooker, Joseph Lister, Ernest
	  Rutherford.
	Major Scientific achievements (some of):
	designing St. Paul's Cathedral
	laying groundwork for classical
	  mechanics
	discovering law of gravity and three laws
	  of motion
	coining word "cell" for basic unit of life
	Hooke's law of elasticity
	Boyle's law
	inventing drinking chocolate
	creating basis of Natural History
	  Museum's collection
	introducing numerous plant species to
	  the Western World
	helping popularize evolutionary theory
	devising antiseptic surgery
	pioneering nuclear physics (etc.)

Yep. No contest. So let's have a look at the Royal Society's website to see what it says about man-made global warming. After all, with such a distinguished history, it's bound have the right answer.

Ah yes. Here it is. On December 16, 2009, following the UN's

Copenhagen Summit, the Royal Society issued an important and definitive statement entitled "Preventing Dangerous Climate Change". How did we know it was important and definitive? Because the Royal Society told us so:

> This statement has been approved by the Council of the Royal Society, and was prepared in consultation with 30 leading climate scientists. It is informed by decades of publicly available, peer-reviewed studies by thousands of scientists across a wide range of disciplines. Climate science, like any other scientific discipline, develops through vigorous debates between experts, but there is an overwhelming consensus regarding its fundamentals. Climate science has a firm basis in physics and is supported by a wealth of evidence from real world observations.

Often, when scientists are trying to communicate their discoveries to the wider world, they can be frustratingly vague, undogmatic, tentative. That's because their job, by its nature, deals more in probability than it does in certainty. But the authors of this particular statement clearly had decided to dispense with such nuance:

> There is no such thing as 'safe' climate change. Even the global temperature increase to date (about 0.75°C) is contributing to effects that are impossible to adapt to in some regions, notably small low-lying islands and coastal areas. As the temperature rises further, so will the risk of more widespread and dangerous climate impacts; from sea-level rise, from increasing frequency and intensity of climate extremes such as heat waves, floods and droughts, especially in vulnerable areas.
>
> A maximum global temperature increase of 2°C since pre-industrial times has been adopted by many nations as a goal to prevent dangerous climate change. If global greenhouse gas (GHG) emissions are reduced at 3–4 percent per year after 2020 it has been estimated that there is a fifty-fifty chance of limiting global temperature

increase to roughly 2°C; but only if GHG emissions begin to decline within the next decade. By 2050 emissions would need to be down to near 50 per cent of their 1990 levels, with continuing reductions in the second half of this century.

It went on:

The Intergovernmental Panel on Climate Change (IPCC) assessment in 2007, which involved a large number of the most eminent climate change scientists in the world, highlighted the severe climate effects that could result from a 'business as usual' approach to global GHG emissions. The balance of scientific research since the IPCC report broadly confirms and strengthens its key findings.

Utter hogwash, of course. But unless you knew already that it was utter hogwash, I think that most likely you'd be inclined to believe it. After all, this isn't just some crappy, two-bit blogger with an Oxford Arts degree giving you his tuppeny hapenny's worth. This is, scientifically speaking, about as close as you can get to the Voice of God.

Nevertheless, several prominent members of the Royal Society effectively forced the organization to issue a retraction, which came in the form of a 2010 update to their 2007 guide to climate science.

Which brings us back to those people we all meet at parties: the ones who say "2,500 scientists can't be wrong". Or "well, the consensus is…." Or "the IPCC says." They're not engaging with your argument because they feel they don't need to. It's like a game of Top Trumps where your card—the James Delingpole or Christopher Booker or Richard North one—has a Science Credibility rating of 2, and their card—the Royal Society, or the IPCC one or the NASA one—has a Science Credibility rating of 800,000. They win every time.

But they shouldn't. What they are doing, though they may not be aware of it, is falling for the logical fallacy sometimes known as *argumentum ad verecundiam* ("argument to respect") and sometimes as *ipse dixit* ("he himself said it"). This is the grown-up version of a debating technique popularly used in playgrounds by eight-year old boys: "My Dad says Father Christmas does exist and my Dad knows because he's been to the North Pole, so there"—the implication being, of course, that "My Dad's" wisdom and authority is so manifestly great it brooks no opposition.

The correct response to the "My Dad says" line is—if only you but knew it when you were eight years old—"Well poo to what your Dad says. What does he know about anything anyway?" It is also the broadly correct response to the use of *argumentum ad verecundiam*. Sure it's quite likely that scientists of the IPCC and the Royal Society have a better grasp of the science of global warming than, say, your Dad. Or even my son's Dad. But likelihood is not the same thing as certainty. No person or institution, however apparently wise, reverend and distinguished, has a monopoly on infallible truth.

Mind you, if you tried to explain this to the person at the party, I doubt they'd be persuaded to change their mind. In fact I know they wouldn't because I tried it once during a heated discussion at a Christmas drinks party with a fellow blogger named Will Heaven. Heaven considered it plain absurd that I dared to quibble with "the vast majority" of the world's most distinguished scientists. "Oh yeah. Use the Appeal to Authority, why don't you?" I sneered. "Of course I'm appealing to authority. What's wrong with that?" replied Will.

Had I been more clever, I would have raised the subject of Post Normal Science (PNS). You probably haven't heard of PNS. I hadn't myself until very recently but you'll find it extremely useful for warding off climate change evil. If the Warmists are Voldemort—and they are—and you are Harry Potter (or Hermione or Ron, if you prefer) then PNS is your Defense Against the Dark Arts. So read this bit carefully. It might just save your life.

So. Post Normal Science: a concept you won't have heard of, invented by two men you've never heard of either—Jerome Ravetz and Silvio Funtowicz. Yet it has proved so secretly influential and so mightily important, that it has affected the course of the whole world. Without it, the whole AGW scare might never have happened.

Before there was Post Normal Science, there must have been Normal Science, right? Right. Normal Science is the process I mentioned earlier, described by Thomas Kuhn in that influential book *The Structure of Scientific Revolutions*—the one where older theories are replaced by newer, better theories, and so on *ad infinitum*.

Normal Science presupposes that scientists are motivated, above all else, by their selfless pursuit of objective truth. Of course, in real life it rarely quite works out that way, as Thomas Spratt pointed out as early as 1667 in his *History of the Royal Society*:

> For whosoever has fix'd on his Cause, before he has experimented; can hardly avoid fitting his Experiment, and his Observations, to his own Cause, which he had before imagin'd; rather than the cause of the truth of the Experiment it self.

In other words, scientists are prone to ignoring inconvenient results. They also need to earn a living, just like the rest of us, and the direction their research takes is inevitably influenced by the funding available. If you want to research grey squirrels and your potential paymasters are only interested in red squirrels, well tough. Unless you want to starve, red squirrels it is.

This was what President Eisenhower warned about over fifty years ago in his "Farewell Address to the Nation" (January 1961):

> Today, the solitary inventor, tinkering in his shop, has been overshadowed by task forces of scientists in laboratories and testing fields. In the same fashion, the free university, historically the fountainhead of free ideas and scientific discovery, has experienced a revolution in the conduct of research. Partly because of the huge costs involved, a government contract becomes virtually a substitute for intellectual

curiosity. For every old blackboard there are now hundreds of new electronic computers.

The prospect of domination of the nation's scholars by Federal employment, project allocations, and the power of money is ever present—and is gravely to be regarded.

Yet, in holding scientific research and discovery in respect, as we should, we must also be alert to the equal and opposite danger that public policy could itself become the captive of a scientific-technological elite.

Here Ike predicted more or less exactly what has come to pass with the massive government-funded climate change industry, on which thousands of scientists depend for their livelihoods. Are they *all* fiddling the data so as to keep their jobs? Of course they're not. As David Michaels noted in a 2008 article in the *Washington Post*, in medical research the corrupting process is usually much more subtle. It's not so much that the research itself is shoddy, as that the questions it seeks to answer are skewed in a particular direction, so that evidence that suits your desired end is talked up—and that which doesn't suit is conveniently ignored.

Of course scientists don't like to admit this. Recently, my "climate skepticism" was challenged on a BBC documentary by the Nobel Prize-winning geneticist Sir Paul Nurse, who was presenting a program that asked why the public was losing its faith in scientists. One reason, I suggested, was the lack of integrity shown by many climate scientists, which might well be the result of the "funding effect". Sir Paul chastely insisted that neither he nor any scientist he knew was so base as to have the integrity of his research distorted by funding. "So when the European Union alone spends more than five Manhattan projects on the global warming industry, you don't think it's going to have a corrupting effect?" I asked. Sir Paul remained adamant it hadn't. But then, he's not a climate scientist.

Just as there are rewards for scientists whose research proves the "right" things for their employers, so a dire fate can await those who reach the "wrong" conclusions. Galileo suffered for this at the hands of the Roman Catholic Church; so too did the Soviet geneticists murdered under Stalin. Their modern day counterparts would include almost any scientist whose research tends towards climate change skepticism. And also James Enstrom and Geoffrey Kabat.

James and Geoffrey *who*? Yes, quite. If they'd been the men who proved that passive smoking really exists, there would no doubt be official statues of them in every square. But they didn't. In fact their research demonstrated just the opposite, which is why their work has been vilified or suppressed by the publicly-funded medical establishment ever since.

And the crazy thing is, they never set out to be the poster boys for smokers' liberty. Quite the opposite. They both hated smoking. That's why when they began to look into the effects of secondary smoke inhalation, they were full of bright hopes that their research would help nail this great social evil once and for all. And in this, they had the full support of their main sponsors, the American Cancer Society and the Tobacco Related Disease Research Program.

Enstrom and Kabat analyzed thirty years of American Cancer Society data (1959 to 1989) that had tracked no fewer than 118,000 Californians and was the world's first major long-term investigation into the effects of passive smoking. But as their study progressed, Enstrom and Kabat began to realize something rather awkward: they weren't going to deliver the results their sponsors wanted. As they discovered, exposure to environmental tobacco smoke (i.e. second-hand smoke or "passive smoking"), no matter how intense or prolonged, creates no significantly increased risk of heart disease or lung cancer.

From being the heroes of the health lobby, Enstrom and Kabat became its number one villains. The American Cancer Society and the Tobacco Related Disease Research Program dropped them like a hot potato. The only way Enstrom and Kabat could afford to complete their research was—irony of ironies—with the backing of the cigarette industry. Of course, this gave their critics the ammunition they needed not to take their work seriously. After all, it was clearly biased: it had been funded by Big Tobacco.

So Enstrom and Kabat didn't get a Nobel Prize for services to the lungs of smokers' families, nor did they get marble busts of themselves on either side of the portico of the World Health Organization. But it would be nice to think their efforts produced something far more rewarding: the warm glow you get when you know you've done the Right Thing.

Mind you, for scientists of Enstrom and Kabat's generation, it would have been unthinkable to do otherwise. To manipulate scientific evidence to particular ends could hardly be called proper—or indeed "normal"—science at all. Why it would be so unorthodox you'd have to call it something else entirely different. You'd have to call it...well, we'll come to that in a minute.

In December 2009, shortly after the Climategate scandal broke, the BBC made an uncharacteristically fair and balanced attempt at examining some of these issues on its Radio 4 debating program, "The Moral Maze".

"Can science ever be truly morally neutral?" the program asked.

The leaking of e-mails from the University of East Anglia Climate Research Unit has raised the issue of where should we draw the line between science and campaigning. In a complex world of competing interests, it's vital that we have an independent and rational method to judge and inform policies. But is it naïve to expect scientists to put their personal views aside when dealing with such an important issue? Do we rely too much on scientific evidence to shape policy and is it driving out political and moral debate in society?

Among the expert witnesses called to testify on the program was Lewis Wolpert, Emeritus Professor in Cell and Developmental Biology at University College, London. Professor Wolpert (born

1929) was quite adamant about a scientist's proper role. "Science is value-free", he has often said. "I regard it as ethically unacceptable and impractical to censor any aspect of trying to understand the nature of our world."

But surely there must be exceptions, Professor Wolpert was asked on the program. Suppose a scientist were to discover something as deadly as the atom bomb or some new secret whose effects on mankind were most likely to be deleterious; surely then he would have a duty to suppress it for the good of humanity? Not at all, Wolpert replied. It is not for the scientist to make moral judgments. His function is to serve only the truth.

Now consider this statement from a *Discover* magazine interview with the late Stephen Schneider (1945–2010), founder and editor of the journal *Climatic Change*, IPCC lead author and Professor of Environmental Biology and Global Change at Stanford University. Schneider was one of the foremost cheerleaders for the AGW scare, apparently having forgotten that back in the 70s, during his tender formative years, he was one of the leading advocates for the perils of global cooling.

At first Schneider appears to be in full agreement with Professor Wolpert:

On the one hand, as scientists we are ethically bound to the scientific method, in effect promising to tell the truth, the whole truth, and nothing but — which means that we must include all the doubts, the caveats, the ifs, ands, and buts.

But then he qualifies his statement:

On the other hand, we are not just scientists but human beings as well. And like most people we'd like to see the world a better place, which in this context translates into our working to reduce the risk of potentially disastrous climatic change. To do that we need to get some broad based support, to capture the public's imagination. That, of course, entails getting loads of media coverage. So we have to offer up scary scenarios, make simplified, dramatic statements, and make little mention of any doubts we might have. This 'double ethical bind' we frequently find ourselves in cannot be solved by any formula. Each of us has to decide what the right balance is between being effective and being honest. I hope that means being both.

Er, right, Professor Schneider. So when, back in 1987, *Time* magazine rang and asked you for a quote for its "The Heat Is On" cover story, and you said "Humans are altering the earth's surface and changing the atmosphere at such a rate that we have become a competitor with natural forces that maintain our climate. What is new is the potential irreversibility of the changes that are now taking place"—which hat were you wearing? Your "science" hat? Or your "human being" hat? And did you ever go to the trouble of pointing out the distinction to the journalist, who presumably rang you for scientific expertise rather than for your propagandizing skills at offering up "scary scenarios"?

Before we get on to Post Normal Science—and we're nearly there, now: close enough to smell the putrescence—I'd just like to dwell briefly on some of Schneider's phrases.

Each of us has to decide what the right balance is between being effective and being honest. I hope that means being both.

Mm. Nice; reasonable; undogmatic; thoughtful.

We are not just scientists but human beings as well.

Yes! Yes! Not one of those horrid people in a white coat, with mad staring eyes and wild hair and crazy labs full of bubbling beakers spewing evil smelling gases—but a warm, lovable kind of guy who probably washes the dishes, writes nice thank you letters and remembers his wedding anniversary and other nice, caring human being kinds of things.

Like most people we'd like to make the world a better place.

Phew! And yay! You are *so* our kind of scientist Stephen. Not one of those world-destroying types, like you find in some labs. But one of the good ones, who really cares. We love you Stephen Schneider!

No, not really. I'm just trying to point up something I've noticed quite a bit among advocates of the AGW agenda. Never mind whether it's Jonathon Porritt, with his Etonian charm, or nice Rajendra Pachauri, with his straggly yogi's hair, or nice George Monbiot with his soft-spoken otherworldliness, or nice Al Gore, with his frayed lovable air of some portly, slightly battered, once incredibly expensive teddy bear bought for one of the Rockefeller kids in the 1930s. They're all very good at presenting themselves as men who—above all else—really, really *care*. They're doing what they do for the good of the world. They have no underlying agenda. They're not dogmatists. Theirs is quite simply the position that any reasonable person would wish to adopt. The nice position.

I got this sensation again when reading one of the guest posts on Watts Up With That? (WUWT). It was a very long, rambling, and slightly obscure post by a determinedly nice-and-reasonable-sounding fellow named Jerry Ravetz, whose name vaguely rang a bell, though I couldn't remember why at first.

Anyway, the commenters at WUWT couldn't get enough of him. "Great read!!! Wonderful analysis!!!" said one. "Stunning, a tour de force," said another. "This is the best article on the subject I have ever read," said a third. By which stage, I was starting to worry.

You see, I'd always had bags of respect for the insight and intelligence and superior understanding of the people who comment at WUWT. (It was one of them, you'll remember, that came up with the name "Climategate.") Yet here they were applauding what struck me as a classic exercise in pseudo-academic obfuscation. This guy, whoever he was, was taking an awfully long time to say very little, and not very clearly at that.

No need for a point-by-point breakdown here. (If you've the time and the patience you can try it yourself, but it'll be like wrestling an eel.) Suffice to say that the truth suddenly dawned when I came to the comment by ScientistForTruth:

> I'm amazed. Looking at the ecstatic comments, I think most of you are about as happy as the Trojans who wheeled the horse, a gift from heaven they thought, within their walls and got drunk, only to find that night that their city had been infiltrated and lost after years of battle. Beware! Ravetz is a very bright guy and very perceptive but Ravetz and Hulme have done their utmost to dispatch "normal" science. Now their ideas will destroy you.

Strong words. But ScientistForTruth was right. A few weeks earlier, I remembered reading his essay on Post Normal Science (PNS). It's by far the most thorough and intelligent demolition of PNS anyone has written and I recommend it hugely.

Here's how the author sets out his stall:

> What has become of science? We thought that science was about the pursuit of truth. Then we became perplexed at how quickly scientists have prostituted themselves in the service of political agendas. We have seen the unedifying spectacle of scientists refusing to share their data, fiddling their results, and resorting to *ad hominem* attacks on those who have exposed their work to be fraudulent. We have seen the Royal Society becoming a shamelessly crude advocacy society. We have seen President Obama choosing notorious climate alarmists and liars to be his personal advisors. We have seen the peer-review process and journal editors colluding to prevent publication of results that do not serve the politically-correct agenda, and scientists

refusing to consider results that demolish their pet theories. What is going on here?

What is going on is that science is no longer what we thought it was. It is now a tool in the hands of socialists, and the smart money is flowing into the pockets of 'scientists' who will serve their agenda. Follow the money. Whilst traditional physics and chemistry departments are closing in British universities, and there is a shortage of science teachers, there is an abundance of cash being poured into departments that will serve socialist ends, and no shortage of acolytes desirous to use this as a route to power. Once there was modern science, which was hard work; now we have postmodern science, where the quest for real, absolute truth is outdated, and 'science' is a wax nose that can be twisted in any direction to underpin the latest lying narrative in the pursuit of power. Except they didn't call it 'postmodern' science because then we might smell a rat. They called it PNS (post-normal science) and hoped we wouldn't notice.

Stirring, crusading stuff. And all the more valuable for the fact so few people were wise to it. If they had been, WUWT readers would not have given Ravetz such unqualified praise to his first guest post. After all, from a climate skeptic's perspective, Jerome Ravetz is essentially the Antichrist. This man framed the moral philosophy which wiped out the scientific integrity so revered by the many decent, upstanding engineers, geologists and physicists who tend to congregate on WUWT. Possibly still worse, he is the man who made the whole AGW scam possible.

"Facts uncertain, values in dispute, stakes high and decisions urgent." This, according to Ravetz—and he should know: he did invent it—is what he calls the "mantram" at the heart of PNS. It presupposes that certain scenarios exist in which the values of Normal science—you know: facts, empiricism, rigor, honesty, that kind of old-fashioned stuff—simply aren't up to snuff, and that a newer, improved more Post-Modern kind of science is needed to get the job done.

Ravetz is a left-leaning U.S.-born academic and Communist party fellow traveler. He formulated his "PNS" theory at Britain's Leeds University in the early 90s with Silvio Funtowicz. In the abstract for their 1993 treatise "Science for the Post Normal Age", they claimed:

...a new type of science—'post-normal'—is emerging...in contrast to traditional problem-solving strategies, including core science, applied science, and professional consultancy...Post-normal science can provide a path to the democratization of science, and also a response to the current tendencies to post-modernity.

No, don't worry if it doesn't make much sense. That's the whole point. This is the language of academia in the finest traditions of Derrida and Foucault and Barthes and De Saussures and Chomsky. Add to it that whole ragbag of monstrously overrated Structuralist, Post-Structuralist and Marxist thinkers whose writings are so labyrinthine and obscure that no one (possibly not even the authors themselves) could unravel them. They are designed not to celebrate old-school values like lucidity and logic, but rather to subvert them. The medium is the message: everything you think you know is wrong; welcome to the new order.

In the case of Ravetz and Funtowicz, this new order (a kind of scientific variant on the post-modernist movement in art and literature) entailed making science less elitist and hierarchical, more democratic and responsive to the needs of the modern age. Instead of pursuing the obsolete and possibly dangerous concept of "truth", their theory posited, a scientist's new duty ought to be towards something called "quality." And by "quality" they meant something more akin to rhetoric—the ability to manipulate evidence and present it in such a way as to achieve particular, desirable political ends.

You can see why this philosophy might have appealed to the cabal of activist-scientists responsible for pushing the AGW scare. Here was Mother Earth—they couldn't be sure, the facts being uncertain but *they felt it in their bones*—facing the greatest threat to her existence in the entire history of mankind. The stakes were so high, and doom so imminent, there simply wasn't time to waste with any of that tedious, old-fashioned researching and debating nonsense. The time for action was *now*, or more preferably, yesterday. It really was that serious.

This you'll remember was the overriding message of Al Gore's "An Inconvenient Truth": "The science is settled." Only cranks and crackpots and weirdoes on the outer fringes, Big Al assured us, now disputed "The Consensus" in AGW. The science had segued, with a haste and urgency that in older times might have been considered indecent, into political process.

That, of course, is the essence of PNS. It belongs less in a laboratory than the Ministry of Propaganda. Among those who certainly understood this early on was Mike Hulme of the Tyndall Centre, who once wrote:

Self-evidently dangerous climate change will not emerge from a normal scientific process of truth seeking, although science will gain some insights into the question if it recognises the socially contingent dimensions of a post-normal science.

In the wake of Climategate, Hulme has often positioned himself in radio interviews and debates as the likable, accessible, undogmatic centre ground between the Warmists and the Skeptics. This seems to me like a ploy of dissembling genius given that

a) as Professor of Climate Change in the School of Environmental Sciences at the University of East Anglia, he has worked closely with most of those implicated in the Climategate scandal, and
b) he's an ardent advocate of the very philosophy that made Climategate possible.

Not unlike Ravetz himself, Hulme sounds nice, plausible, reasonable, moderate—until you work out what it is he's actually saying. At least Joseph Bast in *American Thinker* was wise to his game—as he showed in his review of Hulme's book, *Why We Disagree About Climate Change*:

> More than a few people will be tempted to buy this book based on the promise, implicit in its title, that it offers an examination of the ideas and motives of both sides in the global warming debate. But that is not what this book is about. Rather, it is the musings of a British socialist about how to use the global warming issue as a means of persuading "the masses" to give up their economic liberties.

He went on:

> ...socialists like Hulme can frame the global warming issue in such as way as to achieve seemingly unrelated goals such as sustainable development, income redistribution, population control, social justice, and many other items on the liberal/socialist wish-list.
>
> It is troubling to read a prominent scientist who has so clearly lost sight of his cardinal duty — to be skeptical of all theories and always open to new data. It is particularly troubling when this same scientist endorses lying by others to advance his personal political agenda.

Well indeed. But it's not as though Hulme has ever been coy about his position. Rather, he employs the beguiling technique of hiding his views in plain sight, as when he declares:

> The function of climate change I suggest, is not as a lower-case environmental phenomenon to be solved...It really is not about stopping climate chaos. Instead, we need to see how we can use the idea of climate change—the matrix of ecological functions, power relationships, cultural discourses and materials flows that climate change

reveals—to rethink how we take forward our political, social, economic and personal projects over the decades to come.

"Climate change", in other words, has little if anything to do with "science" as you or I might understand the concept. It's not a genuine problem to be solved, but a handy excuse—with a fashionable green patina—to advance a particular social and political agenda under the cloak of ecological righteousness and scientific authority.

After Climategate, we are entitled to ask: '*Whose* scientific authority?' It's all very well for someone like Lord Rees to defend the Royal Society's position on global warming by brandishing "Nullius in verba" (as in, take nobody's word for it), as if it were still the emblem of irrefutable truth. But the fact is that his institution's integrity—like that of its U.S. cousin the National Academy of Sciences—lies in tatters precisely because it has done the thing its motto says it never does. It listened to a coterie of post-normal scientists who were more interested in political activism than objective truth—and took their word for it.

CHAPTER 6

A FEW THINGS YOU SHOULD KNOW
ABOUT "GLOBAL WARMING"...

DIANE: This generation are disaster junkies....Every day they wake up craving a narrative fix. When they see a photograph of a polar bear, hitching a lift on a passing ice flow, they cannot see a wild animal at ease in its natural habitat. What they see is the last five minutes of Titanic!

From "The Heretic" (2011), a play by Richard Bean

WHO: James Delingpole—but more importantly, dozens of
         eminent oceanographers, economists, geologists, physicists,
         astrophysicists (etc.)
WHAT: Heartland Institute's Fourth International Conference on
         Climate Change
WHERE: Marriott Magnificent Mile, Chicago
WHEN: May 16th to May 18th, 2010

You'd imagine the Heartland Institute's climate conference would be pretty dull, a meeting of 700 mostly male, mostly middle-aged-plus climate skeptics (or "realists", as one of the keynote speakers Richard Lindzen tells us we must learn to call ourselves). We're cooped up in a downtown hotel for two and half days of intense panel sessions

WATERMELONS: THE GREEN MOVEMENT'S TRUE COLORS

("Quantifying the Effects of Ocean Acidification on Marine Organisms"; "Green Eggs and Scam: the Myth of Green Jobs"; "Analysis of the Russian Segment of the HADCRUT3 Database") and lectures (beginning at 7:30am). But I haven't had so much fun in years.

First, the hospitality. They know how to look after you, these right-leaning U.S. think tanks—even modest-sized ones like the free market Heartland Institute. Of course, it suffers the "misfortune" of being largely funded by private donors rather than—contrary to what you've been told by many Greens—"Big Oil", "Big Carbon" or "Big Totally Evil". Food is good. Booze is plentiful. There is little wimping out—especially not from the strong Aussie delegation including Senator Cory Bernardi and scientists Bob Carter and Ian Plimer.

Second, the people. Here I am, a mere blogger and polemicist, rubbing shoulders with some of the world's most eminent oceanographers, economists, geologists, physicists, astrophysicists—even a couple of astronauts. I can't believe it. I am not worthy. But instead of shunning me, they're coming up and shaking my hand and thanking me for the modest service I have done for their cause. *Our* cause.

Little do they know yet that I'm about betray them. Not *horribly* betray them. It's not like I planned to let a bunch of deep green activists through a side-door (anyway, the organizers seem to have employed several burly men to check badges and prevent any foul play). It's not like I'm going to write an op-ed for the *New York Times* saying: "I recant. ManBearPig is real and we're all going to fry."

What I am going to tell them, in the speech I have prepared, is that for all the difference they're going to make in this debate on global warming they might as well go home right now.

Obviously, though, I don't phrase it quite as bluntly as that. These are nice, decent, principled people, after all, several of whom—since I began covering Climategate—have become my personal heroes. Three of them are on my panel: physicist Fred Singer, Ross McKitrick (the Canadian economist who, with Steve McIntyre, exposed the flaws in the infamous Hockey Stick) and meteorologist Joe D'Aleo (whose research into the siting of weather stations and the Urban Heat Island effect has cast serious doubt on the extent of late 20th Century "global warming"). The last thing I'd want to do is make them feel unwanted.

So I begin by declaring how honored I am to be among these experts: "Like a humble shepherd boy who has suddenly found himself translated to Mount Olympus." I mean it, too. Every skeptical climate scientist is, almost by definition, a hero because in order to maintain his stance he will have sacrificed money, job security, and career advancement in return for little more than the slim satisfaction of moral principle.

But I also mean what I say next, which is essentially that the work these fine men is now all but redundant. It really doesn't matter how many more brilliant papers Roy Spencer produces on cloud cover feedback or how many times that Nils Axel Mörner proves that sea levels show absolutely no sign of dangerous increase. This is a debate that skeptic scientists can never possibly win, no matter how much apparently overwhelmingly persuasive evidence they produce. That's because the debate was never about "the science" in the first place. It was, is and always will be about politics.

The Heartland Institute conference took place exactly six months after the Climategate documents were posted onto the internet in November 2009. And almost every day after it provided us skeptics—sorry, "realists"—with yet another humdinger of a story exposing either the flimsiness of AGW theory or the corruption, incompetence, mendacity or malfeasance of the various vested interests pushing that theory.

With tremendous originality (yeah, like I'm in a position to complain) many of these new scandals were christened with the suffix "-gate". One blogger, P. Gosselin, claimed to have counted no fewer than 70 of them.

Pachaurigate exposed the shady dealings of Rajendra Pachauri, the extravagantly bearded, cricket-loving, Indian yogic who has served as chairman—and at the time of writing still bizarrely is—of the IPCC since 2002. The former railway engineer (who has also dabbled in writing soft-porn) famously urged, shortly before Climategate, that in order to correct humanity's "unsustainable" life styles we should all learn to "eat less meat", to do without iced water in restaurants, to pay a special levy for air-conditioning in hotels and to be forced, through high taxes, to avoid the "irrational" decision to fly.

Strangely, none of these rules (apart from the meat one: that's easy enough for vegetarians like Pachauri) seems to have applied to the bearded love guru himself. He clocks up innumerable air miles every year, sometimes on IPCC business, sometimes merely to watch a cricket match, invariably travelling in grand style and staying in the best air-conditioned hotels.

Thanks to the digging of investigative blogger Richard North, we have learned that Pachauri enjoys a millionaire lifestyle, including a house in one of Delhi's most expensive neighborhoods. Pachauri's tangled web of business interests, directorships and advisory positions in the climate change and energy industry represent, at the very least, a clear conflict of interest with his position as head of so politically and economically influential an organization as the IPCC.

There have been questions too, about Pachauri's directorship of a consultancy operation called The Energy Research Institute (TERI) in New Delhi. TERI professes to be a non-profit-making organization, but appears (from its sketchy accounts) to have fingers in all sorts of unlikely pies. Why, for example, given its mission to "work towards global sustainable development, creating innovative solutions for a better tomorrow", does its campus run a golf course in a parched district of India, using up to 300,000 gallons of water a day? And why, given that the land was given to TERI by the local development authority for "institutional or public or semi-public purpose" was TERI found to be selling club membership to rich Indians for Rs. 25,000 (£550)?

Many of the other "Gates" focused on inaccuracies and absurdities in the IPCC's Fourth Assessment Report (FAR). **Africagate**, for example, exposed its dubious claim that climate change could by 2020 cause yields from rain-fed agriculture in some African countries to fall by as much as 50 percent. This claim—as Richard North drily noted on his EU Referendum blog—turned out to have been "a wild exaggeration, unsupported by any scientific research, referenced only to a report produced by a Canadian advocacy group, written by an obscure Moroccan academic who specializes in carbon trading, citing references which do not support his claims."

Amazongate concerned another dodgy claim made in the FAR: that climate change, leading to a reduction in rainfall, was threatening the survival of "up to 40 percent of the Amazonian rainforest." However, on further examination, again by the indefatigable North, the only "evidence" provided to support this claim originated from a non-peer-reviewed paper produced by green activists for the WWF (of aforementioned carbon credit fame in the Amazon). The claim was eventually sourced to a paper by another green activist—ex-WWF employee, Dr. Daniel Nepstad—now working for the Woods Hole Research Center. Nepstad's paper, though peer-reviewed, made no mention whatsoever of climate change. That's because it was about the effects of logging and forest fires.

Most damaging, though, was **Glaciergate**. This was a big deal for numerous reasons, not least because melting glaciers have become such a major symbol in the catastrophists' litany: right up there with melting ice caps, drowning polar bears and the sinking Maldives. Al Gore used melting glaciers to drive home his point in "An Inconvenient Truth", noting how the vast Himalayan ice sheet feeds seven of the world's major river systems, thus contributing to fresh water supplies for 40 percent of the world's population.

So, naturally enough, when the IPCC's 2007 report claimed that the likelihood of the glaciers disappearing by 2035—and perhaps sooner—was "very high", it seemed to confirm all the pants-wetting, pessimistic predictions by eco doom-mongers. If we didn't act soon, then an entire sub-continent would be dying of thirst. And not at some unimaginably distant date, but actually so soon that many of us would live to witness it via satellite on our spiffy new hologram TV sets, quite possibly featuring smell-o-vision and even empatho-pain facilities too (technology permitting).

Except it wasn't true, at all. The year 2035, it emerged, originated from a claim made by Dr. Syed Hasnain in an April 1999 interview with an Indian environmental magazine—"Down to Earth". This in turn was picked up and used almost verbatim in that gold standard of peer-reviewed reliability, the IPCC's Fourth Assessment Report. However, perhaps sensing that a quote lifted from an obscure Indian eco-journal might not quite carry the weight it should, the IPCC instead decided to cite as its reference point a 2005 report by the WWF, which had quoted another, similar, interview Dr. Hasnain had given to the British magazine *New Scientist*. This report wasn't peer-reviewed either.

In fact, the closest Dr. Hasnain's claims came to being peer-reviewed was when an eminent Austrian glaciologist called Dr. Georg Kaser had described them as "so wrong that it is not even worth dismissing." Subsequently, India's leading glaciologist, Dr. Vijay Raina, produced a report called "Himalayan Glaciers: A State-of-the-Art Review of Glacial Studies, Glacial Retreat and Climate Change" which showed these claims to be rubbish. This prompted an ill-advised intervention by IPCC chairman Rajendra Pachauri, who rose to defend Hasnain's claims by accusing Raina of "voodoo science." India's environment minister subsequently asked Pachauri to apologize.

At this point the plot grew murkier when it emerged that Hasnain was one of Pachauri's employees. For the previous two years, he had worked as head of TERI's new glaciology unit, which seems to have been created in order to extract part of a $500,000 research grant being offered by the Carnegie Corporation for research into

Himalayan glacier melt. Dr. Hasnain's alarmist and erroneous claim that glaciers in the region would "vanish within 40 years as a result of global warming" was—it became clear on Carnegie's grant statement—influential in securing the deal.

Finding himself under pressure to resign, Pachauri began backtracking. First he claimed it was a slip-up, adding "I don't think it takes anything away from the overwhelming scientific evidence of what's happening with the climate of this earth." Then he blamed it on "human error", while Hasnain claimed—incorrectly—that he had been misquoted.

According to another IPCC author, however, it was no such thing. Professor Murari Lal told an investigation conducted by the United Nations Environment Program that "it was wrong to assume, as has been done in sections of media, that the year 2035 had crept in the report by mistake." The implication is that a known untruth was inserted into the IPCC report quite deliberately, for reasons we can only guess, but which surely had nothing whatsoever do with TERI's appetite for that handy grant funding.

You may feel overwhelmed by the detail at this point. That's very much how we skeptical bloggers felt in the months following Climategate, as we tried to keep up with it all. It was like a gushing oil strike we couldn't turn off—not at night, not on weekends, not ever. Day after day the black stuff kept coming. Stories about the tangled dealings of the increasingly tarnished Pachauri. Stories that exposed the BBC's Warmist bias. Stories about lying non-profits, lying government ministers, lying advertisements. Stories which exposed so many flaws in the Fourth Assessment Report it seemed no one could take the IPCC seriously ever again. Stories which discussed the various inquiries being conducted on Climategate. Stories detailing the legal actions being considered against Phil Jones, Michael Mann et al., for alleged malfeasance.

The enemy was on the run. Obviously it was difficult on occasion to resist the temptation to gloat—"Climategate goes uber-viral;

Gore flees leaving evil henchmen to defend crumbling citadel" ran one of my more excitable headlines. But generally I remember feeling towards the warmists rather the same pity as for Saddam's trashed and terrified convoys of demoralized troops as they fled back to Baghdad, strafed by A-10 Warthogs, after the first Gulf War. The baddies got their just come-uppance but now the time was fast approaching for magnanimity and forgiveness.

Instead, however, something shocking happened—several shocking things, in fact. Perhaps it was naïve of us to have expected otherwise. Still, I don't think any of us realists believed they were capable of quite such chutzpah. But they were. Rather than throw up their arms in surrender, the enemy fought back. Not with hard facts to counter our hard facts; not with new scientific evidence to bolster their argument, but with a barrage of lies and stonewalling and back-scratching and panel-rigging and appeals-to-authority and bullying and all those other nefarious techniques we'd seen exposed in the Climategate emails and that we imagined (in our innocence) they'd be too embarrassed to try again.

Most disgraceful of all—in a tightly competitive field—were the three inquiries into Climategate. The first, a cursory parliamentary investigation by the UK's House of Commons Science committee, concluded after a short hearing that the CRU had done nothing wrong and that the case for AGW remained intact. Professor Jones's refusal to share data and computer codes was entirely normal practice within the "climate science community", it decided. As for those awkward emails about a "trick" and "hiding the decline": these were merely colloquial terms used in private emails and not part of a "systematic attempt to mislead."

The second inquiry, though, made the first one look tougher than the Spanish Inquisition. It was headed by one Lord Oxburgh, whose appointment by the University of East Anglia to chair an investigation into the scientific aspects of the CRU scandal was likened by an anonymous insider to "putting Dracula in charge of the blood bank."

As well as having financial interests in the carbon trading and wind farming industries, Lord Oxburgh is Director and Vice-Chairman of Globe International (Global Legislators Organization for a Balanced Environment). This cryptic organization is a worldwide network which lobbies governments to take more drastic action on climate change and other environmental issues. Strangely enough, Lord Oxburgh's inquiry found no evidence of any wrongdoing either.

But the third inquiry was different. Thorough, wide-ranging, incisive, scrupulously fair.....No, I jest. The third inquiry, headed by Sir Muir Russell, was also a whitewash. Besides stuffing its panel with avowed Warmists or friends and former friends of the UEA, Sir Muir decided that the most effective way of ascertaining the CRU scientists' guilt was to call them in for a short, friendly chat over a cup of tea and ask them whether they'd done anything wrong. The CRU scientists all said they hadn't. Sir Muir's inquiry then concluded that it had found no "evidence" of any wrongdoing. This was more or less true—but then, it hadn't looked for any.

Yet at the Heartland Institute conference, despite these setbacks, the mood was still euphoric. Climategate, the generality of opinion ran, had been a game-changer—the event which finally drew to the public's attention the skullduggery which skeptics had been trying to expose for years, hitherto with little success. From now on, it would simply be a question of showing our new interested audience that there was more—much more—where Climategate came from. All we needed to do was to win the world over to our side through sheer weight of evidence and force of argument.

But I wasn't so sure, hence the vein of pessimism running through my otherwise upbeat speech. We were, I said, in the midst of a conflict every bit as important as the World Wars fought by our grandfathers and great-grandfathers, and whose repercussions if we lost would be every bit as dire. The battle we were fighting was one between liberty, plenty, joy and optimism on the one hand, and despair, pessimism and tyranny on the other. We so-called "deniers",

I told my audience—and they didn't seem to mind being told this—represented the true forces of goodness and light. It was the pushers of the great AGW lie, perhaps the biggest conspiracy in the history of the world, who were the forces of evil.

As you'll realize when you read on, I wasn't exaggerating. But before I take you on that particular journey, I want first to dispense very briefly with a business some of you have been gulled into thinking is much, much more important than it really is in this debate: the so-called "science" of global warming.

In the early stages of writing *Watermelons*, I visited with my old friend Alain de Botton. We talked about works in progress, as fellow authors do, and I asked Alain which big questions he would most like to see answered by my new book.

"I'd like to know about the science," he said. "Is global warming happening? Is it man-made? What can we do to stop it?"

"Oh," I said, rather disappointed. "You want to know about *that* do you?"

What troubled me was not the thought of having to deal with awkward scientific questions—I'll do so in a moment—but rather the realization of just how big an ideological struggle remained to be fought.

Alain, as you'll know if you've read any of his many splendid philosophy books, is well-informed and no fool. Yet here he was, an intelligent, free-thinking, open-minded political moderate asking the green equivalent of questions like "Is private property permissible in any circumstances?", "How soon can we nationalize the means of production?" and "Will the next five-year plan prove even more ineffably glorious than the last five-year plan?"

By which I mean that all three of those questions come so freighted with cultural assumptions that they're not so much questions as ideological statements.

"Is global warming happening?" presupposes

a) that this is something that might be worth worrying about

b) that it isn't something that has been happening on and off, quite harmlessly and naturally, for millennia and

c) that it's implicitly worse than global cooling.

"Is it man-made?" presupposes that human influence on climate must perforce be an issue of major concern.

"What can we do to stop it?" is the most ideologically-charged of the lot because it takes as a given every single one of the climate alarmists' most extravagant doomsday scenarios. This suggests that the recent period of global warming is not only unprecedented but catastrophic, that it's worse than global cooling, that it's something we are capable of doing something about.

Not, of course, that I'm blaming Alain for thinking this way. After 20 or more years of intensive eco-propaganda, it's how most of us have been conditioned to think. We're like Pavlov's Dogs. Treat us to a "hurrah word" like "sustainable", "renewable", or "organic" and we'll drool and salivate and whimper for more. But at the mention of "climate change" or "global warming", we growl, bark and stiffen in trepidation. We delude ourselves that we're capable of forming rational judgments about "Global Warming" based on our careful sifting of the evidence. But we're not—not least because the "evidence" that has been provided for us by the sources of supposed authority (our political leaders, the media, the scientists...) is so corrupt as to be meaningless. We think we're free agents in all this but we're not. We're green Manchurian Candidates.

To understand the scale of the deception that has been practiced against us, let's consider the four reports produced so far by the IPCC. As Professor Bob Carter notes and summarizes in *Climate: The Counter Consensus*, each report has grown increasingly extreme in its portrayal of the crisis facing us. This especially applies to the "Summary for Policymakers" section of each report which, of course, is the part intended for our political leaders to read, on which they base policy decisions.

* First Assessment Report (1990)—"The observed [20th century temperature] increase could be largely due...to natural variability."
* Second Assessment Report (1996)—"The balance of the evidence suggests a discernible human influence on climate."
* Third Assessment Report (2001)—"There is new and stronger evidence that most of the warming observed over the last 50 years is attributable to human activities."
* Fourth Assessment Report (2007)—"Most of the observed increase in globally averaged temperature since the mid-twentieth century is very likely [= 90 per cent probable] due to the observed increase in anthropogenic greenhouse gas concentrations."

If the IPCC were Pinocchio, its nose would have grown longer and longer in those 17 years between the first and fourth reports. That's because the increasingly alarmist tone of its Summaries for Policymakers has not remotely been borne out by the real-world data. On the contrary, by the time of the Third Assessment, global warming had stopped. In the past ten years, even CRU's data suggests that global warming has halted.

This doesn't, of course, mean that global warming will never happen again (and certainly, the benefits of moderate, slow warming would far outweigh the disadvantages). What it does mean, however, is that there's something very, very creaky about the central plank of the climate alarmists' theory about the relationship between man-made CO_2 levels and rising global temperatures.

Bear this in mind next time you hear a climate alarmist banging on about "the science". What "the science" has shown is that while levels of man-made CO_2 have continued to rise as industrial output around the world has increased, global temperatures have not. The world stopped warming in 1998. This is important. What it means, essentially, is that the theory claiming that catastrophic and unprecedented global warming is linked with man-made CO_2 has been (in science-speak) "falsified". In you-and-me speak, the theory has been torpedoed below the waterline, hit in the magazine and blown out of the water.

"Oh now come, on!" some of you must be thinking. "No way is this problem as easily solved as that. If it were, we would have heard about it. It would be a massive scandal. The repercussions would be tremendous. People would be absolutely *livid* if billions upon trillions of pounds, dollars and Euros were wasted trying to deal with CO_2, if it doesn't cause global warming and global warming isn't happening anyway. Wouldn't they?"

Yep, you'd think. In the rest of the book I'll explain why that assumption is entirely wrong—and how the AGW propagandists have managed to pull the wool over the eyes of so many, for so long, on such precious little evidence.

First though, I want to make sure you're absolutely clear on how very flimsy is the "science" supporting AGW. This open letter sent by 141 scientists to UN Secretary General Ban Ki-moon on the eve of the Copenhagen summit in December 2009, neatly makes the point:

Specifically, we challenge supporters of the hypothesis of dangerous human-caused climate change to demonstrate that:

1. Variations in global climate in the last hundred years are significantly outside the natural range experienced in previous centuries;
2. Humanity's emissions of carbon dioxide and other 'greenhouse gases' (GHG) are having a dangerous impact on global climate;
3. Computer-based models can meaningfully replicate the impact of all of the natural factors that may significantly influence climate;
4. Sea levels are rising dangerously at a rate that has accelerated with increasing human GHG emissions, thereby threatening small islands and coastal communities;
5. The incidence of malaria is increasing due to recent climate changes;
6. Human society and natural ecosystems cannot adapt to foreseeable climate change as they have done in the past;

7. Worldwide glacier retreat, and sea ice melting in Polar Regions, is unusual and related to increases in human GHG emissions;
8. Polar bears and other Arctic and Antarctic wildlife are unable to adapt to anticipated local climate change effects, independent of the causes of those changes;
9. Hurricanes, other tropical cyclones and associated extreme weather events are increasing in severity and frequency;
10. Data recorded by ground-based stations are a reliable indicator of surface temperature trends.

Does this letter disprove the existence of potentially catastrophic man-made global warming? No. But then, as it goes on to point out, it really doesn't need to:

It is not the responsibility of 'climate realist' scientists to prove that dangerous human-caused climate change is not happening. Rather, it is those who propose that it is, and promote the allocation of massive investments to solve the supposed 'problem', who have the obligation to convincingly demonstrate that recent climate change is not of mostly natural origin and, if we do nothing, catastrophic change will ensue. To date, this they have utterly failed to do.

Indeed. At which point, defenders of the Warmist creed wheel out the mighty engine they call the Precautionary Principle. "All right," they say. "Even if the chances of dangerous Man-made Global Warming happening are much, much slimmer than 'the scientists' have claimed, surely it still makes sense to do *something* just in case. After all, the consequences if they are proved right will be so horrific that the price of not doing something could be incalculable."

Sometimes this is called the Pascal's Wager argument. In 1670, the French philosopher Pascal argued that even if there is no proof for the existence of God, it still makes rational sense to believe in him because the potential losses from not believing in Him if He *does* exist are far greater than the potential costs of believing in Him if He *doesn't* exist. Worst-case scenario for an atheist is eternal hellfire; worst-case scenario for a Christian is the discovery that his life spent going to church was completely wasted.

Pascal's Wager was a bad idea in 1670 (what if God is Muslim? Or a giant cockroach who hates Christians every bit as much as he hates atheists?). It's an even worse idea now, because of its dismally feeble grasp of cost-benefit analysis. When applied to AGW, it presupposes that the costs of not doing something are potentially infinite, while the costs of doing something are negligible. This is emphatically not the case.

That's why I prefer to call it the Tin Foil Hat Argument. I do so in honor of all those people out there who believe that evil aliens from outer space are trying to control our minds, and that the only way of preventing this is to wear a tin foil hat. Now I personally don't believe this theory is correct, but I would have to concede that if it did turn out to be true, we would all be in serious trouble. What if bored teenage aliens took charge and possessed us all with a simultaneous urge to jump off a high building or run in front of a bus? What if they took control of our governments and made every country in the world declare war on one another? What if they decided to destroy our countryside by persuading us to abandon effective carbon-based fuels and erect vast barrages of ugly, ineffective, bird-chomping wind farms, instead? Truly the horror possibilities of alien mind control are endless.

For this reason, you might argue based on the *Precautionary Principle*, it makes absolute sense for our governments to pass a decree enjoining that from now on we all wear tin foil hats. Forever. It needn't be too obtrusive. It might even be good for us: men could revive the chic tradition of going to work in bowlers (only tinfoil-lined this time, obviously, and they'd have to wear them at their desks, not put them on a hat stand when they got into the office). Women would love the excuse to experiment with different styles. The millinery industry would benefit hugely. Kids could happily incorporate their new "Foilies" or "Tinfers" in their childish antics, with games like "throw Johnny's hat up a tree and watch him jabber in terror for fear that the aliens will suck out his brain".

Similarly cogent arguments could be made, I'm sure, for the urgent need to enact a massive, worldwide ray-gun-building program. The size of weaponry we're talking about here would be hugely expensive. Not much less than we're planning to spend on Climate Change, probably. But again, the consequences of not doing so could be disastrous. We know, after all, that it would only take one asteroid strike to send us all the way of the dinosaurs.

We also know, thanks to the Drake equation, that there probably is extraterrestrial life out there—and that there's no guarantee they're cute ones with long arms, big eyes, sweet croaky voices and darling little hearts that glow when they're trying to send out a signal to their mothers. It might equally be that they're much more like the scorpion/ant/nightmare horror creatures on "Starship Troopers", hell bent on chopping us in half with their hideous pincers or coating us with acid slime that burns through us like napalm or.... Well that's the thing about outer space. The possible threats when you start thinking about them are legion, and therefore clearly, a very pressing case for the application of that all-important precautionary principle—and to hell with the cost!

I was debating this issue recently with a committed AGW believer, who mocked my realism thus: "And I suppose you think it's a good idea not to look left and right before you cross the road, do you?" This is a classic straw man argument. No one is claiming that it is not sensible to take precautions before crossing the road because, knowledge and experience tell us, roads are full of fast-moving vehicles that could easily knock us over. The precaution is worth taking because the inconvenience (glancing right, left, then right again) is small, while the threat is proven and genuine. Quite the opposite is true with AGW.

In fact, when you stop to think about it, it's amazing the Warmists still dare show their faces in public, let alone have the gall to go on arguing that more and more of *our* money should be thrown at *their* imaginary problem. They lost the debate in 1998. That's when global warming stopped. That's when by rights they should have thrown up their hands and gone: "All right. It's a fair cop, guv. Man-made CO_2 obviously isn't the driver of dangerous global warming. Maybe the sun has more to do with it, after all...."

Yet they continue to defend their threadbare theory, with chutz-pah. It's akin to William Pirrie, co-designer of the Titanic, staging a press conference in late April 1912, to rebut the outrageous claim by certain despicable skeptics that the Titanic did not safely cross the Atlantic on its maiden voyage from Southampton to New York:

Reporter: "Hang on. So what you guys are saying is that, er, the Titanic *didn't* hit an iceberg and sink on the night of April 14th with the loss of 1,517 passengers and crew?"

William Pirrie: "What we are saying, sir, is that the Titanic is unsinkable."

Reporter: "Er, right. But the thing is, Lord Pirrie, we have evidence to suggest it, er, *did* sink. We have eyewitness accounts by survivors. We have reports of the distress signals the Titanic sent before she sank. We have corroboration from the fact that the Titanic never arrived and that no one has seen her since April 14. Are you saying that unbeknownst to us, the Titanic is still currently afloat, full of paying passengers and happily plying her trade back and forth across the Atlantic?"

William Pirrie: "Thank you, but I refuse to take impertinent questions from someone who is almost certainly in the pay of our arch rivals, the Cunard Line. Now, I'll pass you over to expert members of our design team, who will explain why the tensile strength of the steel used in our watertight bulk-heads and the particular quality of the rivets we used render the Titanic impervious to damage from even the largest whale or similar floating marine object. Then our science advisors will explain how the current period of global cooling renders it quite impossible that any icebergs could possibly have strayed into so southerly a latitude."

Reporter: "But –"

William Pirrie: "I am also happy to announce that we are setting up a news agency—RealTitanic—which will provide an invaluable resource for those responsible reporters in the respectable branches of the press in need of swift, detailed, expert rebuttals of the pernicious ongoing myth that our splendid ship suffered any kind of mishap on April 14th."

You think I'm exaggerating? Okay, let's have a look at some of the claims made by climate alarmists to support their case for urgent, concerted and expensive action to "combat climate change" and see how they stand up.

Pacific Islands such as Tuvalu will soon be swamped by rising sea levels, creating thousands of climate refugees.

The "climate refugee" claim, made by Al Gore in "An Inconvenient Truth", was found by a London High Court judgment to be entirely untrue. There is no evidence that Tuvalu has been subject to abnormal or dangerous sea level rises. Independent analysis by Willis Eschenbach gives a best estimate of a MSL (mean sea level) rise of a mere 0.07 mm per year. Paleo-geophysicist and sea-level expert Nils-Axel Mörner says that the seepage of sea water into Tuvalu's inland fresh water is probably the result of environmentally unfriendly activity by the Japanese pineapple industry.

The Maldives are in trouble, though. They must be. What about that dramatic photograph of the Maldives government holding a cabinet meeting underwater?
For anyone who can find a way to milk it, climate change is the cash cow that keeps on giving. So, of course, it makes sense for small nations like the Maldives to hire press advisors and stage publicity stunts in order to extract large sums of guilt-money from the richer industrialized nations—and never-mind awkward details like factual accuracy. No, there is no sea level rise problem in the Maldives. Around 1970, the sea level actually fell about 20cm. In the last 40 years it has not risen at all. This has naturally proved most inconvenient for green campaigners. One of the signs that sea level has not risen in the Maldives used to be an old tree so close to the shoreline it would have been swamped by the slightest sea rise. It was recognized as a marker by locals and featured in a documentary made by Professor Mörner. Unfortunately it's no longer there. According to eye-witness accounts related by locals to Mörner, it was destroyed by an Australian sea-level team of climate change activists funded by the IPCC.

OK—so what about the millions of people threatened by flooding in Bangladesh?
Of course the Bangladeshis are threatened by flooding. Bangladesh sits squarely on the Ganges Delta—it's low, flat and densely populated. A sea level rise of just one meter would flood almost 20 per cent of the country's land area, displacing around 20 million people. But this is an unfortunate fact of geography rather than—as charities like Oxfam would have us believe—a function of the callous indifference by the industrial West to the potential damage created by climate change. Yes, sea level is rising: it has been for several millennia. For the last 150 years, it has risen at an average residual rate of around 1.8mm per year, with no sign of any recent acceleration. This means that Bangladeshis will have plenty of time to do what humans

have always done in response to climate change: adapt. There will be parts of Bangladesh that need to build flood defenses, as would be entirely normal and sensible for any population living on a flood plain. Alarmists rarely mentioned that the land mass of Bangladesh is growing, thanks to sediment carried down the Ganges which settles in the delta and adds nearly 20 km² of coastland every year.

But the poor polar bears....
Nope. They're not in trouble either, unless you count a doubling in the population since the mid-1960s as the sign of an "endangered" species. The reason *Ursus maritimus* landed itself the "Threatened" status in 2008 from the U.S. Fish and Wildlife Service was due to pressure from green activists who recognized the bear's tremendous value as a poster child for the "icecaps-are-melting-and-it's-all-our-fault" lobby. Those four drowned polar bears cited by Al Gore in "An Inconvenient Truth" were the victims not of hunger desperation but—it subsequently emerged—succumbed during a severe storm. Polar bears are strong swimmers and have been found as far as 60 miles from land without coming to any harm. Anyway, it's *Homo sapiens* we should be worried about, not *Ursus maritimus*. Which species, after all, will be better equipped for dealing with the next (overdue) ice age?

The Arctic is Melting!
Yes, it does so every summer. In all, about 3.8 million square miles of sea-ice melts each year. Then, in winter it grows back again, thanks to a complex process known as "freezing". Though it's true that in the summer of 2007, Arctic ice coverage shrank to a near-historic low, it staged a massive comeback in the winters of 2008 and 2009. There is no evidence to support the alarmist claim that the Arctic will be "ice free by 2030".

Ah, then how do you explain the recent opening of the Northwest Passage?

This is another variation on the popular melting Arctic theme. In 2007 Robin McKie, science editor of the left-leaning *Observer* newspaper, reported: "The Arctic's sea ice cover has shrunk so much that the North West Passage, the fabled sea route that connects Europe and Asia, has opened up for the first time since records began." Al Gore's hero Bill McKibben grew similarly excited: "By the end of the summer season in 2008, so much ice had melted that both the Northwest and Northeast passages were open. In other words, you could circumnavigate the Arctic on open water.....Even skeptics can't dispute such alarming events."

But why would they even bother? As New Zealand journalist Ian Wishart records in his indispensible book *Air Con* (2009), Roald Amundsen navigated a ship through the passage in 1903, while in the 1940s—when the Arctic actually was warmer than it is today— the Royal Canadian Mounted Police regularly forged the Northwest passage on patrol duties.

Extreme Weather Events

Yep, there's no doubt about it: during the 20th Century the number of reported natural disasters increased drastically, as did the cost of damage in billions of U.S. dollars. According to the World Bank: "In the aggregate, the reported number of natural disasters worldwide has been rapidly increasing, from fewer than 100 in 1975 to more than 400 in 2005." And according to the IPCC's Fourth Assessment Report, this can only get worse due to our old friend that begins with "C-" and ends in "-limate change":

Projected climate-change related exposures are likely to affect the health status of millions of people, particularly those with low adaptive capacity, through....increased deaths, disease and injury due to heat waves, flood, storms, and droughts...

Case closed then? Hardly. The reason for the increase in reported natural disasters is, fairly obviously, because of the dramatic improvement in communications. And the reason for the increased cost of damage is that the world has become much wealthier, meaning there's more expensive property—often built in more precarious but desirable waterfront locations—to be destroyed by natural disasters.

In fact, there is no evidence to suggest that the so-called "extreme weather events" of the last 30 years—Hurricane Katrina, say, or the flooding in Queensland when monsoons dumped more than 1.2 meters of water in just seven days, or the bush firestorms that ravaged the state of Victoria in southern Australia—are anything other than an entirely normal expression of natural processes which have been occurring for millennia.

This has not, of course, stopped alarmists from claiming otherwise. In 2004, Dr. Chris Landsea (one of the world's leading authorities on hurricanes) was appalled to read a press release from IPCC lead author Dr. Kevin Trenberth titled: "Experts to Warn Global Warming Likely to Continue Spurring More Outbreaks of Intense Hurricane Activity." This entirely contradicted not just Landsea's research, but every other study into the subject of which Landsea was aware. Not even the first two IPCC reports, to which Landsea had contributed, made such a claim.

Despite protests from Landsea, Trenberth went ahead and announced his spurious claim in a press conference held at Harvard Medical School. It was eagerly picked up by the world's media. Reuters reported: "Recent storms, droughts and heatwaves are probably being caused by global warming, which means the effects of global warming are coming faster than anyone had feared, climate experts said on Thursday."

Except most hurricane experts, including Landsea and Bill Gray of Colorado State University, were saying no such thing. Landsea wrote to IPCC Chairman Rajendra Pachauri asking for assurances that this unsupportable claim would not be repeated in its next assessment report. But instead of backing down, Dr. Pachauri took Trenberth's side, arguing that his claims "accurately reflected" the IPCC's Third Assessment Report. Landsea replied that this was hardly plausible given that he himself had written the relevant sections of that report. He then tendered his resignation as an IPCC author.

The IPCC, wrote Landsea, was "subverted and compromised, its neutrality lost...." He went on: "I cannot in good faith continue to contribute to a process that I view as both being motivated by pre-conceived agendas and being scientifically unsound."

Landsea's resignation went virtually unreported. The IPCC caravan trundled on, regardless.

Ocean Acidification

An important topic, not because it is any more real a threat than the other chimeras mentioned above, but because of what it implies about the changing tactics of climate change alarmists. Since global warming stopped in 1998 (invalidating their greenhouse hypothesis), they have been forced to find a new excuse to blame man-made CO_2 for all the world's ills. The handy one they have settled on is "Ocean Acidification", first popularized by a 2005 report by the (fanatically alarmist) Royal Society. This report used computer models to predict that if global emissions continue to rise at present rates, "the average PH of the oceans will fall by up to 0.5 units by 2100." Subsequent reports by well-funded alarmists have predicted that this will result in skeletal thinning in planktonic micro-organisms and the death of coral reefs.

Despite any number of expert scientific rebuttals to all this scare-mongering—studies, for example, showing that coral and plankton have actually benefited from increasing warmth and CO_2—the ocean acidification myth has become yet another article of faith for greenies. Or, as I prefer to think of it, their "Siegfried Line". The Warmists won't give up on their man-made global warming meme just yet, but if (as will most likely happen within the next decade) they are forced into retreat by a succession of freezing winters and miserable summers, they can always fall back on this second line of defense. "All right, so maybe we weren't as right as we thought about that silly idea, whatever it was, oh yeah, 'man-made global warming.' But that doesn't mean all our schemes to have CO_2 designated a form of poison by the Environmental Protection Agency, and have it taxed and regulated as a dangerous eco-hazard, were a waste of time and money. No sirree. Why just look at this scary photo we've taken of a dying coral reef....!"

I could, of course, go on to dispense with some of the 501 other myths and scare stories about climate change so assiduously pushed by the Green lobby: Larsen B in Antarctica, the "melting" Greenland ice sheet, Mount Kilimanjaro, increasing malaria, droughts, plagues, the shutdown of the Gulf Stream. But I hope that I've presented you with more than enough reasons to suspect the fraudulence of so much of "the science" that has been used to fuel the climate change industry.

By this stage of the book, I hope I have managed to persuade even eco-fanatic readers that there is something suspect about the quality of the science that has been used to push the AGW agenda.

Now, if we are to demonstrate convincingly that a crime has been committed, we need to study our alleged culprit's modus operandi to see whether we can establish any kind of motive. This is the subject of the rest of this book.

CHAPTER 7

WATERMELONS

Global Warming is the mother of all environmental scares. In the scope of its consequences for life on planet earth and the immense size of its remedies, global warming dwarfs all the other environmental and safety scares of our time put together. Warming (and warming alone), through its primary antidote of withdrawing carbon from production and consumption, is capable of realizing the environmentalist's dream of an egalitarian society based on rejection of economic growth in favor of a smaller population eating lower on the food chain, consuming a lot less, and sharing a much lower level of resources much more equally.

Aaron Wildavsky, 1992

This chapter is dedicated to Keith Farnish, a deep ecologist whose ideological views couldn't be further from my own, but without whose help this book might never have been written. You see, although I knew I wanted to write about Climategate in some way or another, what I couldn't quite decide was how. But after a brief—and perfectly friendly—email exchange with Farnish, I finally realized what needed to be done. I would set out to answer perhaps the most puzzling and fascinating questions about AGW: the ones to do with the underlying psychology.
Questions like:

"But if AGW isn't true, what would motivate people to make things up?"

and:

"If Greens so love nature, why aren't they more bothered about carpeting unspoiled landscapes with wind farms?"

and:

"Why is it that Greenies, who are supposed to be all 'peace and love', so often sound uptight and angry and shrill?"

Some of my conclusions, I expect, will be offensive to people who consider themselves part of the Green movement, amusing to people who loathe the Green movement, and hopefully enlightening to people who aren't sure exactly where they stand but would like to find out more. I've tried hard not to exaggerate for effect—except occasionally, just for fun. The suicidal, mankind-hating, technology-loathing, apocalyptic vision of the world I'm about to present to you is not something I've invented so as to present the green movement in the worst possible light. Rather, I show the green movement as it chooses to represent itself in books such as *Time's Up* (2009) by our friend Keith Farnish, which describes (with unhealthy relish) the coming apocalypse—brought on, of course, by humanity's selfishness and greed, nay, by its very existence:

> I'm rarely afraid of stating the truth, but some truths are far harder to give than others; one of them is that people will die in huge numbers when civilization collapses. Step outside of civilization and you stand a pretty good chance of surviving the inevitable; stay inside and when the crash happens there may be nothing at all you can do to save yourself. The speed and intensity of the crash will depend an awful lot on the number of people who are caught up in it: greater numbers of people have more structural needs—such as food production, power generation and healthcare—which need to be provided by the collapsing civilization; greater numbers of people create more social tension and more opportunity for extremism and violence; greater

numbers of people create more sewage, more waste, more bodies—all of which cause further illness and death.

Luckily Keith has a solution to the problem. It goes like this:

The only way to prevent global ecological collapse and thus ensure the survival of humanity is to rid the world of Industrial Civilization.

Perhaps, he suggests, we might achieve this through a process he calls "unloading." (Or as we might call it: cutting off your nose to spite your face):

Unloading essentially means the removal of an existing burden: for instance, removing grazing domesticated animals, razing cities to the ground, blowing up dams and switching off the greenhouse gas emissions machine. The process of ecological unloading is an accumulation of many of the things I have already explained in this chapter, along with an (almost certainly necessary) element of sabotage.

Personally I found this a bit disconcerting. Call me old fashioned, but I remain strangely attached to the Industrial Civilization that Keith Farnish is so keen to abolish. It has given me work, transport, entertainment, clean water, healthy children, a nice home, pleasant vacations and much more besides. I think I'd be quite loath to chuck in the towel just because some guy in a book says it's the only way our planet will survive. And it worries me that there are people who read this stuff and agree wholeheartedly: "Yes. Yes. Exactly! This is just what we need to do."

One of these people is a guy named James Hansen, who wrote a puff for Farnish's book:

Keith Farnish has it right: time has practically run out, and the 'system' is the problem. Governments are under the thumb of fossil fuel special interests—they will not look after our and the planet's well-being until we force them to do so, and that is going to require enormous effort.

Unfortunately, this is not some random guy who coincidentally shares his name with a climate scientist of the same name. It is the same Dr. James Hansen who—as head of NASA's Goddard Institute for Space Studies (GISS)—happens to control one of the world's four main climate data sets. The same Dr. James Hansen whose supposedly "unbiased" scientific authority has been instrumental in pushing global warming alarmism.

Now I suppose it's possible that Hansen was too busy actually to have read and understood the book. But those slightly sinister phrases—"the system is the problem" and "until we force them to do so"—rather suggest he shares Farnish's views on Industrial Civilization, and agrees with the activist measures which Farnish recommends to destroy it. They are, in any case, consistent with Hansen's behavior elsewhere: his extravagant claim that coal-fired power stations are "death factories" that should be closed, and his court testimony offered in defense of Greenpeace activists accused of criminally damaging Kingsnorth Power station in southeast England. This rather invites the question: if this is the kind of stuff Hansen seriously believes, how can we trust him to give a reliable, honest, detached scientific view on *anything*?

Anyway, shortly after writing this story up on my blog, I had a nice email from Keith Farnish. It said: "I am *genuinely* interested to know where your skepticism arises from—in my experience it is generally people not wanting to have to change how they live; money only comes into it in the most public cases."

"Too right, I am a person not wanting to change how I live," I was tempted to reply. But I realized that this would misrepresent my position. For Farnish it would merely confirm what he and his fellow greens have long suspected of people they label as "deniers": that our actions and opinions are the result of a mixture of greed, selfishness, complacency and knee-jerk conservatism. It would simply never occur to them that the reason we choose not to change the way we live is because we've looked at the world, studied the facts, and realized there's absolutely no *need* to. And the reason it would never occur to them is that, like religious zealots everywhere, the Greens believe they have a monopoly on revealed truth.

Now I appreciate that this statement is pretty much guaranteed to raise the hackles of the more "fair-minded" reader. I think, for instance, of my lawyer friend Helen who doesn't yet know what she thinks about climate change, but suspects there's probably merit on both sides of the argument. "How can you possibly make the sweeping accusation that Greens are religious zealots?", I can just imagine her saying. "All they are is people who care about nature. And what's so wrong with that?"

Hmm, well that's an interesting point I've just put into your mouth there, Helen, and my reply is this: "There's absolutely nothing wrong with caring about nature. Most of us do, me very much included. But the big problem with the green movement is that it doesn't really love 'nature'. It loves 'Nature', which is something else entirely. Let me explain…."

Nature with a small 'n' is the sort of thing you or I might enjoy when we go for a long country walk. We'll climb a hill and admire the view. We'll pick blackberries or—if we're lucky and they're in season—wild raspberries and strawberries. We'll show our kids the galls made by wasps on oak leaves. We'll pull out ferns, strip off the leaves and make swords or spears and have fights. We'll spot a red squirrel and say, "Wow! That was amazing! I just saw a red squirrel." Or maybe a native Australian Fierce snake: "Jeez, mate. That was close. If he'd got your ankle you'd have been dead before you hit the ground." Or maybe even a grizzly bear: "Easy now. Don't run. And if he comes any closer, play dead, and try to avoid having your face torn off by his claws…"

Nature—with a small 'n'—is something we drink in, admire, respond to, commune with, feel good in, seek solace in and thoroughly cherish. None of us, I feel sure, looks at a remote, pristine beach crawling with newborn turtles and thinks: "What this bastard needs is a juicy oil slick!" We all believe in conservation. We're all grateful for the natural wonders God—or the happy accident of Big Bang, or however you prefer to rationalize it—has given us. We all like biodiversity. None of us wants the tree frogs to die.

For your serious Green, however, the enjoyment you or I derive from nature is not just trivial but essentially wrong-headed, because it is grounded in selfishness and anthropocentricism. When you watch Chris Packham quivering with ecological righteousness on the BBC's hugely popular nature series "Springwatch", the distinct impression he gives as he treats us to yet more spectacular close-ups of feeding swallows and nesting otters is: "You don't deserve to see this. These animals really would be better off if you weren't here!" Of course this could just be my imagination, based on my reading of his fervent advocacy of man-made global warming and his slightly overzealous manner. But then again, when asked by the *Radio Times* which animal he wouldn't mind seeing extinct, Packham did reply: "Human beings. No question. That's the only one."

I detect a similar puritanical intensity in my old sparring partner George Monbiot. When Monbiot and I debated in public for the first time, shortly after Climategate, I approached him trepidatiously to shake his hand, and to try to establish that for all our disagreements we did at least have something in common. What I settled on is the fact that we both adore the mid-Welsh countryside. Monbiot lives in a rural town called Machynlleth. Every year, I rent a holiday cottage with my family not too far from there. We're simply never happier than when striding across the near-deserted hills, foraging for bilberries, looking for adders, gawping at the unspoiled views towards the Brecon Beacons (a mountain range in South Wales) and the Black Mountains (southeast Wales), and thinking: "God! How lucky we are to have all this!"

Though I know that Monbiot is capable of responding to the natural world with similar fervor, there remains a vast gulf between our understandings of it, guaranteeing we shall always be at loggerheads. That gulf, essentially, is the product of our diametrically opposed views on the role of man within nature. I take the positive line that, for all our myriad faults, we humans have created much that is beautiful and good on our planet, and that as we grow richer and more technologically advanced, we'll continue to achieve more good. Monbiot seems to embrace a far more pessimistic view of humanity, technology and "progress", seeing our presence on earth as deleterious to the planet's interests.

I think this may be why Greenies are able to gaze on the same beautiful Welsh views that I love, and yet not be horrified at the idea of ruining so glorious a prospect with fields of ugly white wind turbines. It's because, in their puritanical eyes, the concept of "a nice view" is an entirely human construct, dependent on aesthetic judgments which no other members of the animal kingdom would or could make. Nature—real Nature, with a capital N—is 'red in tooth and claw'—it doesn't care whether a view is pretty or not. All that matters is the bigger picture: the balance of the eco-system. And it's this balance, Greens believe, that the human species threatens to destroy at any moment.

It's surely no coincidence that some of the most ardent naturalists are often quite violently misanthropic. Consider this statement from the late professional 60s gambler-turned-zookeeper John Aspinall:

Some of us are now drawn to believe that a demo-catastrophe will be an eco-bonanza. In other words, a population readjustment on a planetary scale from 4,000 million to something in the nature of 200 million would be the only possible solution for the survival of the eco-system or systems that nurtured us.

Aspinall loved his capuchin monkeys, his Himalayan brown bears and his tigers—which killed three of his keepers, with another two killed by elephants—but was decidedly less enamored of his own kind.

The same is true—if to a lesser degree—of that nice fellow David Attenborough, doyen of nature documentary presenters. With his whispery, caressing voice and gentle manner, Attenborough exudes kindness, sympathy and avuncular warmth. But that's because when we see him on TV he's usually communing with gorillas and the like, which he obviously adores. Yet his views on his own species we can infer from his position as a trustee for the Optimum Population Trust—a British organization which up until 2011 argued on its website that the world's 6.8 billion population must, at the very minimum, be reduced to a more "sustainable" 5.1 billion. Attenborough subscribes to the view, in other words, that there are at least 1.7 billion of us on this planet who just shouldn't be here.

I was first alerted to the green movement's curious psychopathology during a live discussion with environmentalist the Hon. Sir Jonathon Porritt on BBC Radio 4's topical news debate program "Any Questions". Until you meet him, he's the sort of chap you imagine will be disarmingly nice. And though at dinner beforehand he was perfectly cordial, if a bit grand and diffident, in the debate itself he rather lost his cool.

What really seemed to get his goat when was when I had a dig at his enthusiasm for a proposed scheme to build a tidal barrier across the River Severn, which flows through Wales and Western England and finally empties into the sea in the Bristol Channel. Not only would this be a massive waste of money—at least £30 billion to produce an average of perhaps 1.9 gigawatts of electricity, about the same as a single, considerably cheaper coal-fired power station—but its effects on Britain's historic landscape would be devastating. It would deprive Britain of one of its most remarkable natural phenomena—the annual Severn Bore tidal wave, which enables surfers to surf miles up the river—but would also flood the mud flats which provide the habitat for millions of wading birds.

At my invocation of the mud flats, Porritt flew off the handle, with a long, spluttering diatribe about rising sea levels (as high as seven meters, Porritt claimed, though on what evidence he never made clear) and about "a very grim future for mankind" unless we reduce carbon emissions by 80 percent by 2050. "Wonderful that James is such an ardent defender of the *mud flats*," he sneered, in a tone that would make Alan Rickman's Professor Snape in the "Harry Potter" movies sound more like Julie Andrews in "The Sound of Music". "At last he's found a cause worth defending."

I must say I was taken aback. You might not give much of a damn about the biodiversity of mud flats if you were the executive of an oil company working in the Niger delta. Or if you were some aggressively conservative, cigar-chomping capitalist father who just learned from his precious daughter's new idiot Berkeley boyfriend that he was President of the Mud Flats Preservation Group. But surely one might expect better from an individual who has spent his whole career speaking up for environmental causes, whether as an advisor to the Prince of Wales, leader of the Green Party or chairman of the Sustainable Development Commission? You know—holism, butterflies beating their wings in the Amazon rainforest, and all that. Since when did spoonbills and plovers and curlews digging for food in the Bristol Channel get to be ruled as ineligible?

What I witnessed in Porritt is an attitude surprisingly common among members of the Green movement—the watermelons. It's what I call the "In order to save the City we have to destroy it" mentality. Or, if you like, the "Nature trumps nature" orthodoxy. Or—if you prefer to invoke Lenin, which I'm sure we quite reasonably can, given the authoritarian tendency of so many Greens—the "You can't make an omelet without breaking eggs" stratagem. And if I'm making it sound scary, that's probably because it *is* scary. The more closely you examine the core tenets of its faith, the more you realize that there is nothing cuddly, fluffy or bunny hugging about the watermelons' religion. In fact you might not unreasonably describe it as a pagan death cult, rooted in hatred of the human species, hell bent on destroying almost everything man has achieved, slavishly, weirdly, insanely devoted to a heartless goddess who offers nothing in return, save cold indifference.

Does that sound mad and extreme? Of course it does. I've lost count of how many friends—even normal, sentient, vaguely conservative-leaning friends—who've said to me before an election: "You know what? I think I'm going to vote Green this time." And the point they're trying to make is not to show how radical and loony they are—it's not like saying "I'm voting for the Ku Klux Klan"—but to indicate that, rather than continue to play the tired, adversarial game between left and right, they've decided to opt for the caring, innocuous middle ground.

So let's have a closer look at what the watermelons really believe. A good place to start is Rachel Carson's 1962 bestseller *Silent Spring*. "Without this book, the environmental movement might have been long delayed or never have developed at all," wrote Al Gore in an introduction to a 1994 reprint of the book. Gore went on to claim that Carson had an equally transformative effect on U.S. environment policy as Harriet Beecher Stowe had on slavery. Except, Gore argued, Carson was probably even more significant because while Stowe "characterized an issue that was already on everyone's mind", Carson warned of a "danger that hardly anyone saw".

Carson's book shook an entire generation's faith in the very notion of scientific progress. Doubts that were sown seventeen years earlier by the events at Hiroshima and Nagasaki were now crystallized by her claims: technology was going to kill us all. She argued that the main danger lay in wanton use of the pesticide DDT. This would cause a cancer epidemic that would hit "practically 100 percent" of the human population. It would also wreak almost unimaginable havoc on the earth's fragile eco-system by wiping out bird life—leading to Carson's titular "Silent Spring".

Surely Gore had a point, for once? Well, it's true that *Silent Spring* was the scare story that put green issues on the map. The book inspired thousands of young men and women to join the Green movement. It led to the creation of the Environmental Protection Agency in 1970, and the furor generated by the book certainly was a catalyst in the banning of the pesticide DDT in 1972.

Yet Gore and his ilk seem blissfully ignorant of the Environmental Protection Agency's seven-month hearing (and more than 9,000 pages of testimony) prior to the ban being enacted, in which EPA Judge Edmund Sweeney concluded:

> DDT is not a carcinogenic hazard to man... DDT is not a mutagenic or teratogenic hazard to man... The use of DDT under the regulations involved here do not have a deleterious effect on freshwater fish, estuarine organisms, wild birds or other wildlife.

Or might it be, perhaps, that for committed watermelons like Gore, it doesn't much matter whether the likes of Carson get their facts wrong or right—that as long as the "correct" environmental message is put across, any convenient untruth will do?

Bizarrely, despite Sweeney's recommendation, two months later the head of the EPA, William Ruckelshaus, still proceeded to ban DDT in the U.S. Many other countries succumbed to activist pressure and followed in America's wake—thus depriving the world of its most effective pesticide against malarial mosquitoes. Since malarial mosquitoes were then and continue to be one of the world's biggest killers—responsible for over one million deaths a year and countless human suffering besides—it has not unreasonably been argued that Carson's book, by inspiring the ban, has been responsible for more deaths than Adolf Hitler.

Yet none of this awkwardness has deterred Greens from using Carson as their poster child. On Earth Day in 2007, thirteen prominent environmentalists (among them Al Gore) paid tribute to her legacy in an essay collection called *Courage to the Earth*. Several wildlife reserves and conservation areas have been named after her, as have at least one school, a bridge, a hiking trail and three environmental prizes, while her birthplace in Springdale, Pennsylvania, is on the National Register of Historic Places. Every year, a feast (a "sustainable" one, naturally) is held there in her honor by the Rachel Carson Homestead Association.

Perhaps when Paul Ehrlich is finally clutched to Mother Gaia's bosom, he too will be similar feted. After all, he did at least as much fine work towards the cause of environmental catastrophism as Carson. And in his predictions of doom, he was also equally mistaken.

Ehrlich is best known for *The Population Bomb*, the 1968 bestseller that terrified hippies—their parents, children and dealers too—with such claims as this:

> The battle to feed all of humanity is over. In the 1970s and 1980s hundreds of millions of people will starve to death in spite of any crash programs embarked upon now. At this late date nothing can prevent a substantial increase in the world death rate.

In another—fictional—account of the world in the future published in Ramparts magazine, Ehrlich envisioned that the "sea would be virtually emptied" of fish. In that world, by 1980, thanks to toxic pesticides, the average age of death in the U.S. would be just 42. The canny Ehrlich also hedged his bets as to which direction this "disastrous" climate change would take. "With a few degrees of cooling a new ice age might be upon us," he argued in the *Population Bomb*. But "with a few degrees of heating, the polar ice caps would melt, perhaps raising ocean levels 250 feet."

Colder or warmer? Fish or no fish? Birdsong or no birdsong? Ah, what the hell, it didn't matter any more for now the floodgates of EnviroHysteria™ were wide open. Then a Democrat Senator called Gaylord Nelson got in on the act. In 1970, horrified by a massive oil spill he witnessed a year earlier off the coast of Santa Barbara,

California, he founded Earth Day to raise awareness of environmental issues through a series of 'Nam-War-protest-style "teach-ins" across the U.S.

Twenty million Americans took part in the first Earth Day event, a million of them (including celebrity guests Ali McGraw and Paul Newman) at a rally in New York City, whose mayor agreed to shut down Fifth Avenue and offer the use of Central Park for the occasion. The inevitably massive media coverage it garnered, including a one-hour prime time CBS news special presented by voice-of-the-nation Walter Cronkite, placed eco-issues very firmly on the political agenda. That same year in December, President Nixon created the U.S. Environmental Protection Agency (EPA).

The EPA's guiding philosophy was—and remains—very much the product of the culture from which it sprung. That culture, hippiedom embodied, was inspired by the teachings of radical academic and anti-nuke protester Barry Commoner, who helped pioneer the notion that progress is the enemy of the environment.

Commoner propounded his theory in his 1971 book *The Closing Circle*, in which he proposed four laws of ecology. They are:

1. Everything is Connected to Everything Else. There is one ecosphere for all living organisms and what affects one, affects all.
2. Everything Must Go Somewhere. There is no "waste" in nature and there is no "away" to which things can be thrown.
3. Nature Knows Best. Humankind has fashioned technology to improve upon nature, but such change in a natural system is, says Commoner, "likely to be detrimental to that system."
4. There Is No Such Thing as a Free Lunch. Everything comes from something. There's no such thing as spontaneous existence.

Around the same time, the British research scientist James Lovelock was formulating his "earth feedback hypothesis", later renamed the "Gaia Hypothesis". The entire planet, he argued, is one giant living organism whose various constituents—biosphere, atmosphere, oceans and soil—constitute a "feedback or cybernetic system which seeks an optimal physical and chemical environment for life."

See if you can guess which of the myriad elements in Lovelock's self-sustaining biosphere is about as welcome as a tramp who's climbed out of a dustbin smelling of rotten fish and staggered into your beautiful daughter's wedding ceremony just as she's about to say "I do"? Well, I'll give you a clue. You're one of them. I'm one of them. And for those of you at the back who are a bit slow, Lovelock spells it out in a recent book, *The Revenge of Gaia*. In an interview about the book, he crows: "It would be hubris to think humans as they are now are God's chosen race." Because we're not. We're doomed, he tells us. We're *all* doomed. And it's no more than we deserve, either, for being such a filthy blight on Mother Gaia's otherwise perfectly balanced ecosystem.

And *The Ecologist* was with him all the way. Founded in 1970 by Lovelock's good friend "deep ecologist" Teddy Goldsmith—brother of billionaire financier Sir James, uncle of eco-friendly billionaire Conservative MP Zac Goldsmith—the magazine made clear from its first editorial exactly how it viewed man's role in the great scheme of things. We are, Goldsmith argued, just a "parasite"—or a "disease which is still spreading exponentially". We have "long since ceased to play any useful ecological role". We are, in fact, "waste".

In the next chapter I shall examine the most influential of all eco-alarmism handbooks—*The Limits to Growth*—and the most influential of all eco-alarmist organizations, the Club of Rome. But before that, I should like (with your permission) to bludgeon you over the head with just a few more examples of how bizarre, destructive, misanthropic and unashamedly extremist the green mindset really is. And where better a place to do that than by visiting the paradigm of green values in excelsis—Nazi Germany?

It would be unfair to blame the Nazis for every last facet of environmental ideology. Edward I of England beat them by seven centuries to create the world's first Clean Air Act with his 1272 interdiction on the burning of sea coal. King James I beat Hitler to the claim of the world's first celebrity anti-smoking campaigner. John Muir, and before his time the Romantic poets, were ahead of the game on deifying Nature.

Nazi Germany took a stronger approach to pushing eco-ideology. It was the first nation to ban smoking on public transport (Hitler thought it a filthy habit: tobacco, he believed, was "the wrath of the Red Man against the White man, vengeance for having been given hard liquor"). It was also the first to take the concept of "animal rights" seriously (in 1933 Goering—ah, the big cuddly softie—said that anyone found guilty of animal cruelty or experimentation would be sent to the concentration camps). It passed the first national environmental laws—the Reich Nature Protection Law of 1935—and was the first to champion organic food (a special obsession of Heinrich Himmler) and vegetarianism (another of Hitler's fads). Above all, it was the first to address, with rigorous planning and mechanized efficiency, the issue that tends to concern eco-minded catastrophists more than any other: what to do about the world's population "problem."

The Nazi expression for this problem was "*Lebensraum*"—living space—a phrase which, not uncoincidentally, was borrowed from ecological theory. There being not enough *Lebensraum* available in Germany, it was only logical that the Reich should expand its frontiers, drive out—or exterminate—the native *Untermenschen* and replace them with hearty, healthy, racially pure Nordic types. In his December 1942 decree "On the Treatment of the Land in the Eastern Territories", Himmler expressed it thus:

> The peasant of our racial stock has always carefully endeavored to increase the natural powers of the soil, plants, and animals, and to preserve the balance of the whole of nature. For him, respect for

divine creation is the measure of all culture. If, therefore, the new *Lebensräume* [living spaces] are to become a homeland for our settlers, the planned arrangement of the landscape to keep it close to nature is a decisive prerequisite. It is one of the bases for fortifying the German Volk.

Note how the concepts of nature, folk tradition, racism and national unity were intimately bound in the Nazi ideology. The Germans—inevitably—had a phrase for this: *Blut und Boden* (Blood and Soil). It was invented by one of the party's leading green ideologues, Richard Walther Darre (Hitler's first Minister of Agriculture) who, like many eco-minded folk, was a great campaigner against urban decadence and a champion of rugged self-sufficiency.

For understandable reasons, modern greens have sought to distance themselves from the Nazis. But as the authors of the essay collection *How Green Were The Nazis?* argue, this won't quite wash:

The green policies of the Nazis were more than a mere episode or aberration in environmental history at large. They point to larger meanings and demonstrate with brutal clarity that conservationism and environmentalism are not and have never been value-free or inherently benign enterprises.

Precisely. Nazi Germany did not represent some grotesque perversion of green values; rather it represented their purest, most honest form of practical expression. If—as the modern green movement does and the Nazis did—you want to create a depopulated, almost "Garden of Eden" world where small numbers of chosen people live in a state of rustic, deindustrialized, organic bliss, then clearly the two key questions you must ask are "Which people?" and "How?" The Nazis simply took the most direct and honest route: they decided who the *Untermenschen* were, exterminated them on an industrial scale, then attempted to repopulate their territory with the sturdy Nordic types they believed were most fit to inherit their New Jerusalem.

In the post-World War II years, the Green movement was a bit more circumspect about its desires and intentions. But its instincts remained little changed—just look at books like Harrison Brown's *The Challenge of Man's Future* (1954), which looked forward to solving the world's population problems with a New World Order run on remarkably similar lines to the experiment which had ended in a Berlin bunker just nine years earlier:

> In the first place, it is amply clear that population stabilization and a world composed of completely independent sovereign states are incompatible....Given a world authority with jurisdiction over population problems, the task of assessing maximum permissible population levels on a regional basis need not be prohibitively difficult.

And according to what kind of criteria might this "world authority" make its judgments? Harrison proposes that it might "prevent breeding in persons who present glaring deficiencies clearly dangerous to society and which are known to be of a hereditary nature":

> Thus we could sterilize or in other ways discourage the mating of the feeble-minded. We could go further and systematically attempt to prune from society, by prohibiting them from breeding, persons suffering from serious inheritable forms of physical defects, such as congenital deafness, dumbness, blindness, or absence of limbs.

Elsewhere in his unpleasant book (quite clearly indebted to the Eugenicist philosophy that supposedly died in disgrace with Nazi Germany), Brown speaks of the human species in disgusted tones that, as we've seen earlier, would have been most heartily applauded by Teddy Goldsmith, James Lovelock and John Aspinall. Having speculated with horror on a world inhabited by 200 billion people, Brown writes:

> At this point the reader is probably saying to himself that he would have little desire to live in such a world, and he can rest assured that the author is thinking exactly the same thing. But a substantial fraction of humanity today is behaving as if it would like to create such a world. It is behaving as if it were engaged in a contest to test nature's willingness to support humanity and, if it had its way, it would not rest content until the earth is covered completely and to a considerable depth with a writhing mass of human beings, much as a dead cow is covered with a pulsating mass of maggots.

Urrgggh! All those people—yellow, black and brown ones especially—*breeding.* The horror!

If Harrison Brown were just some crackpot from the outer fringes of the environmental movement, I would not quote him at such length. Unfortunately, just like Rachel Carson and Paul Ehrlich, he is hailed as one of the greens' great gurus. Among his biggest admirers is John Holdren, the green activist who is now President Obama's Director of the White House Office of Science and Technology Policy, also known as his "Science Czar".

In 1986, Holdren edited and co-wrote an homage entitled *Earth and the Human Future: Essays in Honor of Harrison Brown,* in which he claimed:

> Thirty years after Harrison Brown elaborated these positions, it remains difficult to improve on them as a coherent depiction of the perils and challenges we face. Brown's accomplishment in writing *The Challenge of Man's Future,* of course, was not simply the construction of this sweeping schema for understanding the human predicament; more remarkable was (and is) the combination of logic, thoroughness, clarity, and force with which he marshaled data and

argumentation on every element of the problem and on their inter-connections. It is a book, in short, that should have reshaped permanently the perceptions of all serious analysts....

You wait with baited breath for the moment in the essay where Holdren blushingly dissociates himself from Harrison Brown's borderline Nazi Eugenicism. Or at least, from Brown's sinister advocacy for a new world government in charge of population control. But the moment never comes. And there's probably a good reason for that: because Holdren was arguing for very similar policies in a book he wrote in 1977 (with Paul and Anne Ehrlich) called *Ecoscience*.

Besides advocating state-enforced abortions for undesirables and the mass sterilization of humans through drugs in the water supply, the book argues for the creation of a "Planetary Regime". This Planetary Regime—perhaps run under the auspices of "UNEP and the United Nations population agencies"—would "control the development, administration, conservation and distribution of *all* natural resources, renewable or non-renewable, at least insofar as international implications exist." (I particularly dig that so-extreme-and-scary-it's-funny use of the italicized "all", in the original.)

And there's more. This Planetary Regime "might also be a logical central agency for regulating all international trade....including all food on the international market." And, of course, it would be given responsibility "for determining the optimum population for the world and for each region and for arbitrating various countries' shares within their regional limits." Oh and obviously, in order to ensure the New World Order runs smoothly, there would need to be "an armed international organization, a global analogue of a police force"—just in case formerly free citizens around the world started getting uppity about the "partial surrender of sovereignty to an international organization."

With luck, by this stage, I've helped you form a pretty clear picture of what the watermelons stand for. And by this I don't mean the nice, fluffy associations "green" has developed over the years—nurturing, caring, cherishing, preserving, cleansing, and so on. I mean, rather, the core beliefs on which the green religion is based, as expressed in the writings of its most influential philosophers.

These core beliefs, though often dressed up as concern for nature and the future of mankind, are rooted in the most bitter misanthropy and direst pessimism. They care little for the human species' myriad achievements, preferring to see our race as a blot on the landscape, a parasite, a disease which threatens the eco-system's otherwise perfect balance and which should at best be reduced by natural means—at worst ruthlessly culled.

Are these really the kind of people you want to control your children's future?

CHAPTER 8

WELCOME TO THE NEW WORLD ORDER

It may be better to live under robber barons than under omnipotent moral busybodies. The robber baron's cruelty may sometimes sleep, his cupidity may at some point be satiated; but those who torment us for our own good will torment us without end, for they do so with the approval of their own conscience.

CS Lewis

Evil men don't get up in the morning saying 'I'm going to do evil'. They say: 'I'm going to make the world a better place'.

Christopher Booker

No it doesn't involve sinister bald men with scars on their faces. Or white Persian cats. Or secret trap doors that drop you into the shark tank. Or deep, exultantly malevolent, echoing laughter that goes "Mwa ha ha ha ha ha haaa!"

On the contrary, the people who would like to deprive you of your democratic rights, wipe out a sizeable chunk of the global population, destroy Industrial Civilization, and rule the planet according to their own agenda could hardly be more considerate or nice. They're doing it for all of us, you understand. Because they care. Because, unlike you or me, they have been granted the wisdom to realize that our ailing planet is on a fast track to hell and that only through radical intervention by an enlightened elite can it hope to survive the next millennium.

Or, as Aurelio Peccei once put it:

> Phenomenal increases, rapidly approaching critical maxima, are happening in population, pollution, energy release, speed, automation and other areas revolutionized by technology. In the changed dynamics of these interacting factors lie the reasons why mankind is confronted with such an unprecedented complex of explosive problems. But we do not yet seem ready to realize that the time has come to plan and act on a scale and in ways capable of matching the new thrust and threat of events. Considering the situation in these broad and essential terms, we must recognize that very little is being done to redress it and set human fortunes on a sound and reasonable course. [Very] bleak situations will undoubtedly meet us during the next decades, unless a supreme effort is made now to get out of the present global impasse.

Peccei was the co-founder of an obscure organization called the Club of Rome. Now, you might find this reassuring: "Well I'm sure if he were that big a menace I would have heard of him." Or you might, as I do, find it rather unnerving: "Yikes! How can such obscure people wield so much influence?" But if you want to understand how deep green ideology has managed to penetrate so far into modern Western culture, Peccei is your man. Peccei, and yet another man you might well not have heard of called Alexander King.

Peccei, a wealthy Italian industrialist, was an anti-fascist resistance fighter during World War II, captured and nearly tortured to death by the Nazis. Afterwards he worked for Fiat, then Olivetti, where he rose to become president. King was a distinguished Glasgow-born research chemist, who during the war had recognized the insecticidal potential of the moth-balling agent dichloro-diphenyl-trichloroethane, which he rechristened "DDT" and which went on to be used against lice and mosquitoes. It was a discovery that, as we shall see, he would later regret.

King first contacted Peccei in the mid-1960s, impressed by a speech Peccei had given, which oozed the kind of ecological catastrophism we saw in the previous chapter. On meeting, they hit it off instantly because they shared a belief system that would form the ideological basis for a shadowy new organization they decided to call the Club of Rome. These beliefs were:

1. That the planet was getting dangerously overcrowded;
2. That resources were fast running out and must somehow be conserved;
3. That economic growth was the problem, not the solution; and
4. Urgent action needed to be taken, through the creation of some form of pan-global authority, to deal with 1, 2, and 3.

Now it's possible that many of you reading this will share King's and Peccei's belief in the first two propositions. (Though I hope I've disabused you of these notions by the time you've finished the next chapter.) Some of you—perhaps in a nostalgic nod to the abundant 90s when it was fashionable to think this way—might even agree with proposition 3. And yes, much though it pains me to imagine it, I expect there will even be one or two among you who aren't totally, one hundred percent averse to the New World Order alluded to in 4.

But it's OK, don't worry, I'm not going to get cross and accuse you of being stupid, muddle-headed, naïve, closet Marxists, or anything like that. All I'm trying to do is show how two men you've probably never heard of—King and Peccei—turned out to be stunningly successful and influential propagandists. Add 1, 2, 3 and 4 together, after all, and what you have is the blueprint for an eco-fascist tyranny so powerful and all-encompassing it makes Nazi Germany look like Mary Poppins' nursery. Yet King and Peccei managed to persuade people like you—and if not you, then definitely many of the people you know, like and respect—all around the Western world that such a belief system is eminently reasonable, sensible and benign.

How? The catalyst was the Club of Rome's first publication, a seminal 1972 book called *The Limits to Growth*, which was remarkable for at least three reasons. First, its title made you understand the message even if you hadn't read the book: that—duh!—maybe economic growth isn't such a great thing, maybe there should be, like, *limits* to it. Second, it sold at least 10 million copies, making it probably the most successful environmental bestseller ever. Third, it was the first book to make proper use of the eco-lobby's deadliest and most effective terror weapon: the scary computer model.

From a propagandist's perspective, the brilliant thing about computer models is that they can be made to "predict" whatever fantastical scenario you want them to "predict" while yet imbuing the exercise with a plausible but entirely spurious air of scientific authority. Not only are these models highly dependent on the quality of the information you choose to feed into them ("Garbage In; Garbage Out"), but (even today, let alone back in 1972) they are not advanced enough to capture the almost infinitely-layered complexity of the real world.

None of which is likely to have troubled the audience for *The Limits to Growth*. Computers were, after all, the hot new thing. The spiffy flow charts in the book, based on modeling by Professor Jay Forrester of MIT, seemed more than adequate confirmation of the book's thesis: that the planet was incapable of supporting economic and population growth on the scale it had experienced since the war; that therefore modern industrial society must come to an end.

Some people knew right away that *The Limits to Growth* was a crock. Among these was John Maddox, editor of *Nature*, who in the same year (1972) published a counterblast called *The Doomsday Syndrome*, in which he weighed in against "irresponsible exaggerations which may cause unnecessary public alarm and divert attention from really important problems".

But Maddox was swimming against the tide. The groundwork was done by Carson and Ehrlich; the late Sixties and early Seventies—with their oil crises, back-to-nature hippie values and drug-induced paranoia—were in any case fertile territory for grand universal theories of environmental apocalypse. With *The Limits to Growth*—perhaps the greatest piece of Seventies fiction this side of "Jaws" or "Chariots of the Gods?"—the Club of Rome established a vital bridgehead in its war on Western Industrial Civilization.

One of the curious paradoxes about the Club of Rome is that it is at once highly secretive and brazenly transparent. On the one hand, its meetings are all held behind closed doors, with none of its minutes published; on the other, it has a friendly website—complete with remarkable list of distinguished members (see below)- and it regularly publishes books that quite unambiguously promote its doctrines.

Here is the most infamous Club of Rome statement:

> The common enemy of humanity is man. In searching for a new enemy to unite us, we came up with the idea that pollution, the threat of global warming, water shortages, famine and the like would fit the bill. All these dangers are caused by human intervention, and it is only through changed attitudes and behavior that they can be overcome.

The real enemy then, is humanity itself.

The bit that comes later is also pretty sinister:

> Democracy is not a panacea. It cannot organize everything and it is unaware of its own limits. These facts must be faced squarely. Sacrilegious though this may sound, democracy is no longer well suited for the tasks ahead. The complexity and the technical nature of many of today's problems do not always allow elected representatives to make competent decisions at the right time.

R-i-g-h-t. So what you're telling us, Club of Rome, is that you loathe humankind, that you applaud lying, that you don't believe in democracy and that you want to impose some kind of New World Order on us all, against our will?

What's weird is that instead of keeping this information hidden in a steel-lined inner sanctum accessible only to acolytes at Operating Thetan level or above, the Club of Rome is happy to lay out its agenda for anyone who's interested. Those quotes come from its 1993 publication *The First Global Revolution*, co-written by Alexander King and Bertrand Schneider—which was freely available in all good book stores and is available online.

These people can't be for real, surely? That was my first reaction when I read those quotes. I thought: "Probably just some obscure bunch of Situationist pranksters. Or one of those crackpot fringe eco-fascist groups that says stupid things to grab everyone's attention but makes no difference to anyone because they've only got about three and a half members."

But you only have to look at the membership list of the Club of Rome and its sister organizations—the Club of Budapest and the Club of Madrid—to appreciate otherwise. If these Clubs are a joke, they must be extremely high-level and sophisticated. Their membership (full, honorary, associate) includes senior diplomats, ex- and current world leaders, religious leaders, billionaire CEOs, scientists, pop stars, ex-wives of Rolling Stones and environmentalists including: Al Gore, Jimmy Carter, Vaclav Havel, Romano Prodi, Kofi Annan, the Dalai Lama, Jean Chretien, Mikhail Gorbachev, Bill Clinton, Peter Gabriel, Bianca Jagger, Paolo Coelho, Mary Robinson, Deepak Chopra, Daisaku Ikeda, Aung San Suu Kyi, Jacques Delors and not to forget, of course, Guy Verhofstadt, the former Prime Minister of Belgium...

It's possible, of course, that being such busy people none of these luminaries had time to bone up on what the Clubs actually represent. No doubt, too, there was some sort of cozy gang-joining peer group thing going on. You can imagine Vaclav Havel saying: "Gabriel's a member, you say? *The* Peter Gabriel? Bloody hell. The Lamb Dies Down on Broadway is my all time *favorite* album. Count me in!" And the Dalai Lama saying: "The ex-Prime Minister of Belgium? You're kidding? I've spent my whole life *dreaming* of meeting the ex-Prime Minister of Belgium."

There's also an argument to be made that for all their dubious pronouncements, all of these Clubs are only talking shops where the great and the good (and their entourages) gather to enjoy agreeable lunches in delightfully civilized old buildings in beautiful cities. They put the world to rights over a glass or two of fine claret, before heading off back to their day jobs—as innocuous as your local Shriners or Rotary Club.

And indeed when you read inside accounts of the Club of Rome, that is pretty much the modus operandi. "That evening the group was invited to Gvishiani's suite in the Imperial Hotel in Vienna. He served his favorite fruit vodka," runs an entirely characteristic sentence from *Memoirs of a Boffin* by J. Rennie Whitehead, who joined the Club in 1970 and attended many of its early meetings. Whitehead's tone, throughout, is that of an agreeable, easygoing, gentle old cove who just happens to belong to a group of like-minded chums who possess bags of money, the highest level connections and the certain knowledge of exactly what needs to be done to save the world.

Only, the fact that "what needs to be done" involves depriving people of their democratic rights, destroying their livelihoods, preventing them from reproducing and stealing their every liberty seems to bother Whitehead not one jot. There is no apparent malice in him. He simply believes—in the manner of EU *fonctionnaires* and UN bureaucrats and Whitehall mandarins throughout the ages—that "the gentleman from the Club of Rome knows best."

Discretion bordering on invisibility, power without responsibility were very much part of the original plan. As Whitehead has it:

[The Club of Rome] provided the climate in which new ideas were generated; it catalyzed the meeting of researchers with common interests from different countries; it sought out interested funding agencies and helped negotiate funds for the newly-conceived projects; and it provided a forum for discussion and reports on progress. It was by adherence to this brilliantly simple "non-organization" concept that Aurelio Peccei and Alexander King established and maintained the independence and the stature of the Club of Rome.

The Club of Rome is Macavity the Mystery Cat of the global green movement. Its invisible paw prints are all over everything, but by the time you get to the scene of the crime, the sinister feline has vanished.

Or has it? Probably the best analysis of the Club of Rome's tangible effects on global environmental policy comes courtesy of a website called "The Green Agenda":

While researching [...] and during my academic studies, I have come across many references to the Club of Rome (CoR), and reports produced by them. Initially I assumed that they were just another high-level environmental think-tank and dismissed the conspiracy theories found on many websites claiming that the CoR is a group of global elitists attempting to impose some kind of one world government.

I am not a conspiratorial person by nature and was faced with a dilemma when I first read their reports. But it's all there—in black and white.

Indeed. Here, for example, is the Club of Rome's Master Plan— and yes, amazingly, it really does call it a Master Plan—from its 1974 publication *Mankind at the Turning Point*:

In Nature organic growth proceeds according to a Master Plan, a

Blueprint. According to this master plan diversification among cells is determined by the requirements of the various organs; the size and shape of the organs and, therefore, their growth processes are determined by their function, which in turn depends on the needs of the whole organism. Such a 'master plan' is missing from the process of growth and development of the world system. Now is the time to draw up a master plan for organic sustainable growth and world development based on global allocation of all finite resources and a new global economic system.

Note that use of the word "sustainable." By the mid-90s it would become a commonplace, "sustainability" having entered the vernacular of every middle class household as one of those unimpeachably desirable life-goals you could only possibly disagree with if you were the kind of Neanderthal who didn't care whether your tuna fish was caught with skein nets or dolphin-friendly rod and line.

Few people who used the word had any idea of its origin or meaning. But it seemed to embody a multiplicity of equally wondrous concepts including:

* Make-do-and-mend, just like grandma did in the War.
* Our marvelous new compost heap which Charlie will insist on peeing on—jolly disgusting if you ask me, but he read somewhere in some magazine that it speeds up the composting process.
* Fish, yes oh-my-god fish: aren't you worried about them? I am. We won't touch cod nowadays. And haddock's even more of a no-no. Unless it's Icelandic, of course, which is a blessed relief because I've tried Charlie out on mackerel and whiting and he's not having it. He says that when he was a child, fish like that were only good for crab bait.
* Chunky-knit, oiled woolen sweaters which will never go out of fashion and jolly good too because we're so horribly wasteful as

a society, don't you think? Me, I'm seriously thinking of giving up fashion altogether. For Lent at least. Though I do rather have my eye on those marvelous new pony skin numbers Emma Hope's doing. And I haven't yet told you about that new Marni coat...

(Etc.)

Forgive me if I sound slightly cynical about the "s" word. Problem is, I *do* know what it means and how it entered the language, and I'm afraid it embodies an ideological principle that is far from nice: Sustainable Development.

Yes, Sustainable Development sounds like a good thing too—but that is only because we've been culturally programmed to think that way. We associate it with pleasant notions like wild flower meadows left to flourish and Icelandic waters teeming with cod (unlike the poor, overfished, never-to-be-restored Grand Banks), but in fact its underlying philosophy has much more to do with taxation, regulation and control.

As the Green Agenda website puts it:

It is an all-encompassing socialist scheme to combine social welfare programs with government control of private business, socialized medicine, national zoning controls of private property and restructuring of school curriculum which serves to indoctrinate children into politically correct group think.

This was certainly the context in which Maurice Strong used the "s" word in his role as Secretary-General of the United Nations Conference on Environment and Development when he wrote in a 1991 report:

Current lifestyles and consumption patterns of the affluent middle class—involving high meat intake, use of fossil fuels, appliances, home and work-place air-conditioning, and suburban housing—are not sustainable. A shift is necessary which will require a vast strengthening of the multilateral system, including the United Nations.

See how easy it is for an innocent word to mutate into something nasty? You thought "sustainability" meant desirable, manageable life-goals like giving your favorite old sweater another year by patching up the sleeves, or paying over the odds for misshapen organic vegetables. As Strong understands it, however, sustainability is a concept that gives unelected bureaucrats from the UN the right to decide how much meat you eat, how much fuel you use, even how habitable your home is in the sweltering heat of high summer.

And Strong, unfortunately, is closer to the mark than you. That's because of all the dramatis personae in our story—more so than James Hansen, Rajendra Pachauri, Crispin Tickell, Bert Bolin and perhaps even Al Gore—Maurice Strong is the man most responsible for turning the Green agenda into world-changing reality.

Maurice Strong was born in 1929 in Canada during the Great Depression, into a family with strong socialist leanings. His cousin Anna Louise was a Marxist and a member of the Comintern who spent two years in China with Mao and Chou En-Lai at the height of the Cultural Revolution. Her burial in China in 1970 was supervised personally by Chou En-lai. This family connection is partly why Strong enjoys such a close relationship with the current Chinese regime. It was to China that Strong scurried after being implicated in Saddam Hussein's "oil for food" scandal. He now advises the Chinese government on climate change and carbon trading.

Young Maurice left home at 14 and quickly discovered he had two great gifts—the first for making money (variously as a fur trader, investment analyst, oil company VP, cattle rancher, landowner and most recently, as a carbon trader, all of which have contributed to his enormous personal wealth) and the second for social networking (before the days of Facebook), especially within the orbit of the United Nations where he first worked in 1947 in New York, as a lowly assistant pass officer in the Identification Unit of the Security Section.

Strong's main interest, however, was—and has been for many years—the idea of global governance by a self-appointed elite. He spotted early on that quite the best way to achieve this was by manipulating and exploiting international concern about the environment. As he once put it: "Our concept of ballot-box democracy may need to be modified to produce strong governments capable of making difficult decisions, particularly in terms of safeguarding the global environment."

Though it was the Club of Rome that invented the weasel concept of "sustainability", it was Maurice Strong who made it real. He wormed his way through the UN system for years. As early as 1972, he chaired the first UN Conference on the Human Environment, which in turn led to his appointment as first director of the new UN Environment Program (UNEP). In 1983, he was handpicked by UN Secretary-General Kofi Annan to serve as a key member on the "World Commission on Environment and Development." The Brundtland Commission (as it became better known, after its chairwoman, former Norwegian Prime Minister Gro Harlem Brundtland) produced a report called *Our Common Future*. Its central theme will no doubt be familiar:

Sustainable global development requires that those who are more affluent adopt life-styles within the planet's ecological means—in their use of energy, for example. Further, rapidly growing populations can increase the pressure on resources and slow any rise in living standards; thus sustainable development can only be pursued if population size and growth are in harmony with the changing productive potential of the ecosystem.

The idea that began a decade earlier as a twinkle in the eyes of Alexander King and Aurelio Peccei finally was made flesh. Few were capable of spotting at this stage that this oh-so-nice-looking, bonnie, bouncing, gurgling babe had a birthmark on its scalp that read "666". But they might have gotten an inkling from the next paragraph: "We do not pretend that the process is easy or straightforward. Painful choices have to be made."

To find out how painful, the world would have to wait till Strong's report at the May 1992 Earth Summit in Rio de Janeiro. This was Strong's finest hour: the culmination of twenty years' maneuvering and positioning. Here, at last, he had gained sufficient clout to be able to persuade 179 nations to surrender their sovereignty by signing up to perhaps the most far-reaching and constrictive code of environmentally correct practice in the history of the world: a document known as Agenda 21.

Taken at face value, though, Agenda 21 is innocuous to the point of dullness—as you can tell from the first paragraph:

1.1 Humanity stands at a defining moment in history. We are confronted with a perpetuation of disparities between and within nations, a worsening of poverty, hunger, ill health and illiteracy, and the continuing deterioration of the ecosystems on which we depend for our well-being. However, integration of environment and development concerns and greater attention to them will lead to the fulfillment of basic needs, improved living standards for all, better protected and managed ecosystems and a safer, more prosperous future. No nation can achieve this on its own; but together we can—in a global partnership for sustainable development.

All sounds jolly agreeable. What kind of killjoy would you have to be not to want "improved living standards for all", "better protected....ecosystems" and a "more prosperous future"? But then you reach that phrase "global partnership for sustainable development" and your antennae might just start to quiver. Would that be a polite way of saying "One World eco-fascist government?"

Agenda 21 effectively puts an end to national sovereignty, abolishes private property, elevates Nature above man, and places a host of restrictions on what we've come to accept as our most basic freedoms—everything from how, when and where we travel to what we eat.

This is what Maurice Strong presumably meant in that chilling UN report about "unsustainable" lifestyles. In the bright new future envisioned by Agenda 21, your behavior will be determined by the diktats of an enlightened elite over which you have absolutely no democratic control. Strong knows some of you might not like it. But if a world government dictatorship is the price we all must pay for saving our planet, then that is what needs to happen. As he admits:

> The concept of national sovereignty has been an immutable, indeed sacred, principle of international relations. It is a principle which will yield only slowly and reluctantly to the new imperatives of global environmental cooperation. It is simply not feasible for sovereignty to be exercised unilaterally by individual nation states, however powerful. The global community must be assured of environmental security.

OK—you get the idea. Except some of you still aren't convinced because you're thinking

a) Agenda 21 sounds way too much like Area 51, the place where "They" keep the bodies of the "Aliens" they found after the "Roswell Incident" in New Mexico, and must consequently be another of those conspiracies only nut jobs believe in. Or,

b) that if a document signed as long ago as 1992 really were that much of a problem, you'd definitely have heard of it by now. Or,

c) that no sovereign nation, no matter how many free *caipirinhas*
its representatives downed at the Rio shindig, would have been
mad enough to commit itself such a stringent and binding international treaty ... so I must therefore be exaggerating.

Well, I quite agree with you about a): Agenda 21 does indeed
sound so villainous it couldn't possibly be for real, but this is just an
accidental by-product of bureaucratic literalism. Its name originated
simply because it represented an "agenda" for the 21st century. As
for b) yes, I'm with you again. It is astonishing how little coverage
has been granted to a document right up there in significance with
the Declaration of Independence and Magna Carta (though with
exactly the opposite effects).

And on c) what you must realize is that Agenda 21 is a wolf in
sheep's clothing. The reason governments found it easy enough to
sign is because it contains no legally binding obligations. But then, it
doesn't need to, for its apparently voluntary codes can be enforced—
and *are* regularly, scrupulously enforced—via a mechanism over
which sovereign governments have little control anyway: the vast,
labyrinthine, democratically unaccountable behemoth that is the
United Nations.

One of the great mistakes many of us make with the dear old UN
is to view it as an utter shambles of corruption, venality, muddled
thinking, needless waste, political correctness and monumental
incompetence. In our minds, it's an institution so ineffectual that
its blue-helmets could do nothing to stop all those hapless Bosnians
being massacred under their noses at Srebrenica. It's so wrong-
headed that two of the member states on its Human Rights Commission are Libya and Sudan.

While this analysis is entirely fair and justified, it often leads to
the misleading conclusion that the UN is nothing more than a glo-
rified and highly expensive talking shop designed mainly to give
Third World kleptocracies, obscure island states, Islamo-fascistic

dictatorships and Banana Republics a slightly smaller sense of griev-
ance and inferiority.

But that's just the bickering, self-defeating apparatus of the UN
General Assembly. There's another, much larger and more extended
part of the UN that is considerably more effective and directed, and
a lot more dangerous. It comprises bodies such as the Economic
Commission of Europe (ECE)—a green activist wing of the UN
that uses its $30 million annual budget to campaign for "rational
use of resources and sustainable development"; as well as the International Council of Scientific Unions (ICSU), the World Meteorological Organization (WMO) and the United Nations Environment
Program (UNEP)—which between them were responsible for
setting up the IPCC.

We have to be careful here. The danger is that, exposed to all these
initialed UN offshoots, your eyes will glaze over and you'll drift into
complacent indifference. But this, of course, is one of the UN's secret
weapons, just as it is one of the European Union's. Either you're committed to the project, fully cognizant of and sympathetic to its aims,
or you're so far removed from it that the whole damned thing might
just as well not exist. In this way does the UN spread its tentacles,
grabbing ever more power for itself and ever more control over your
daily life—until by the time you become aware of what it's doing,
you've left it far too late to stop it.

To give you a rough idea of the UN's spread, a 2004 UNEP study
estimated that the UN system had over the years initiated 60,000
environment-related projects. Over a dozen UN agencies have
their own environmental operations. Then there's the Economic
and Social Council (ECOSOC), a large umbrella group prioritizing
science and renewable energy, responsible for subgroups including
Committee for Sustainable Development (CSD). The CSD, in turn,
meets annually to monitor the efficacy with which member states
are implementing—yes—Agenda 21.

But really it doesn't need to, for the apparently "voluntary" codes are enforced in such a way as to pass unnoticed by those outside the system. Those within the system include politicians, European Union and UN technocrats, green activists and environmental NGOs. Those outside the system are people like you and me. *We don't know how Agenda 21 works because we are not meant to know.*

This becomes clear in a 1998 UN discussion document, "The Future of Local Agenda 21 in the New Millennium". Here, a man called Gary Lawrence (former Director of the Centre for Sustainable Communities at the University of Washington, Chief Planner in the City of Seattle, and an advisor to the President's Council on Sustainable Development) outlines how best to outfox all those dangerous liberty-lovers who might seek to frustrate the noble work of the United Nations:

> Participating in a UN-advocated planning process would very likely bring out many of the conspiracy-fixated groups and individuals in our society such as the National Rifle Association, citizen militias and some members of Congress. This segment of our society who fear "one-world government" and a UN invasion of the United States through which our individual freedom would be stripped away would actively work to defeat any elected official who joined "the conspiracy" by undertaking LA21. So, we call our process something else, such as comprehensive planning, growth management, or *smart growth.*

Note that Lawrence doesn't even try to deny the anti-democratic nature of this "UN-advocated planning process". His sole concern is how best to slip this one-world government agenda under the radar of any pesky concerned citizens. And the best way, he suggests, is through lies, deception and a form of Orwellian Newspeak in which once-innocent words are subverted to promote the controlling agenda of the left.

That phrase "smart growth" is a good example. A key element of this urban planning philosophy is "intensification"—i.e. more dense building. This is not only ironic—since many of those who promote "smart growth" are also population pessimists—but paradoxical. As noted in a recent study, "in locations where intensification occurs, greater concentrations of traffic tend to occur, and this worsens local environmental conditions." Duh! Perhaps it should be called dumb growth. How on earth did we get here?

Well, you must remember that Agenda 21 was launched in Rio two decades ago, and it's been 25 years since the Bruntland Commission advanced the concept of "sustainable development", and four decades since the Club of Rome idealized "limits to growth". This is more than enough time for those who believe in the Project to act, in true Gramsci-ite fashion, to infiltrate and take over the system.

Agenda 21 is enforced mainly at the local government level. Here is how it works:

1. Local environmental activists create a Local Agenda 21 (LA21) lobby group. Spouting the mantra "Think Global, Act Local", they urge their town/city/district government to sign up to the "voluntary" code of Agenda 21.

2. Often the local government agrees, encouraged from within by the kind of "watermelons" who tend to be drawn to careers in "public service". Around the world, 1,200 districts have signed up—from Finland to Zimbabwe (whose starving, tyrannised people, you might think, have more immediate pressing concerns than, say, introducing a low-carbon, sustainable transport system or greater gender equality in the workplace).

   The biggest take-up has been in the U.S., where over 600 districts have signed up. And not just the usual suspects, like Berkeley, California, but even places in red states such as Dallas, Texas.

3. The local government signatory is welcomed to the fold of ICLEI— Local Governments for Sustainability, the UN-funded pressure group responsible for promoting Agenda 21. (It was founded as

the "International Council for Local Environmental Initiatives" but changed its mission and name in 2003.) ICLEI bestows accolades on the local government—such as its "Star Community Index" rating—for its efforts in advancing the valuable cause of sustainability. In turn, the local government entity can then boast about its achievements in publicity handouts, showing voters how sensitive and caring it is. These ratings also make it far more likely that the local government will receive grants and/or other financial inducements from any number of UN- , EU- or federal and state government-sponsored initiatives.

4. In return for attaining this shiny new green status symbol, the local government feels honor-bound to promote the "sustainability" agenda it has committed to (at least, on its website). This can take myriad forms: converting public transportation from diesel to biofuels (thereby subsidizing corn growers, making food more expensive, and increasing emissions to the environment); issuing fines for incorrect recycling; penalizing drivers of sports utility vehicles with higher parking permit charges; and greater restrictions on car use generally. In the U.S. its effects are felt especially through town planning. Zoning regulations are changed to encourage "high-density" housing in town centres and to prevent suburban development on farmland.

5. And there ain't nothing you can do about it.

It's the last part that makes Agenda 21 so scary, of course: the utter lack of democratic accountability. It's a little like returning home after a long vacation to your local church. You discover that it has been decorated with pentacles and that the minister is now wearing a black cloak and preparing to sacrifice a goat where the altar used to be.

"What's going on?" you ask, in horror. "Well, it's what we all agreed on," says the minister. "*When* did we agree to all this? No one asked me!" "We put a message on the notice board. We held consultation meetings for anyone who was interested. Did you not get a call from young Damien, on our steering committee? The general feeling was that Christian worship was too old-fashioned, patriarchal and Western for our younger members, and that Satanism was a more vibrant, diverse and inclusive way forward for the community."

"But I want the old church back. I liked the old church!"

"I'd love to help but I'm afraid it's out of my hands. You see, as a signatory of Agenda 666 this church is now statutorily committed to our new code of practice..."

But wait a second: isn't this a slightly over-the-top analogy to apply to a series of measures which, after all, were designed by good, well-meaning people to make the world a kinder, fairer, cleaner, more socially just and, yes, more *sustainable* place?

What, exactly, is so wrong with following Portland, Oregon's appeal for "20-minute neighborhoods", where everything you need is within convenient walking distance? Why shouldn't local governments reduce housing costs by encouraging the development of high-density urban communities? What's not to like about reducing our reliance on cars, cutting carbon emissions and protecting our natural environment from urban sprawl? And why shouldn't the vast majority of the U.S. landmass be set aside for designated wildlands, and wildlife corridors and other protected zones so as to preserve the raw beauty of nature for future generations to enjoy for all eternity?

In fact, what kind of evil, snarling, selfish monster would you have to be *not* to want all this wondrous stuff? Well, for one thing, you might be concerned about the fact that Portland's eight percent increase in population density between 1990 and 2000 contributed to a 65 percent increase in traffic congestion. (By comparison, on average large urban areas in the U.S. experienced a 6 percent decrease in density and a 42 percent increase in congestion.)

Welcome to the passive-aggressive world of global watermelons—socialism hiding behind the guise of environmentalism. If you disagree with the "consensus" pushed through by the watermelons: tough. It serves you right for being such a freak.

And of course, this is why beneath their smiling, nurturing, consensual façade, the watermelons represent such a ruthless totalitarian outlook. All those zoning regulations, for example, and wildlife corridors—they may appear to be sensible gestures. But what about the interests of the farmers whose land they steal? What about all the property owners whose investment values fall and whose rights are undermined and/or stolen?

As for "eco-friendly" measures such as government-mandated recycling initiatives, and penalties for car use: what about those hard-working families who believe that local government should ensure that the streets are safe and the trash is cleared—rather than police their residents' levels of ecological correctness? What about all those people who have considered the evidence, and question the whole premise of global warming?

Sure, there's a case to be made for some aspects of "sustainability". But as free citizens, we surely ought to be able to vote for these things, rather than have them foisted on us by a handful of watermelons who know how to game the system.

Yet this is exactly how Agenda 21 operates. While paying lip-service to grassroots "people power", it circumvents the democratic process entirely. You didn't vote for all these stringent new rules and taxes; you don't remember being consulted about them. Yet somehow, these values—which may be alien to everything you believe in—seem to have been absorbed by your local government, as if by osmosis, and now form the basis of policy decisions which will have a major impact on your life.

In an article for the website "Big Government", James M. Simpson described it well:

In "*Sustainable Development*" [Marxists] have found a magic mantra. It has allowed them to insinuate *all* their socialist fantasies into our legal code, under our noses, with little or no fanfare, scant public debate and graveyard noises from our treacherously AWOL mass media, right down to the local level—*with our permission.*

Let's be absolutely clear: this "sustainable development" is not the wholesome, cozily innocuous thing a succession of glossy magazine lifestyle articles have persuaded us it is. It is born of the pessimistic *Weltanschauung* ("worldview") we see in such pieces as Teddy Gold-smith's first editorial in *The Ecologist,* where he variously describes the human race as "parasites", a "disease" and "swarming masses"; the *Weltanschauung* that led the Club of Rome to declare in a 1974 report—"Mankind at the Turning Point"—that "the Earth has a cancer and the cancer is Man"; the worldview that enabled Maurice Strong to describe in his autobiography the prospect of billions of environmental deaths as "a glimmer of hope."

And inextricably bound with this *Weltanschauung* is a very specific belief as to how Earth's problems must be remedied. Might this involve trying to make everyone wealthier so they can afford to pollute less and are tempted to breed fewer children? Nope. Might it involve making energy cheaper, so that fewer of the world's poor suffer from fuel poverty? Nope. Might it involve making governments more democratically accountable so that people are freer? Nope. For all the green doomsayers wedded to a belief in dangerous overpopulation and diminishing resources, the proposed solution is always the same: less freedom, less consumption, higher taxation, more regulation and bigger government.

Now at this point in the chapter, just when you think it can't get any worse, I want to do the equivalent of the scene in the movie where the camera cuts away from the close up—and you realize that the outcrop they're standing on is but a tiny promontory of a mountain so high and vast, amid a range so enormous it truly beggars your feeble imagination, utterly transforms your perspective and makes you go: "Wow! The wonders of CGI!"

I'm going to do this by introducing you (just briefly, for we're in danger of conspiracy shock overload here) of just a few more of the big names and organizations involved in promoting exactly the same One World Government agenda.

Let's start with Mikhail Gorbachev. Yes, that's right: dear Gorby, with the endearing birth mark on his bald pate and the habit of performing folk songs at private fundraising soirees (I've heard him). The same man who did so much make the world a safer, better place when—in happy partnership with Ronnie Reagan and Margaret Thatcher—he helped bring about the end of the Cold War with Glasnost and Perestroika. Well, he's now involved with this conspiracy. Big time.

In 1991, he established the Gorbachev Foundation (motto: "Toward A New Civilization") as "a think tank whose purpose is to explore the path that global governance should take as mankind progresses into an interdependent global society." Most of his green activism, though, is conducted through another organization which he founded—Green Cross International (GCI)—which has 31 national affiliates around the world and whose honorary board members include former UN head Javier Perez de Cuellar, actor Robert Redford and media mogul Ted Turner. The organization's stated mission is to "help ensure a just, sustainable and secure future for all." [Hmm. Now where have we seen that "s" word before?]

Gorby was also responsible, in collaboration with Maurice Strong, for the Earth Charter (2000). This is a collection of principles— described on Strong's website as "a widely recognized, global consensus statement on ethics and values for a sustainable future" and officially endorsed, natch, by the United Nations—which starts out like a fluffy, New Age wish list (Principle no. 1: "Respect Earth and life in all its diversity") but which turns out on closer examination to be yet another master plan for global, socialist eco-tyranny.

Principle 10, for example, asks that we "Ensure that economic activities and institutions at all levels promote human development in an equitable and sustainable manner." Not just that, but also we must: "Promote the equitable distribution of wealth within nations and among nations." And "Ensure that all trade supports sustainable resource use, environmental protection, and progressive labor standards." And even: "Require multinational corporations and international financial organizations to act transparently in the public good, and hold them accountable for the consequences of their activities."

And who will be defining and enforcing these progressive ideals? No one over whom you have any kind of democratic control. That's because the aim of the Earth Charter is to eliminate national sovereignty and place us all under the control of a single "Earth Government."

As Gorby himself said in a speech,

> One of the worst of the new dangers is ecological....Today, global climatic shifts; the greenhouse effect; the "ozone hole"; acid rain; contamination of the atmosphere, soil and water by industrial and household waste; the destruction of the forest; etc. all threaten the stability of the planet... I believe that the new world order will not be fully realized unless the United Nations and its Security Council create structures... authorised to impose sanctions and make use of other measures of compulsion.

This is made explicit on the website of Dr. Robert Muller, former UN Assistant Secretary General, who declares, in the course of several long, imaginary dialogues between himself, God and Earth:

> Please stand up, delegates of the world, hold each other's hand and let us swear together that we will accomplish this historical miracle before it is too late: to save this Earth, to save humanity with a new world order. All the rest is secondary. Let us strengthen and reform the United Nations into a United States of the World or a World Union like the European Union.

All of which would be easier to dismiss as the kooky ramblings of an eco-nut of no consequence if Dr. Muller hadn't been responsible for drafting and overseeing vast swathes of UN environmental policy. He is founder of the United Nations University of Peace (which he sited on a mountain in Costa Rica in honor of an ancient prophecy) where the original Earth Charter document is kept in a specially constructed "Ark of Hope", painted with panels representing the flora and fauna of the world "as seen through the images of the world's traditional artists."

Besides the Earth Charter, the Ark contains over 1,000 "Temenos Books"—handcrafted books "made by artists, schoolchildren, and citizens around the world, expressing their individual and collaborative prayers and affirmations for Earth." These regularly tour the world's schools and universities, spreading the message of a "just, sustainable and peaceful society."

Not only does the New Age religion of the New World Order have its own Ark, but also its own Tower of Babel. Or, if you prefer, its Rosetta Stone. It's called the Georgia Guidestones, and comprises five mighty granite slabs, each nearly twenty feet tall, that were created in 1979 at the behest of an "elegant gray-haired gentleman", Robert C. Christian (operating under a pseudonym). At first, Christian wasn't taken seriously by the local contractor he commissioned for the job. But when he mentioned that money was no object and produced his first check for $10,000, all of this changed.

Since their erection on a hilltop in the U.S. state of Georgia in 1980, the Georgia Guidestones have attracted a deal of controversy. Given the "ten commandments" that are inscribed on the slabs, in eight different languages, this is not altogether surprising. The first, for example, gently hints that the majority of the human population should be culled:

MAINTAIN HUMANITY UNDER 500,000,000 IN PERPETUAL BALANCE WITH NATURE.

Even when the stones were erected in 1980, to fulfill this injunction would have entailed killing eight out of every nine humans. Today, it would involve executing closer to 12 out of 13. Not, of course, that the Guidestones put it quite so crudely. But you can guess their ideological bent from one of the other commandments: "BE NOT A CANCER ON THE EARTH" says one. Hmm. Now where have we heard that phrase before?

Among those who have been fingered as the mysterious "elegant gray-haired gentleman" is the media mogul Ted Turner. This seems unlikely. If he had grey hair in 1980, he'd surely be older than Turner is now. But the message of the Guidestones certainly chimes with Turner's own deep green ecological views, particularly regarding the human race. "A total world population of 250–300 million people, a 95 percent decline from present levels, would be ideal," Turner once famously said, having apparently temporarily forgotten that with five children of his own, he has done more than most to contribute to the "problem".

Presumably that means he'd get on like a house on fire with the Duke of Edinburgh, who—in a foreword to a book called *If I Were an Animal*—wrote: "In the event that I am reincarnated, I would like to return as a deadly virus, in order to contribute something to solve overpopulation." Perhaps too, Turner would have found a kindred spirit in the late Alexander King (who besides co-founding the Club of Rome, you'll recall, was the man who popularized the use of DDT as an insecticide during the war). In his memoirs, King confided somewhat chillingly: "My chief quarrel with DDT in hindsight is that it has greatly added to the population problem."

You'll find quotes like this repeated endlessly on the internet, as often as not on conspiracy sites warning of the coming New World Order. This, of course, makes it much, much easier for their significance to be downplayed by green opinion-formers in the mainstream media: "Oh you don't take that kind of thing seriously, do you? It's just a bunch of 9/11 Truthers and Alex Jones nuts and right-wing fruitcakes, indulging in their c-r-azee conspiracy theories."

So before we close this chapter, I'd like to address this issue in more detail. Perhaps we should start by trying to decide what, exactly, is a conspiracy theory. I quite like the definition offered by (green MSM opinion former) David Aaronovitch in his conspiracy-theory-debunking book *Voodoo Histories*. Aaronovitch says that a conspiracy theory is "the attribution of deliberate agency to something that is much more likely to be accidental or unintended."

What's useful about this definition is that it expresses proper contempt for many of the more idiotic urban myths of our time such as the one—which prompted a time- and money-wasting official inquiry—that Diana, Princess of Wales, did not really die as a result of an unfortunate car accident in a Parisian tunnel, but was bumped off by British security forces, perhaps on the orders of the Royal Family, because she knew too much or she was secretly pregnant with a Dodi Fayed's illegitimate Muslim love child or…

Well, it's a nonsense and was obviously a nonsense from the start. The British Royal Family hasn't been in the business of bumping off awkward members for at least four centuries. The intelligence services are so hamstrung by political correctness these days they're not even allowed to do "wet jobs" on evil, vicious enemies of the state, let alone well-loved and beautiful English princesses. And just suppose she had been pregnant with Dodi's love child (which the inquest showed she wasn't): what would it have mattered, when the succession to the throne had long since been decided with the births of Princes William and Harry?

Sure, a deeper investigation might have been merited had it emerged that the brakes of the Princess's car had been tampered with, or that traces of ricin had been found in her body, or someone suddenly noticed on taking her to hospital that there was a huge stiletto between her shoulder-blades with Prince Philip's crest on the haft. But none of this transpired. Instead what emerged fairly quickly was that the driver of her car was drunk, that the car was going very fast when it crashed, that Princess Diana had chosen not to wear her

WATERMELONS: THE GREEN MOVEMENT'S TRUE COLORS

seat belt: all indications, any reasonable person might conclude, that this was all very much a case of cock-up, not conspiracy.

But just because conspiracy theories tend by nature to be more convoluted and less immediately plausible than the alternative explanation doesn't mean that they're all untrue. This is where Aaronovitch's definition—and his book too, for that matter—falls down. Built into it is a metropolitan liberal's sneery assumption that conspiracy theorists are all deeply deluded, socially inadequate, mostly sinister right-wing whackos, and that conspiracy theories never turn out to be conspiracy fact because, well, they just don't.

So where does that leave this chapter? Is it all just smears and innuendo? Did I pick as many big names as I could find on the internet—Mikhail Gorbachev! Robert Redford! The Dalai Lama! The ex-Prime-Minister of Belgium!—then trawl for a few scary quotes and loony-tune websites, and join the dots in a random way so as to concoct an entirely spurious web of intrigue?

I wish.

Look, when I began researching this book, I thought it was going to be about Climategate and global warming—not some massive international plot to destroy Western Civilization and replace it with a grisly New World Order based on rationed resources, enforced equality and the return of the barter system. The last thing I'd choose would be for such a conspiracy to exist because a) the thought is so depressing and b) it would run the risk of undermining the rest of my argument, by characterizing me—at least in some readers' eyes—as a paranoid nutjob.

Unfortunately, though, the weight of evidence was against me. So brazenly open are the leading ideologues of the green movement about their plans for a New World Order, I'm not even sure that the word "conspiracy" properly applies. When you think of a conspiracy, you think of something clandestine, underground, hidden. But these "conspirators" are happy to shout their intentions from the rooftops. Whether it's Maurice Strong on his road to Rio, John

Holdren calling for the "de-development" of the United States or Britain's Tyndall Centre urging a "managed recession"; whether it's a Friends of the Earth campaign leaflet, or a Club of Rome policy document, or a report published by the UN-sponsored Commission on Global Governance, the message that emerges is always the same. Economic growth must be reined in, resources rationed, personal liberties curtailed, wealth redistributed, private property abolished and a new era of—yes—"global governance" by experts and other unelected bureaucrats be ushered in. You don't need to be a conspiracy theorist to believe in the green movement's master plan for a New World Order, only to possess the basic ability to read and listen.

This is why I find it hard to be sympathetic when, say, a figure of the stature of the Prince of Wales flies with his entourage to Rio to tell a conference of businessmen that "We have only 100 months left to save the world from Climate Change". Or when, a few months later, he boards his biofuel-powered royal train to tour Britain, lecturing his future subjects on the need to live "sustainably."

It was just this kind of well-meaning idiocy that prompted me to write a catty denunciation of my future king in the *Spectator*. Like one of his predecessors AEthelred the "Unready", I argued, Prince Charles is "unraed"—Anglo Saxon for "ill-advised". But more than that he is spoiled, petulant, irresponsible and thick.

Not all my readers agreed. Some of the criticisms I got were pure snobbery—on the lines of "Who are you, you disgusting little oik, to be calling our future King a prat?" Others were on the similarly predictable grounds that Prince Charles is a nice, well-meaning chap, doing his best, and if he wants to talk about preserving scarce resources, and reducing carbon footprints and living more sustainably, well what's wrong with that?

What's wrong with it is that there are no-half measures in the modern green movement. To join it simply because you like trees, flowers and birdsong is the rough equivalent of joining the Nazi party in the mid-Thirties just for the smart uniforms, restaurant discounts and more efficient train time tables. Which is to say that the eco-fascistic elements are *not* optional extras. The anti-capitalism, the hatred of economic growth, the curtailment of personal liberty, the disdain for the human race, the yearning for a one-world government of rule by "experts"—these are all as integral to watermelons as *Lebensraum* and extermination camps were to Nazism.

I'm sure that the Prince of Wales, Ted Turner, Robert Redford, Leonardo DiCaprio, Deepak Chopra, Ed Begley Jr. and the rest of the green movement's long, long list of celebrity useful idiots are awfully nice people once you get to know them. And I'm sure they have the very best of intentions, But I'm afraid the time has long since passed when ignorance or naivety could in any way excuse their support for so thoroughly malignant a cause.

In its self-righteous eagerness to save the world, the watermelons are ideologically committed to the path most likely to destroy the world. That's not nice. That's not caring. That's pure insanity.

CHAPTER 9

MALTHUS & CO.

The enormous amount of coal required to run our great ocean steam-
ships, our leviathans of the deep, and the innumerable factories of
our cities is making such inroads upon the available store that nature
cannot forever supply the demand. When all the coal of the earth is
used, what then?

Lord Kelvin, mathematical physicist and engineer, 1902

So you now you know it's a neo-Marxist plot to take over the world,
and it's all rooted in the deepest of misanthropy. You know that
many of the proposed solutions to what may well be an imaginary
problem are quite stupidly, self-destructively wrong. Yet still you
have your doubts.

You're thinking: "Well all right, maybe the science supporting AGW is a bit dodgy. And maybe the motives of all the different vested interests pushing it aren't as kosher as they might be. But
that doesn't mean the green movement is wrong about everything. I
mean, overpopulation *is* a serious problem. And resources *are* finite.
And we *do* need to take care of the planet for future generations. And
we *can't* go on consuming the way we do because it just leads to so
much waste. And all that pollution we pump into the air, you can't
tell me it's having no effect whatsoever. And what about GM? And
surely you must agree that organic agriculture is better? And…."

Yep. I hear this a lot. Even from people who consider themselves hard-headed rationalists and who are highly skeptical of the so-called "consensus" on man-made global warming. And it's entirely understandable, not only because of the cultural brainwashing process I've described in earlier chapters but also because it all seems like the most basic common sense.

Stands to reason, doesn't it? We all know that the world is made of *stuff.* ("Scarce resources", as an economist might call it). We all know that from our personal life experience using a range of materials such as beer, light bulbs, condoms, tires, running shoes and so on, that once we've used up *stuff* we can't really use it again, unless maybe it's a glass bottle or some other recyclable item. We've all stood in a crowded lift or train carriage and felt how unpleasantly claustrophobic it is. And we've all been to our favorite stretch of coastline and gone: "Oh no! Last time I was here there was just a couple of beach shacks and a tiny guest house and a few turtles laying their eggs. And now look at it: ruined! Totally ruined!" We've all been stuck in a traffic jam (a lot more often than we used to). And we all know that population is growing, especially in the Third World. And of course, we all know about what happened at Easter Island—as those of us who have read Jared Diamond are fond of reminding everyone else *ad nauseam.*

This is what I call the "I reckon" fallacy. That's "I reckon" as in the words that you normally use to introduce your heart-felt—but entirely unsupported—opinion when you offer an argument in a pub. And "fallacy" because, well, that's exactly what it is.

Let's consider a few examples beginning with the case of 18th-century doom-monger Thomas Malthus. In his "Essay on the Principle of Population" (1798), Malthus observed "the constant tendency in all animated life to increase beyond the nourishment prepared for it" and feared that human populations would be subject to the same problem, resulting in a life of perpetual famine, disease, pestilence and vice. Yet Malthus failed to see the Agricultural Revolution happening around him in Britain, which saw rapid advances in agricultural production. He failed to foresee the Industrial Revolution which had just begun.

As history subsequently proved, Malthus was talking out of his tri-corner hat. Between 1780 and 1914, Britain's population swelled more than four-fold—while between 1780 and 1914, her economy grew thirteen times larger. Standards of living rose accordingly, with almost everyone better fed, better clothed and better housed than at any time in British history. Malthus, understandably, fell somewhat out of fashion.

By the mid-20th Century, however, the discredited doom-monger was creeping back into fashion. Among the first to take up his noble cause of cussed pessimism against all objective evidence was one Harrison Brown, aforementioned author of the 1954 book *The Challenge of Man's Future.* In it he wrote:

> ......we are now living in a phase of history which is destined never to be repeated. For the fifth of the world population that lives in regions of machine culture it is a period of unprecedented abundance. And most of us who are a part of that fortunate one-fifth are so enamored with the achievements of the last century and with the abundance which has been created that we believe the pace of achievement will continue uninterrupted in the future. However, only a cursory investigation of the present position of machine civilizations needed to uncover the fact that it is indeed in a precarious position. A cosmic gambler, looking at us from afar, would, in all likelihood give substantial odds in favor of the probability that it will soon disappear, never again to come into existence.

Maybe it's just as well that Brown's cosmic gambler was imaginary. Otherwise he might have lost a great deal of money, possibly being forced to sell the weekend getaway by the fire lakes of Quegglqx, his cherished Blurtwangglle, and perhaps even the anterior fuel-sacs attached to the under-spines of at least 239 of his 842 children.

That's the incredible thing about made-up speculation of an imaginary future based on nothing more than your passionate strength of feeling as to what ought to be true. (Yes, that means you, computer modeling.) Absolutely anything is possible!

So what has really happened to our doomed race in the disastrous 50-odd years since Brown wrote his book? Well, says author Matt Ridley in *The Rational Optimist*, the average human being now earns nearly three times as much money, eats one-third more calories of food, buries one-third fewer of her children and can expect to live one-third longer. She is less likely to die as a result of war, murder, childbirth, accidents, tornadoes, flooding, famine, whooping cough, tuberculosis, malaria, diphtheria, typhus, typhoid, measles, smallpox, scurvy or polio. She is more likely to be literate and to have finished school. She is more likely to own a telephone, a flush toilet, a refrigerator and a bicycle. All this during a period in which the world population has more than doubled.

This doesn't mean that Brown is definitely wrong, particularly if he was using "soon" in the cosmic sense of, "any time in the next three or four million years." What we can say, with confidence, is that he has been wrong so far. As wrong as all those other doom-mongers who have made similar predictions throughout our history, such as the fellow who made this one:

Our teeming population is the strongest evidence our numbers are burdensome to the world, which can hardly support us from its natural elements. Our wants grow more and more keen and our complaints more bitter in all mouths, while nature fails in affording us our usual sustenance. In every deed, pestilence and famine and wars have to be regarded as a remedy for nations as the means of pruning the luxuriance of the human race.

No, not Paul Ehrlich 1968. Nor the Prince of Wales 2010. This was the utterance of Carthaginian priest Tertullian in his "Treatise of the Soul" in 210 AD, when the world's population was a mere 250 million. Since then it has grown to over 6.5 billion. Frankly, which planet would you rather inhabit? Tertullian's blissfully uncrowded car-free zone? Or our current congested hell of long life-expectancies, modern dental care, paid holidays, iPods, contraception, literacy and penicillin?

These are the kind of historical comparisons we don't make nearly often enough. If we did, we might be more grateful and more realistic. Ridley offers a delicious example in *The Rational Optimist*, with an idyllic portrait of a family in Western Europe or eastern North America ca. 1800: gathering around the hearth in their timber-framed house, father reading from the Bible while mother prepares to dish up a healthy stew, daughter is feeding the horse, son pours water from a pitcher into earthenware mugs, and outside there is no noise of traffic, and there are no dioxins or radioactive fallout—only tranquility and birdsong.

Then Ridley puts this fantasy into its correct historical context. Paraphrasing Ridley: Father will be dead at 53 (and he's lucky: life expectancy in England in 1800 is less than 40); baby will die of smallpox, the water tastes of cow manure, mother is tortured by toothache, the stew is grey and gristly. There is no fruit or salad at this season, candles cost too much so the only light comes from the fire, the children sleep two to a straw mattress on the floor.

Is this what eco-lobbyists yearn for when they argue that we must reduce our CO_2 output to "pre-industrial levels"—the bracing pleasures of cold, hunger, discomfort and grinding poverty?

Well, no, obviously not. They believe that massive lifestyle changes are the least worst solution to the Armageddon that awaits us if we don't stop consuming scarce resources *soon*. And let's be honest here: we cannot be sure that they are not correct. The future is a mystery to us all. Anything could happen: asteroid strike, outbreak of World War III, Elvis coming back to Earth to rule over us all with peace, harmony and gentle crooning, Obama being elected for a second term.

So yes, within that multitude of infinite possibilities it is entirely conceivable that our planet's future will pan out along the same disastrous lines envisaged by green doom-mongers: pullulating masses of humans consuming the planet's resources like locusts, melting ice caps, flooding cities, three ark-like ships being prepared in China in order to preserve a select group of humans from the disaster that the Mayans prophesied...etc.

What we can, however, say with absolute certainty is this: if they *are* right it will be a historical first. From Tertullian to Thomas Malthus, from Harrison Brown to Paul Ehrlich, from the Club of Rome to James Hansen—every one of the catastrophists who has predicted doom, gloom and disaster for our planet as a result of expanding populations and burgeoning economic growth so far has been proven entirely wrong. Those few brave "Cornucopians" who have dared to venture the opposite view—that the more people there are on earth the better things get—have so far been proven spectacularly right.

Greatest and most influential of these optimists was a brilliant U.S. economics professor called Julian Simon, a.k.a. "The Doomslayer". In 1980, he put the two competing theories to the test in a famous wager with Stanford biologist Paul Ehrlich, co-author of *The Population Bomb*. Simon challenged Ehrlich to choose any five commodities he liked. Ehrlich bought $200 of each, for a total of $1,000.

Simon's view was that by the end of the decade, the inflation-adjusted prices would fall for each of the five commodities. Ehrlich, of course, could scarcely believe his luck. As any fool knew, when population increases and scarce resources approach their depletion point, naturally the price of commodities will increase. The bet was that exactly ten years after the index date (September 29, 1980), either Ehrlich or Simon would write the winner a check for the inflation-adjusted difference.

With the help of two like-minded friends (John Holdren and John Harte), Ehrlich picked five metals most likely to skyrocket: chromium, copper, nickel, tin and tungsten. Then they waited for the inevitable clean-up—which, humiliatingly, never came. Though the world's population grew by more than 800 million between 1980 and 1990, the prices of all the chosen metals were lower at the end of the decade than at the beginning. Simon won the bet, and Ehrlich wrote him a check for $576.07 in October 1990. More importantly, he had won a moral victory for the cause of Cornucopianism.

Simon died in 1998 and never got the credit he truly deserved. While Ehrlich continued to be feted as an environmental seer (in 1990, the same year he lost the bet, he won a MacArthur Foundation "genius award"), Simon was invariably dismissed during his lifetime as a right-wing crank. As a profile of Simon in *Wired* put it:

> There seemed to be a bizarre reverse-Cassandra effect operating in the universe: whereas the mythical Cassandra spoke the awful truth and was not believed, these days "experts" spoke awful falsehoods, and they were believed. Repeatedly being wrong actually seemed to be an advantage, conferring some sort of puzzling magic glow upon the speaker.

The reward for being right, on the other hand, seems to be mainly derision, hatred and custard pies in the face. This certainly was the experience of one of Simon's acolytes—a young Danish statistics professor called Bjorn Lomborg—when he published an influential bestseller called *The Skeptical Environmentalist*.

Lomborg started out as a member of Greenpeace, fully sympathetic to the cause of the eco-doom-mongers. One day, as a class project, he gave his students the task of analyzing the nonsensical theories of right-wing economist Julian Simon. The intention was to expose them as bunk. Instead, much to Lomborg's surprise, Simon's theories turned out to be scrupulously researched, solidly grounded and entirely plausible.

This gave Lomborg the idea for his book. He would put his academic specialty to use by analyzing all the statistics used by campaigning organizations such as Greenpeace and the WWF, and see how they measured up. What Lomborg found, in almost every case, was that the hard scientific facts had been twisted, distorted and exaggerated by green activists to trump up what he called a "Litany" of man-made eco-disaster scenarios from acid rain to melting ice caps to the effects of the 1989 Exxon Valdez tragedy in Prince William Sound.

Like all oil spills, Exxon Valdez was manna from heaven for green campaigners: shocking, moving photos of seabirds—and better still in this case, oh-so-cute and special sea otters, distraught fishermen protesting about ruined livelihoods; angry political cartoons in newspapers ironically captioned "The Price of Oil?", and nasty, evil, heartless capitalists in the fossil-fuel industry, ripe for scapegoating.

Lomborg's analysis put all of this in its proper context. The number of seabirds killed in the spill—250,000—was no greater than the number of birds that die every day in the U.S. as a result of flying into plate glass window, nor the number of birds that are killed in Britain every two days by domestic cats. As for the $2 billion clean-up operation, well that was probably a waste of money too. Subsequent research had shown that while beaches that were expensively and elaborately cleaned of oil took four years to recover, the beaches that were left alone took just eighteen months.

All of which went down with the greenies like a plate of *steack tartare* at a vegan birthday party. What upset them even more, though, was Lomborg's truly unforgiveable attack on their favorite cause célèbre—the 1997 Kyoto Protocol. As Lomborg pointed out, even in the unlikely event that the Protocol's signatories were to implement its proposals, the effect would merely be to reduce the world's surface temperature by just 0.07°C over 50 years—at a cost to the global economy of $150 billion per annum. Yet for just a single year's worth of that pointless expenditure, Lomborg calculated, it would be possible to ensure that every person on earth had access to clean drinking water and sanitation.

To all this, the green movement responded in its predictable way:

not with factual counterarguments but with a good old-fashioned smear campaign. An ad hoc, quasi-official pressure group calling itself the "Danish Committee on Scientific Dishonesty" declared his book "unscientific". Lomborg was vilified in numerous science journals—one of which called him "anti-Christ"—and at an Oxford book signing he had a custard pie splattered in his face by an activist.

Unfortunately, these smear tactics worked. Ask any green about *The Skeptical Environmentalist* and you'll be assured that it was entirely discredited by an official Danish government inquiry. What they conveniently forget—if they ever knew in the first place—is that the criticisms of the Danish Committee on Scientific Dishonesty were subsequently found to be invalid by an official government inquiry carried out by less partisan officials.

You can see something similar happening today with the latest book to adopt a Cornucopian line—Matt Ridley's *The Rational Optimist*. Though praised by many reviewers, it mightily peeved green campaigners such as George Monbiot, who managed two angry articles on it in the space of a fortnight. After the statutory outburst of petulant ad hominem arguments (dwelling on Ridley's allegedly "disastrous" performance as the chairman of failed bank Northern Rock), Monbiot dismissed Ridley's arguments as a case of "telling the rich what they want to hear."

There's something about Cornucopianism that really seems to get under the skin of greenies. It makes them writhe and shriek and protest as violently as vampires suddenly exposed to light. Just what is it that they find so offensive?

I'd suggest that there are a number of factors at play here, from the green movement's natural, chunky-knit, ingrained husks-and-all pessimism to its puritanical abhorrence of any grand universal theory that celebrates personal liberty, to sheer purblind ignorance. But in essence, I think, it's just another manifestation of that eternal political divide which separates conservatives from left-liberals: head versus heart.

We've touched on the "heart" part already. It's that "I reckon fallacy" that misleads many of us into thinking that just because we feel in our bones that something is true we've no need to support our theory with any real-world evidence.

Take "overpopulation". We all know the world is running out of space. How do we know? Well, because people are always telling us it is—environmentalists, politicians, newsreaders, the guy we sat next to at a dinner party, everyone. It's just so obvious that it must be true. The current world population is nearly seven billion—which is a lot!—and by the middle of this century it will have risen to maybe nine billion, which is a whole heap more. Where are we going to fit all those people? Isn't our planet pretty much filled to bursting, already? Quick, quick, something must be done before the whole world ends up like a Japanese subway train in rush hour!

Or so you might think, until you look at the hard data. You could, for example, fit everyone in the world into the state of Texas, and with plenty of room for each person. Texas is 268,581 square miles, so with a world population of 7 billion, you'd have a density of about 26,000 people per square mile. That is about the same as New York City and is considerably less than Union City, New Jersey (about 53,000 per square mile.). Many other cities around the world have even higher population densities, from Delhi, India (about 75,000 per sq. mi.) to Manila, Philippines (over 110,000 per sq. mi.). Since the world's landmass is 732 times the size of Texas, this would leave enough room for population expansion, farmland and pristine wilderness—you'd hope—to allay the fears of even the most fanatical Malthusian doom-monger.

And how about "food miles"? Until quite recently I believed—as I'm sure many of you do—that the further food products travelled the worse it was for "the environment"; that therefore it made sense to eat fresh, healthy, local produce grown just down the road than, say, green beans flown in from Kenya or raspberries from Chile.

But the facts simply don't bear this out, as blogger Stephen

Budiansky (aka "Liberal Curmudgeon") noted in a controversial *New York Times* article called "Math Lessons For Locavores".

....It is sinful in New York City to buy a tomato grown in a California field because of the energy spent to truck it across the country; it is virtuous to buy one grown in a lavishly heated greenhouse in, say, the Hudson Valley.

The statistics brandished by local-food advocates to support such doctrinaire assertions are always selective, usually misleading and often bogus. This is particularly the case with respect to the energy costs of transporting food. One popular and oft-repeated statistic is that it takes 36 (sometimes it's 97) calories of fossil fuel energy to bring one calorie of iceberg lettuce from California to the East Coast. That's an apples and oranges (or maybe apples and rocks) comparison to begin with, because you can't eat petroleum or burn iceberg lettuce.

It is also an almost complete misrepresentation of reality, as those numbers reflect the entire energy cost of producing lettuce from seed to dinner table, not just transportation. Studies have shown that whether it's grown in California or Maine, or whether it's organic or conventional, about 5,000 calories of energy go into one pound of lettuce. Given how efficient trains and tractor-trailers are, shipping a head of lettuce across the country actually adds next to nothing to the total energy bill.

This is the same rigorous technique Lomborg employed in his analysis of the Exxon Valdez—and you can quite see why greens find it so nerve-grating: its cool rationalism sounds so despicably heartless. How dare Lomborg make light of the deaths of those 250,000 beautiful, feathered creatures—many of them rare and endangered (probably)! Every one of those birds had a mother and father! Every one was a beaked child of Gaia! By introducing those unhelpful plateglass and niggling analogies, Lomborg was draining the tragedy of its underlying emotional truth: that man is evil, that oil companies are even more evil, that something must be done—and soon!—to save the planet from our vile depredations.

No doubt this green tendency towards "emotionalizing the issue" comes in terribly handy when trying to persuade idealistic young souls to make campaign donations, or venture out on boats only to be hosed down by Japanese whale fishermen. But in the field of government policy-making, you might reasonably hope that the decision-making process were based on something a little more concrete. Like, say, hard factual evidence and rational analysis.

This, certainly, was always the view of the great Julian Simon. Starting in his early childhood in Newark, New Jersey, Simon became well versed in the habit of researching facts, thanks to a father who had an annoying habit of intentionally making outlandish statements which young Julian was then expected to rebut. Interviewed by Ed Regis in *Wired* magazine, Simon recalled how his father might insist that the price of butter was 8 cents a pound, even though Julian knew full well it was more like 80 cents. But his father would stubbornly insist otherwise until Julian did his research and came back with reams of incontrovertible proof.

Simon admitted that he himself had begun life as a "card-carrying anti-growth, anti-population zealot" but had changed his mind on realizing that the "data did not support that original belief." The problem with Neo-Malthusian doomsayers like Paul Ehrlich, Simon used to complain, was that their arguments lacked scientific rigor. Rather than sift through historical data and go to the trouble of making complex calculations (such as adjusting for inflation), they preferred to rely on their nebulous computer models, which could predict anything they wanted to predict but which bore little correlation with observed reality.

Another trick the doomsayers would use—still do, especially with regard to global temperature records—was to extrapolate from "conjectural trends". This is where, in order to get the desired result, you pick a short-term trend on a graph (a ten-year period showing apparently dramatic and unprecedented warming, say) and deliberately ignore the long-term trend that puts it into its proper context.

Simon neatly illustrated this point in a 1996 public debate with Hazel Henderson, an author who was trying to make the case for government regulation. It was London's 1956 Clean Air Act, she argued, which we had to thank for a remarkable decline in pollution levels. And to prove it, Henderson produced a graph showing a clear, downward sloping line. Simon, no fan of big government, responded with a graph of his own—this one stretching right back to the 1800s and with a line from the 1920s showing a constant and uniform downward slope. "If you look at all the data," he said, "You can't tell that there was a clean-air act at any point."

But what was it about hard factual evidence that Neo-Malthusians found so threatening? According to Simon, it was that the environmental movement had taken on the qualities of a secular religion to which any form of dissent, however grounded in fact, was viewed as an abominable heresy. Conventionally in religious tradition, nature had been seen as something that God had created for man. In the new green religion, said Simon, man was no longer at the centre of things: "Ecology teaches us that humankind is not the center of life on the planet. Ecology has taught us that the whole earth is part of our 'body' and that we must learn to respect it as we respect life—the whales, the seals, the forests, the seas."

Simon traced this dramatic shift in attitude by comparing old and new scientific textbooks. In the past, he noted, "the descriptions of many birds included evaluations of their effects on humanity in general and on farmers in particular; a bird that helped agriculture was more highly valued than a bird which harmed it." By contrast, the current textbooks "often evaluate humankind for its effect upon the birds rather than vice versa". In the old religion, the human species was enjoined to be "fruitful and multiply"; under the terms of the new one it was little more than a "cancer for nature". But the old one, Simon argued, had it right. Counterintuitive it might be, but it also happened to be true: population growth wasn't the problem—population growth was the solution.

You wouldn't have won a popularity contest by making this point to the Indian government in the mid-1960s, though. With a population that had swollen to over 400 million, the country was on the brink of starvation—and relied for its survival on the five million tons of food aid it received annually from the US.

But all this was about to change thanks to the genius of a man called Norman Borlaug, "the father of the Green Revolution"—surely the most deserving recipient (indeed quite possibly the *only* deserving recipient in a field which has included Yasser Arafat and Barack Obama) of the Nobel Peace Prize.

It's quite an ironic title, really, given that Borlaug was responsible for at least two of the very worst crimes in the green penal code:

1. Feeding the world's starving masses so that they could go on breeding even more.
2. Doing so with flagrant use of mutant crops, using artificial fertilizer.

Through selective breeding of mutant seeds in Mexico in the 1950s, Borlaug had created a short-stemmed strain of wheat that grew less tall but yielded far more than conventional wheat varieties when fertilized. After some initial opposition, Borlaug prevailed on both the Indian and Pakistani governments to try his new wheat strain. Production trebled and by 1974, the food crisis was over. India had become a net exporter of wheat, not necessarily to the advantage of Paul Ehrlich. In *The Population Bomb* he had airily declared:

I have yet to meet anyone familiar with the situation who thinks India will be self-sufficient in food by 1971.

And:

India couldn't possibly feed two hundred million more people by 1980.

Now there are two further points worth making about the Green Revolution. The first is the absurd fact that Borlaug, the man who saved more lives—perhaps a billion—than anyone who ever lived, is now a virtual unknown. (He died in 2009.) He's considerably less renowned, say, than the green movement's mass-murdering poster girl Rachel Carson. This speaks volumes for the warped priorities of our era. Because Borlaug's methods involved large quantities of fertilizer, he has become the bête-noire of all those environmentalists who believe our future lies in the more traditional, eco-friendly "trust-to-nature-and-starve" agricultural model.

And the second point is that Borlaug's Green Revolution was not the first. In 1909, similar transformations were yielded by the discovery of the Haber-Bosch process, which enabled industrial quantities of inorganic nitrogen fertilizer to be made from steam, methane and air. Once again, in the 1920s, plant breeders developed a vigorous and hardy new strain of wheat ('Marquis') which could survive at higher northern latitudes, and could be grown in places such as Canada. It's almost as if God—or Gaia, if you prefer—has been trying to tell us something: that built into our species is a survival mechanism so strong and a capacity for adaptation so powerful, that no matter what crisis nature throws our way, we shall always emerge smelling of violets.

This, essentially, was what Simon believed. It lay at the root of his optimism about the human race. He never much liked the term "Cornucopian", saying "I do not believe that nature is limitlessly bountiful". He did believe, however, that the world's possibilities were sufficiently great that, when combined with "human imagination and human enterprise", we and our descendants would always have more than enough for our needs.

Were Simon alive today, he would have found himself vindicated yet again by the advent of shale gas—an energy revolution as vital and exciting and game-changing as coal was during the Industrial Revolution, as oil was in the early Twentieth Century.

If shale gas didn't exist, it might sound like it originated in the over-active imagination of a deranged, liberty-loving fantasist. At a stroke, it resolves so many of the world's perceived energy problems: it's abundant, it's cheap, it's environmentally benign and it's widespread. (The latter being a particular source of relief to those of us who don't want to be held to ransom by domineering natural gas suppliers like Russia or scary oil suppliers like Saudi Arabia and Iran.)

Shale gas is not a new discovery, of course: it has existed since time immemorial under the ground, trapped within fine-grained sedimentary rock. What has changed, though, is technology. Previously shale gas was thought unviable. But in 1999, a mining engineer named George Mitchell combined the techniques of horizontal drilling with hydraulic "fracking" (creating hairline fractures in the rock) and suddenly, this miracle energy source was rendered commercially extractable.

Its potential benefits are enormous, not least to the U.S. As recently as 2003 then-Federal Reserve Chairman Alan Greenspan claimed the U.S. was running out of natural gas, and urged it to prepare for the worst, saying: "We are not apt to return to earlier periods of relative abundance and low prices any time soon."

By 2010, however, the U.S. was producing more natural gas than Russia, and is currently sitting on nearly two Saudia Arabias' worth of natural gas reserves. But Greenspan was hardly the first great man to fall into the "peak energy" trap. As Matt Ridley has noted, throughout history the "experts" have been warning us that the key energy source of their day was on the verge of running out. In the 1970s, it was Jimmy Carter, channelling E.F. Schumacher, who warned of "peak oil". In the mid-19th Century, it was British Prime Minister W.E. Gladstone who made dire prognostications about the coming coal crisis. And in 1922, President Warren Harding's U.S. Coal Commission—after consulting 500 experts over 11 months—declared:

Already the output of [natural] gas has begun to wane. Production of oil cannot long maintain its present rate.

The mistake made by Greenspan, Carter, Gladstone, Harding, Schumacher (and not to mention M. King Hubbert, the Godfather of peak oil theory) was to ignore the power of human ingenuity. As scarce resources (coal, oil, gas, whatever) are exhausted, so their market price rises. This higher price sends a signal to mining and drilling companies that hitherto inaccessible resources—e.g. deep sea oil—might now be profitable to extract. It also sends a signal to entrepreneurs and inventors that the time may have come to try and find a rival energy source. If humans really behaved in the unimaginative way that the "peak energy" experts seem to imagine we do, then we'd all still be living in caves. Simon understood this perfectly—and it led him to a daring conclusion: that population growth, far from being our most pressing problem, is in fact the very thing that rescues us from disaster. In Simon's words:

One cannot disentangle from human numbers the effects of the human brain and its contents—call it human capital—any more than one can disentangle the effects of the human digestive or pro-creative anatomy from human numbers. It is a crucial element of the model ... that population growth and density affect the structures of markets, law, tradition, and political institutions.

The more people that exist, in other words, the greater the opportunity for the division of labor and the specialization of skills that enable our species to thrive.

And this doesn't even need to be at the expense of the environment. The more efficiently we are able to utilize the land, through technologies such as GM, the more we will be able to leave it in (or return it to) its natural state:

As Stephen Budiansky puts it:

In India alone, improvements in wheat farming alone have spared 100 million acres of additional cropland that would otherwise have had to be slashed out of forests somewhere over the last 50 years to produce the same amount of wheat that Indian farmers produce today thanks to technological advances. That's the equivalent of three Iowas or 50 Yellowstone National Parks. Without modern farming, we literally would have already cut down every acre of rainforest just to grow the staple food crops that feed the world. Would that be "sustainable"?

When I read that passage I was as surprised as you probably are. Skeptic I may be but I'd long assumed—without ever having thought particularly hard about it—that there must be something intrinsically wrong with "intensive farming", that organic food just has to be better for us than artificially fertilized food, and that there's probably something ever so slightly dodgy about GM. (Certainly when I fed my first born his soya milk to cope with some sort of lactic intolerance, I remember being quite relieved to see on the packet of powder that the soya was "guaranteed non-GM.")

This, of course, is the great difficulty with the "Cornucopian" view of the planet. It goes against a profound instinct that we know from Tertullian has been with us for at least 2000 years, and most likely since the days when Ug grunted to Uglugug that caves were becoming far too crowded and there didn't seem to be nearly as many mammoths to kill as before. The Romans called this sense "Ubi Sunt". Today, we call it nostalgia. The past, we tend to believe, was golden and idyllic. The old, traditional ways were better. Ahead lies only misery. And of course, it's all our fault.

Now whether or not you choose to follow this atavistic impulse is entirely up to you. It might be that if you do, you will be quite marvelously vindicated and rewarded with a series of apocalyptic scenarios so spectacular they make "The Day After Tomorrow" look like "High School Musical III". But my advice, if you're a betting man or woman, is: Don't—for the entire weight of history is against you.

CHAPTER 10

PROPAGANDA AND DISSENT

As far as I can tell, the debate is not, by and large, a debate about science. There is broad agreement over major scientific facts among experts who therefore have difficulty even understanding the existence of the popular view. There is broad misunderstanding by many, including nonspecialist scientists. The debate is largely a matter of spin control and intentional misrepresentation. The bulk of relevant information suggests little warming.

Richard Lindzen, Sloan Professor of Meteorology, MIT

I'm willing to acknowledge that the vast majority of those campaigning in their various ways to save the world from AGW are decent, well meaning, lovely people who are kind to children and animals and always stop to help old ladies across the road.

Just occasionally, though, the mask slips and you do start to wonder. Consider the case of the "No Pressure" video (search for it on YouTube) made by writer/director Richard Curtis for a resolutely genteel pressure group called 10:10. (That's as in "let's all reduce our carbon footprint by 10 per cent in 2010".)

The film is set in an English school classroom where an easygoing, lovably kooky teacher (played by Gillian Anderson from "The X-Files") asks her pupils how they plan to reduce their carbon dioxide emissions in support of an eco-campaign called 10:10. Obviously, she adds, participation isn't compulsory. If the children don't want to play ball, that's entirely up to them. "No pressure," the teacher says.

But most of the children do want to participate. One little girl sticks up her hand to say that from now on she'll be cycling to school instead of travelling by car. "That's fantastic, Jemima!" says the teacher. She asks for a show of hands from all those children who want to join the 10:10 campaign. Only two children abstain: a glum-looking pair called Philip and Tracy. "That's absolutely fine," the teacher reassures them. "Your own choice."

Then the bell rings, signaling that the lesson is over. "Okay class, thank you so much for today and I will see you all tomorrow," says the teacher, remembering one last point. "Oh, just before you go, I need to press..." (the teacher absent-mindedly searches among the papers on her desk to reveal a black box with a red button) "...this little button here."

The teacher presses the button and in an instant, the scene turns to horror. First Tracy explodes in a hideous mush of deep red gore. Then, at a second push of the button, Philip is exterminated too. Their classmates scream in terror, recoiling in panic and disgust at the bloody remnants of Philip and Tracy now smeared all over their white school shirts, their exercise books, their faces. A dismembered limb lands with a thump on a desk. Entirely unperturbed the teacher wipes a smear of blood from her glasses. "Now everybody please remember to read chapters five and six on volcanoes and glaciation. Except for Philip and Tracy, of course."

Within hours of its internet release in September 2010, the video went viral. But not quite for the reasons its makers intended. Instead of raising laughs—and money and support—from its target audience, it led to a wave of public outrage. A planned cinema release was cancelled, several companies withdrew their sponsorship and the team responsible had to issue a public apology on the *Guardian* website.

We skeptical bloggers gleefully christened it "Splattergate"—and also, "the gift that goes on giving." Besides providing material for a good half-dozen posts (on everything from 10:10's frantic damage limitation exercises to all the Downfall-style parodies which were cropping up on YouTube), it confirmed something some of us had struggled to get across for years: that beneath the warm, cuddly, caring exterior of the modern green movement lurked a set of razor-sharp fangs and a heart of pure venom.

Of course, as we saw in Chapter 9, environmentalism has long attracted its share of misanthropic cranks with totalitarian yearnings for global eco-fascist domination. "No Pressure" showed just how far these attitudes have penetrated into the cultural mainstream.

Remember, this film was not made for some whacko fringe outfit— Earth First!, say, or the Voluntary Human Extinction Movement. The 10:10 campaign was run by nice, middle-class people with names like Franny and Eugenie. Its sponsors—at least before the furor—included Sony, the mobile phone company O2 and the *Guardian* newspaper. The campaign had been endorsed by everyone from Prime Minister David Cameron to food writer Delia Smith to fashion designer Nicole Farhi. And of course, it had Richard Curtis, writer and director of such eminently lovable and unimpeachably safe, middlebrow comedies as "Four Weddings and a Funeral", and "Notting Hill".

This was what made the video so shocking. Not the content per se, but the fact that a collaborative team of at least fifty film professionals and forty actors, led by so assured and bankable and cozy a director as Curtis, could remain so blissfully unconscious of just how toxic the video's underlying message actually was.

"Wouldn't it be great if instead of having to argue the pressing urgency of our cause with all those pesky, stubborn, selfish Climate Change deniers we could just—teehee—press a red button and kill them all?" it ventured. And *of course* it didn't "mean" it. *Of course* it was all done in a spirit of fun. But suppose for a moment that some campaigning group had made a similar "joke" video in which the troublemakers to be righteously exterminated were homosexuals. Or Muslims. Or disabled people.

WATERMELONS: THE GREEN MOVEMENT'S TRUE COLORS

Well of course, that would never happen—and for reasons that are quite obvious. So why does this same obviousness not apply in the case of Climate Change "skeptics"? Is ecological correctness really so firmly established and all-encompassing now that the civilized majority of decent people can afford to cease further discourse with dissenters?

In the eyes of the "No Pressure" team, the answer was apparently "yes!" It was a cultural assumption they believed would be shared by a significant proportion of their prospective audience. And indeed a significant proportion of alarmists do share this assumption: as I know from the viciousness of the emails I get almost every day; from the bitterness and nastiness of some the comments below my blog; from the hatred I experience on Twitter and Facebook. These people aren't interested in engaging with my arguments. They just want to insult me, belittle me, crush me, destroy me. It's brutal, it's exhausting and I'd be lying if I said it fills me with warmth, well-being and joy.

According to my opponents this makes me an appalling hypocrite. After all, is not my *Telegraph* blog infamous for the colorful invective I throw at Warmists? Did I not once describe Dr. Rajendra Pachauri, esteemed head of the IPCC—at least at the time of writing—as a "cricket-loving, jet-setting, soft-porn-writing, ice-shunning, vegetarian troll-impersonator"? Have I not, in the pages of the *Spectator*, denounced my future king—the Prince of Wales—as a "poisonous loon" and a "terrible prat"?

Guilty, I'm afraid. Guilty as charged on all counts. But in mitigation, I should like to point out something that is invariably overlooked in the black propaganda campaign mounted against skeptics by the powerful, richly-funded AGW alarmist lobby. There is no moral equivalence *whatsoever* between the kind of casual insults we skeptics level at our opponents and the sustained character assassination we get in return.

Let me explain why.

Suppose—heaven forfend!—but just suppose, that the great

statesman and man of science Al Gore were to find himself in a situation where he'd gone for a massage in Portland, Oregon, and suddenly found himself exposed, in a police affidavit, as a blubbery, bullying oaf who had (allegedly) attempted to molest his young, terrified masseuse.

Well now, obviously, as one of Al Gore's ideological opponents I might well revel in this delicious story and chuckle over it with like-minded friends and send the website link (describing all the juicy details) to everyone I know. What I wouldn't do, though, is use it as the basis for an assault on Gore's policies on global warming.

Why not? Because whether Al Gore is indeed a disgusting, many-tentacled, masseuse-abusing pervert, or whether he is a wholesome family man with the sex drive of a eunuch has no bearing on the subject of AGW. His priapic urges do not affect by one jot or title deed the vexed issue of whether temperature rises *preceed* or *follow* CO_2 levels. Gore's libido in no way impinges on the corruption or otherwise exposed in the Climategate emails. When it comes to climate change and climate change policy, Al Gore's sex life is a complete and utter irrelevance.

The same applies to Dr. Rajendra Pachauri. Of course, I'm tickled pink by the hilariousness of the fact that he once dabbled in soft-pornographic literature. Yes, I do detect a certain hypocrisy in the fact that while jetting around the world and staying in the ritziest hotels, Dr. Pachauri urges the rest of us to put on hair shirts and abandon most of the fruits of Western civilization (from ice in our drinks to air conditioning). But my beef with Pachauri has nothing to do with the comical incongruities of his private life; it has to do with his competence and honesty as head of the world's most powerful Climate Change advisory body.

This is why, whenever I do succumb to the temptation to ridicule Warmists in my blog, I never do so except as a decorative adjunct to a serious political argument. I'm never going to write a piece that goes: "Yah boo sucks. The Prince of Wales smells and he's very silly and I hate him, so there." If I'm going to accuse the Prince of Wales of being a fool, I'll always make it perfectly clear why I think he's a fool. I'll explain, for example, that his public pronouncements that we have "100 months left to save the world" are overstated, that I believe it's irresponsible for a future constitutional monarch—a role which requires him to remain politically neutral—to take such a nakedly biased position on an issue as fraught as climate change and that his airy dismissal of "so-called climate skeptics" is ill-informed and an abuse of privilege.

And the reason I adopt this policy is not because I'm an unusually high-minded person. Every climate skeptic I have ever met or read feels exactly the same way. We may ridicule our opposition, we may scoff at their integrity, but never, ever would we use personal invective as a substitute for a reasoned critique of the flaws in their arguments. That would be evasive, shifty, and intellectually dishonest. It would imply we had something to hide—and we don't.

Now compare and contrast this with the techniques all too frequently used by climate alarmists against skeptics. The two main ones are the "appeal to authority" ("the National Academy of Sciences, NASA and the IPCC all say AGW is true, so who are you to doubt them"?) and the argument *ad hominem*. Strictly speaking, the *ad hom* isn't simply about being rude. (Hey I already admitted: I can be rude sometimes too.) Rather it's about ducking the issues altogether with a wholly irrelevant assault on the man's character.

Memo to climate alarmists: my teeth are too big, I've got blubbery lips, my hair's falling out, I wear glasses, my daughter thinks I'm old and ugly, my son thinks I'm deeply uncool, both kids hate my taste in music, I was once on a BBC TV program where a Nobel Prize-winning geneticist put to me a weird analogy about climate change skepticism and cancer treatment—and I hesitated for a moment before answering, I was privately educated, I'm middle class, I read English at Oxford not, ahem, Climate Science at the vastly superior University of East Anglia… These are all facts that you may find in some way detrimental to my claims to be a fully paid-up member of the human race. But what they don't do, really they don't, is in any way invalidate the columns and articles I write on climate change.

You'd be amazed by how many of my critics think they do, though. And by no means am I the only skeptic who gets this treatment. We saw earlier how, in the Climategate emails, Michael Mann refused to take Steve McIntyre seriously because he was a "mining engineer"— as if this had any bearing whatsoever on McIntyre's ability to criticize the Hockey Stick. And here was a typical response from one of my blog readers when I wrote a piece about the AGW skepticism of Professor Freeman Dyson: "James—are you really that stupid. When you have heart disease do you seek out an expert on dermatology? You are just so incredibly dumb about science it's not funny. He's a *theoretical physicist*—an old one. Not a climatologist."

Perhaps the most egregious example was the alarmist response to the public resignation letter written by Hal Lewis, Emeritus Professor of Physics at the University of California, Santa Barbara, to the President of the American Physical Society. Professor Lewis gave this reason for his resignation:

> It is of course, the global warming scam, with the (literally) trillions of dollars driving it, that has corrupted so many scientists, and has carried APS before it like a rogue wave. It is the greatest and most successful pseudoscientific fraud I have seen in my long life as a physicist. Anyone who has the faintest doubt that this is so should force himself to read the ClimateGate documents, which lay it bare. (Montford's book organizes the facts very well.) I don't believe that any real physicist, nay scientist, can read that stuff without revulsion. I would almost make that revulsion a definition of the word scientist.

Devastating stuff. And did the alarmist community seek to rebut it by proving that, contrary to Professor Lewis's claims, the

American Physical Society had not been hijacked by shills for the global warming industry? Or by demonstrating that the "science" underpinning AGW was entirely reliable?

Of course it didn't. Instead, its propagandists sought to portray the distinguished professor as a man of no significance. ("Who is Hal Lewis? I've been studying physics for 30 years and I've never heard of him," wrote a blogger called David Appell.) Another blogger, William Connolley—a green party activist and, until he was banned, a ferociously dedicated Wikipedia spin merchant—sought to dismiss him as a time-serving second-rater:

> So, where are the papers? You can't have a scientific career without papers. There are some early ones—The Multiple Production of Mesons from 1948 with Oppenheimer, no less. Or Multiple Scattering in an Infinite Medium, 1950—worthy maths-ish thing, I'd guess. But past the late-50's early 60's it suddenly gets very thin indeed. I'd guess, without knowing more, that he gave up science and moved into admin.

In English football, this is what we call "playing the man, not the ball."

And by no means do the dirty tricks end there. I had a taste of this myself when a young member of the (virulently Warmist) British Antarctic Survey bought the website address www.jamesdelingpole. co.uk so that he could direct casual browsers, via hyperlink, to the arch-alarmist website RealClimate. My actual website address is www.jamesdelingpole.com—and I can't pretend I was particularly harmed by this sneaky ruse. What did puzzle me, though, was the mentality behind it. Surely if the AGW believers' case is as strong as they persistently claim, there would be absolutely no need to engage in this kind of black ops.

Other skeptics have had it far worse than me. Children's TV presenter Johnny Ball—much beloved in Britain for popular science and math series such as "Think of a Number"—discovered that websites containing pornographic images were set up in his name, inciting bloggers to run campaigns against him saying he should not be allowed near children; an imposter even tried to cancel his booking at a training day for math teachers.

Something similar happened to botanist David Bellamy, another popular British children's TV presenter and science communicator. His work dried up completely once he began publicly expressing certain "unforgivable" views. And what were those offensive, career-destroying views: an admiration for the work of Charles Manson? A penchant for pedophilia? Why no. Like Ball, Bellamy had made the fatal error of speaking out against the nonsense of "Global Warming."

Now you hardly need to be Einstein to work out what all this means. It means that believers in AGW are resorting to increasingly desperate measures to defend their cause. Here are just a few examples of stories from around the world in early 2011 that show how they're getting desperate (see endnotes for references):

In Queensland, Australia, terrible floods have killed dozens of people and caused billions of dollars worth of damage. Of course it was a natural—not a man-made—disaster. Like the even more dreadful floods in 1974, it was caused by a cyclical ocean-atmosphere phenomenon called La Niña. But what so infuriated the victims is that much of this new tragedy was avoidable. After the '74 floods, action was taken by the state of Queensland to ensure that next time, it would be prepared.

So why wasn't it? Because state officials—persuaded by their green activist advisors that "global warming" was now the real threat, and that drought was more to be feared than excess rainfall—had either cancelled or neutered flood defense programs, such as the Wivenhoe Dam. Instead, they pumped public money into supposedly more "urgent" projects, such as Australia's $13 billion desalination plant program.

In Israel, the country's worst-ever fire blazed for four days in December 2010, destroying over 5,000 hectares of forest. Greenpeace blamed the fire on global warming. "Israel must cancel its plans to construct another coal plant, reduce use of fossil fuels, and realize that we are dealing with an international struggle," said Greenpeace in a statement which described the fire as "a direct expression of the effects of climate change." However, a subsequent investigation revealed the real cause of the fire: a global warming activist at a Rainbow Festival was trying to burn her used toilet paper in order to protect the environment.

Britain, the US and many other countries in the northern hemisphere recently experienced their third successive bitter winter, with heavy snowfalls causing transport chaos. Among the many victims of the extreme weather were the millions of British households compelled by new government eco-regulations to install condensing boilers with external pipe work, which froze, then burst, causing much misery and expense. The weather would appear to contradict claims made in 2000 by Dr. David Viner, a talking head from the Climatic Research Unit at the University of East Anglia. Viner was quoted, in a newspaper article entitled "Snowfalls are now just a thing of the past", as saying that in the future "children just aren't going to know what snow is."

In the Sea of Okhotsk, between Russian and Japan, a massive rescue operation was underway to free a Russian factory fishing ship that became stuck in ice more than six feet thick. The ship was stranded on one of those sea routes which, not so long ago, climate alarmists promised would become more easily navigable thanks to the alleged runaway melting of the polar ice caps. The first ice-breaker sent to rescue the ship also got stuck, so another ice-breaker had to try to rescue that one.

In the U.S., NASA announces that 2010 was the third hottest year since records began in 1880. Shortly afterwards, an article appears in the *Guardian* newspaper by Bob Ward, spokesman for the Grantham

Institute (mission: "to drive climate related research and translate it into real world impact"), bemoaning the fact that this shocking "news" was so under-reported in the media.

Had Bob only asked, I could have provided him with a multitude of reasons why NASA's latest shock-horror story didn't grab quite the attention he might have liked. (As indeed could have many of those who tried commenting on his piece but whose comments were blocked by the website moderators.) Among those would be:

1. By curious coincidence, those parts of the world where NASA detected the most significant "anomalous" warming in 2010 were also those where it had no weather stations. With no real world confirmation, how can its estimates be trusted?

2. Since 1850, the world has been emerging from the Little Ice Age (LIA) when average temperatures were significantly lower than they are now. It should not be surprising then, if many of the warmest years in the last hundred years should have been measured in the last decade.

3. The ranking "third hottest year" is all but meaningless, as even Hansen himself admitted when he said: "It's not particularly important whether 2010, 2005 or 1998 was the hottest year on record." That's because these claims are based on year-to-year temperature data that differs by only a few hundredths of a degree. The idea that something as complex and ever-changing as global mean temperature can be calculated to this level of accuracy is nonsense. In other words, Hansen's ranking announcement was a political statement, not a scientific one.

4. Even if 2010 was the third hottest year since 1880, so what? We're talking about a global temperature increase in that period of barely 1°C. This hardly sounds like an imminent climate apocalypse.

Well, you get the idea by now I hope. The Warmists' case looks weaker and weaker by the day. But instead of doing the decent thing and conceding honorably, they're becoming ever more vicious,

WATERMELONS: THE GREEN MOVEMENT'S TRUE COLORS

bullying, devious and authoritarian. And for the most part, they're getting away with it too.

Sure they've had their setbacks: Climategate, the Hal Lewis resignation letter, the embarrassing farrago of Splattergate, the decision by the U.S. Congress to defund the IPCC.

But they're nowhere close to admitting defeat. Not while they've still got so much money on their side. Not when they still have the full support of every Western government. Not when they command most of the world's print and broadcast media—Fox News being an honorable exception. Not when they control most of the world's scientific institutions too.

In some ways, you cannot help but admire their chutzpah. By rights, Climategate ought to have been the end of everything. Game over. Instead, just look at the speech delivered to the American Meteorological Society in January 2011 by Dr. Kevin Trenberth.

That's Trenberth as in the IPCC lead author best known for the now infamous Climategate email that revealed AGW to be an essentially political issue rather than a scientific one:

> The fact is that we can't account for the lack of warming at the moment and it is a travesty that we can't.

Now you'd think, after being caught red-handed like that, Trenberth would never dare show his face in climate science circles again.

Instead, here he is a little more than a year after Climategate, haranguing the American Meteorological Society for their stubborn skepticism, using the word "deniers" no fewer than six times (in the online printed version), and demanding that the "null hypothesis" on AGW theory be reversed. That is, instead of having to prove that AGW exists, what people should now be required to prove is that it *doesn't* exist.

Trenberth's audacity is quite breathtaking. Proving a negative is a scientific impossibility. Ergo, what Trenberth suggests is that the very concept of AGW should be afforded the special protected status usually only granted to snail darters, slipper orchids and the Texas Sand Dunes Sagebrush Lizard. It's like saying: "We can't win this game. We should be allowed to change the rules so that from now on we never lose."

As Willis Eschenbach noted in a scathing essay at Watts Up With That?, this is not just "meaningless" nonsense—it is "pernicious, insidious, and dangerous nonsense." Indeed. While Dr. Trenberth's attitude might be expected of, say, an Italian Renaissance princeling or an African president-for-life, we in the democratic West surely ought to be able to demand rather higher standards of openness, honesty and accountability from men supposedly of science whose salaries we pay and who exert such control over our future.

In climate change terms, Dr. Kevin Trenberth's status as an IPCC lead author makes him one of the most powerful men in the world. He has been entrusted to provide impartial advice to our governments so that they may make the best policy choices on our behalf. It follows therefore that if the word of Dr. Trenberth—and climate scientists like him—is compromised by political activist leanings, we are all in deep, deep trouble.

What concerns me—and should concern you too—is how few people seem to understand this point. The other day I had an anguished phone call from one of my colleagues. "Don't you think you've blogged about climate change enough, now? And when you do blog about climate change, why do you have to sound so angry, so extreme?"

I think the post he particularly objected to was entitled: "Why do I call them Eco Nazis? Because they are Eco Nazis." It drew on research by Mark Musser in *American Thinker*, showing that one of the pioneers of apocalyptic global warming theory was an Austrian Nazi called Günther Schwab. This tied in with a discussion I had about the German Green Party with Dr. Benny Peiser, one of its early members. "Many of our most enthusiastic members were Nazis," Dr. Peiser told me. (Peiser now runs the skeptical Global Warming Policy Foundation based in the UK.) Given the deep ecological leanings of Hitler, Goering and Goebbels documented in Chapter 9, this should hardly come as any surprise.

Yet the truth, apparently, is no defense. The long-running British satirical magazine *Private Eye* juxtaposed my Nazi headline with that of another recent story I had written called "How the Green lobby smears its enemies". Its implication, of course, was that I was a deranged extremist no better than the people I was criticizing.

The Green establishment (of which—to its shame, given its satirical pretensions—*Private Eye* is part) is very good at playing this game. Though guilty of the most outrageous abuses of power, the blackest dirty tricks, the most cynical, barefaced lies, cheating and obfuscation, it yet seeks to portray itself as a modest, decent alliance of concerned citizens, eminent scientists, principled campaigners, high-minded businessmen and responsible politicians who are all just trying to get on with the job of rescuing the world from climate change apocalypse. And being frustrated at every turn by a small, ignorant group of pesky climate change "deniers".

This was the narrative promoted, for example, by a BBC Horizon documentary of January 2011 called "Science Under Attack". Its purportedly open-minded presenter Sir Paul Nurse (Nobel prize-winning geneticist; President of the Royal Society) was shown marveling at the wondrous technology used by NASA to produce its climate data, then nodding sympathetically as a subdued and pitiful-looking Dr. Phil Jones of the Climatic Research Unit recounted how he'd been harassed and persecuted by vicious skeptics during the Climategate affair.

In a concerned and sorrowful voice, Nurse read an extract from a joint letter that had been published in *Science* magazine, signed by many of the world's leading climate alarmists, including Stephen Schneider and Paul Ehrlich. It began, "We are deeply disturbed by the recent escalation of political assaults on scientists in general and on climate scientists in particular." The letter claimed that these assaults were led by "climate change deniers" who are "typically driven by special interests or dogma, not by an honest effort to provide an alternative theory that credibly satisfies the evidence."

The documentary went on, somewhat disingenuously, to bracket climate skeptics (or "deniers" as Nurse casually referred to them) with anti-GM protestors and people who believe that AIDS is not caused by HIV. In a key section of the program, Nurse was shown smirking as a prominent climate skeptic writhed uncomfortably when presented with a difficult analogy involving cancer treatment. The program's message was clear: expert scientists such as amiable, Nobel Prize-winning Sir Paul Nurse and cruelly maligned Dr. Phil Jones are being unfairly persecuted by evil, politically motivated bloggers who don't know what they're talking about because they don't even have science degrees.

Obviously there's an element of sour grapes here. As you may have guessed, I was the blogger singled out by the documentary to represent Evil, Ignorant Denierdom. (Was I naïve to agree to take part? You bet I was, given the BBC's track record and Nurse's association with the fervently Warmist Royal Society!) Indeed, I still find the memory of it all so dreadful, that just writing about it is like pulling teeth. I'm forcing myself to do so because it represents such a perfect paradigm of how the propaganda war between climate alarmism and climate skepticism is now being waged.

In propaganda terms, the documentary was a mighty success. Great was the "Ding dong, the witch is dead!" rejoicing in the left-liberal media and Twittersphere at the abject humiliation of know-nothing literature graduate James Delingpole by a proper, actual Nobel Prize-winning "expert." For days afterwards, I found myself harassed by emails from anonymous strangers telling me how much they loathed me and how much they enjoyed my come uppance. Apparently it was my just deserts for my vicious, ill-informed abuse of all those climate scientists and environmentalists.

Was it really, though? At the risk of driving the point home with a sledgehammer, the debate on AGW is most definitely not one between two parties of equal moral merit. It is not one that will easily be resolved the moment everyone learns to find the "reasonable centre ground." It is, at its most fundamental, a battle as straightforwardly black and white as the one between good and evil.

This isn't to say there aren't lots of wonderful, nice, caring, decent, family-loving, puppy-stroking people on the Warmist side. Nor am I saying there aren't one or two rude, intemperate, outspoken, arrogant, infuriating people on the Skeptical side—e.g. me. But let us be under absolutely no illusions about the nature of the positions adopted by the two competing factions.

On the one side are the skeptics. They value empiricism, openness, and freedom of expression. None of them denies that climate changes naturally. Few, if any, deny that human activity may have some influence on the climate. But they are concerned that the connection between human activity and climate change may have been dramatically overstated by various interest groups. Of course, if the planet really is threatened by man-made climate change, then they will be as eager as anyone else to take remedial action. So far, however, they are not convinced that the evidence of human impact justifies the hugely expensive measures being adopted to "combat AGW". Indeed they believe the measures are doing harm out of all proportion to the nature of the problem. This is why they are prepared to lay their necks on the line and speak up with their unfashionable views, even at the risk of their careers and public opprobrium.

On the other side are the alarmists. They believe that human activity—especially through the release of CO_2—is having a dangerous effect on the climate, and perhaps other things besides, such as ocean acidification. They are convinced their cause is so just and urgent that it relieves them of the need to observe normal standards of probity and decency. In order to Save the Planet, they tacitly accept that it is okay to: rig public enquiries, hound blameless people out of their jobs, breach Freedom of Information laws, abuse the scientific method, lie, threaten, bribe, cheat, adopt nakedly political positions in taxpayer-funded academic and advisory posts that ought to be strictly neutral, trample on property rights, destroy rainforests, drive up food prices (causing unrest in the Middle East and starvation in the Third World), raise taxes, remove personal freedoms, artificially raise energy prices, featherbed rent-seekers, blight landscapes, deceive voters, twist evidence, force everyone to use expensive, dim light bulbs, frighten schoolchildren, bully adults, increase unemployment, destroy democratic accountability, take control of global governance and impose a New World Order.

Call them Eco-Nazis; call them what you will. But however agreeable they may be on a personal level, there's something you cannot fail to admit: what they stand for just isn't nice.

CHAPTER 11

THE PERFECT STORM

"The way to crush the bourgeoisie is to grind them between the millstones of taxation and inflation."

Lenin

It is the 4th Century AD and the Barbarians are at the Gates of Rome. Around the Imperial capitol, the citizens of the greatest civilization the world has ever known are tearing at their togas, quite unable to agree as to what—if anything—should be done.

Some, peering over the ramparts towards the hairy hordes encamped across the Tiber decide they rather like what they see. There's something wonderfully echt and earthy about these splendidly unkempt men with their rich, musky smell and their delightfully untutored table manners. Also, having dwelt so long away from the corrupting influence of the City and having imbibed the purifying spirit of the deep forests, these so-called Barbarians are very likely nice, caring, nurturing types. Probably all they want to do is say "Hello" and share some of their woodcraft skills.

Other Romans, more fatalistic, take the view that the reason the hordes are carrying spears and swords and are now busy spit-roasting a captured legionary is that they *are* here with hostile intent. But perhaps this is no more than Rome deserves. Yes, it may well be that the Barbarians have come to impose on the Romans one or two significant lifestyle changes, possibly including violent death.

But the truth is that Rome has had it far too good for too long. It has expanded its empire way farther than is natural for any reasonable society. It has developed far too many wholly unnecessary technologies, such as underfloor heating, straight roads, aqueducts and municipal bathing facilities, which will almost certainly deplete the world of the scarce resources that future citizens of the planet will need to survive. Sure, the coming Dark Ages may result in the odd century or so of extreme misery and hardship, but a planned recession like this may regrettably be necessary to secure the long-term future of the planet.

Others, more rapacious and cynical, watch with a barely concealed delight. That fake beard and those Barbarian-style furs and trews they bought from the costume shop the other week are increasingly looking like a canny investment. Sure it will be a nuisance when the Pax Romana is finally over, the economy's in chaos and it's every man for himself. But think of all the business opportunities that are bound to arise as Western Civilization crumbles: private security contracts for all those newly unsafe roads, monopolies to be bought and exploited, alliances to be forged with the new regime, etc. As a wise man from Judaea once said: "With crisis comes opportunity."

Still others—and perhaps these represent the majority—glance towards the gathering hordes with a brief tremor of concern before turning to look away to look what's showing this afternoon at the Coliseum. "Nah," they've decided about the alleged Barbarian threat. "Never going to happen. After all, we're not inhabiting some poxy little provincial capital in the arse end of beyond. This is Rome, mightiest and most enduring civilization the world has known. It has lasted over a thousand years and is destined to last just another thousand, wait and see."

Finally, there are the Realists– and unfortunately they're very much the minority—who can see what's coming. They don't like it one bit and believe something should be done before it's too late. Of course, they are not at all popular with most of their fellow Romans, who variously consider them to be hysterical, naïve, or tiresome reactionaries unhealthily wedded to the old ways and too selfish to make the radical lifestyle changes that will be necessary if Rome is to progress with the times.

"But what was so wrong with the old Rome?" plead the Realists. "Didn't we have a good thing going, what with all the trade and abundance and order and peace and prosperity and comfort and sanitation and cleanliness and under-floor heating and learning and technology?"

No one else, though, is much interested in what the Realists have to say. In the unlikely event the Barbarians do prevail, well, all good things must come to an end and there are bound to be at least as many benefits as there are downsides. Why, already, there are rumors in the agora that the new Barbarian economy will result in a whole slew of new Barbarian jobs. Once the pampered Romans get used to the more austere Barbarian lifestyle, fuel costs and living expenses will fall dramatically. Their diet will be a lot healthier because now food will be grown locally rather than transported laboriously and decadently from the far reaches of the Empire.

And if Western Civilization does come to an end, well, what the hell. Western Civilization was always so terribly overrated, anyway.

If you've reached this point in the book, you know which camp you're in. You understand what's at stake and you understand the vastness of the challenge we face. Here we are on the brink of an economic and socio-political precipice. And instead of saying: "Whoa! Let's stay away from there!", most of our political leaders are competing to see who can carry their people soonest and farthest into the stygian void of eternal doom. A pliant science establishment, a rapacious business lobby, a cheerleading media, a hell-bent green lobby and a sizeable portion of the blissfully ignorant populace (giving up their wallets along with their common sense) all stampede towards the cliff yelling: "Wheeeeee!!!"

It's a situation so bizarre that if it weren't actually true, you'd think it could only exist in the fevered brain of some whacko, paranoid fantasist. Which, of course, is exactly how the many critics of this book are likely to label me.

"Conspiracy theorist James Delingpole..." they'll begin. And they really won't need to say any more because already they will have "closed down" my argument. After all, if global warming really were a conspiracy it would have to have involved the complicity of: Tony Blair; Barack Obama; Al Gore; Greenpeace; the WWF; the United Nations; almost the entire mainstream media; the Royal Society; the National Academy of Sciences; almost the entire specialist scientific press from *Science* and *Nature*; the Intergovernmental Panel on Climate Change; Goldman Sachs; the Rothschild family; the Prince of Wales; George Monbiot; Big Oil; the Climatic Research Unit at the University of East Anglia; and most likely the Illuminati, the Freemasons and the Lizard Headed Master Race too...

As we've seen, this isn't a charge that can be answered in one easy sentence. Nor can questions like:

* If global warming isn't happening, then why are the polar ice caps/glaciers melting and my daffodils coming up earlier?
* Why would *the world's top scientists* all agree there was a problem if there wasn't one?
* But surely you must agree we have to rein in our greed and consumption to *preserve scarce resources* for future generations?
* Can't you see we *have* to do something, even if its just on the *precautionary principle*?
* All right, so it may be that the risks of man-made global warming have been exaggerated, but don't you think the measures we're taking to deal with it, and all of these new jobs and technologies will be good for us anyway?

It has taken me an entire book to try to address these common questions and even then, I've barely scratched the surface. This has always been the great challenge for those of us trying to explode the great AGW myth: you're grappling not only with complex facts but also with emotions and passions as powerful, deep-seated and irrational as you'd find among the adherents of a religion.

AGW *is* a religion. It has its high priests and prophets: Al Gore, James Hansen. It has its temples: the National Academy of Sciences, the IPCC. It has its warrior monks: Leonardo DiCaprio, Ed Begley Jr. It has its concept of original sin—the Carbon Footprint—which can be bought off with the help of indulgences—Carbon Offsets. It is motivated by an overwhelming guilt that we are all sinners but that we can redeem ourselves through mortification of the flesh (e.g. replacing bright light-bulbs that work with flickering, yellowish, eco-friendly ones that give you a headache but are apparently better for the environment, so long as you forget about all the mercury they contain) and self-abnegation (taking fewer vacations, paying more money to the government, sacrificing present pleasures for the sake of future generations).

And most important of all it is based on no hard evidence whatsoever. Only on faith. Pure, blind faith.

This lack of factual basis ought to be a weakness. Unfortunately, though, it's what gives the religion such enduring strength, for how can anyone ever disprove something that was never provable in the first place?

Even without this faith element, AGW was always going to be a tough nut for us Realists to crack, for in so many ways it passes the test of Occam's Razor.

William of Ockham was the 14th century monk and logician who formulated the influential principle—*entia non sunt multiplicanda praeter necessitatem*. Loosely translated this means: the simplest explanation is the best one.

Now apply Occam's Razor to AGW and ask yourself which is the more likely explanation:

1. That, as countless respected scientists have noted, our planet is warming as a direct consequence of the increasing amounts of CO_2 man is pumping into the atmosphere, and that unless something is done to contain our CO_2 output, the planet will experience catastrophic overheating.
2. The whole thing is little more than an outbreak of mass hysteria on a scale unprecedented in human history. It was cooked up over a period of decades by an unlikely cabal of scientists, politicians, ecological activists, corporate fat cats, newspaper editors, diplomats and quasi-Marxist ideologues. Its ultimate goal—unbeknownst to most of the useful idiots participating in the scam—is the destruction of Industrial Civilization, the end of national sovereignty and democratic government, and the governance of the world by a new order run by faceless technocrats and shadowy plutocrats.

I know which position I'd prefer to defend in a 30-second soundbite.

Then, there's the question of motivation. And again the argument seems to point in one direction only. After all, which side appears to be more virtuous and trustworthy:

1. The side that cares so much about the health of the planet and the security of future generations that it considers no act of self-sacrifice too great to preserve Mother Gaia?
2. The side so wedded to the comforts of the Western lifestyle that it refuses point blank to amend its selfish ways, because it believes that the planet and future generations can take care of themselves?

Yes, all right, so I've cheated slightly by phrasing it in a loaded way. But this is what happens all the time in the debate on AGW, and it's why for years the Warmists were able to push their agenda almost unchallenged. When one side has such raw, visceral emotion and ardent belief, and the other side has little more than arid facts and cautiously expressed uncertainty, it's inevitable that the side with more passion will capture the public imagination.

And so it will continue to do until reality overtakes it in the form of higher taxes and energy costs, increased regulation, and weather that stubbornly refuses to accord with the climate doom-mongers' apocalyptic predictions. By then, though, it may already be too late. Governments find it much easier to make laws than repeal them, much more satisfying to raise taxes than to lower them. Long after the urgent threat of climate change has been replaced by a more fashionable scare, the stringent regulatory measures taken to deal with that now-non-existent urgent threat will remain firmly stuck in the statute books.

If you don't believe this, consider one example provided by Chris Horner in his book *Power Grab*: "It took until 2006 for Congress to get around to repealing the three percent telephone excise tax originally imposed (at one percent) to pay for the Spanish-American war conflict in 1898."

The great climate realist Christopher Booker says that "We have two very powerful allies on our side: time and weather."

The weather especially seems to have a mischievous sense of humor where climate alarmists are concerned. Remember the flurries of snow that swathed Air Force One as President Obama arrived at the 2009 Copenhagen Summit to discuss the deadly peril of "global warming"? Remember the "climate awareness" march that was cancelled in Washington, DC, that same winter because of an unseasonal, heavy blizzard? It's almost as if Nature is trying to tell us something. Gosh. What could it possibly be?

If we are to believe the meteorologists, polar experts, climatologists, geographers, geologists at the 2010 Heartland Conference in Chicago, the biggest joke of all is yet to come. Many of the signs are there—low sun-spot activity, changes in the Pacific Decadal

Oscillation, increased volcanic activity, global temperatures that have been flat then in slight decline since 1998—that we are entering a prolonged period (perhaps 30 years) of global cooling. The question now is not "Will it happen?" but "Just how bad will it get?"

If we're lucky, perhaps it will just afford us a nostalgia trip to the bitterly cold winters some of us remember from the period between the mid-1940s to the mid-1970s. If we're less lucky, we'll be revisiting the Little Ice Age, perhaps recapturing the pleasures of the Maunder Minimum (1645 to 1715) when ice fairs were held on the River Thames or perhaps the Dalton Minimum (1790 to 1830), which gave us Napoleon's Retreat From Moscow and the terrible "Year Without a Summer." Alternatively, just supposing Mother Gaia really wants to rub our noses in it, we could be entering a proper new ice age—just like the one James Hansen and Stephen Schneider were predicting in the 1970s before the weather started getting warmer and they changed their minds.

So the world is getting colder—uncomfortably, perhaps dangerously so. Historically, periods of cooling have led to poor harvests, food shortages, starvation and civil unrest. Despite the advances we have made in biotechnology, the world's total grain production still operates at no more than a 15 percent surplus. If the wheat- and corn-growing regions of the Northern hemisphere were affected by prolonged cooling—and they would be—surplus could turn to deficit in no time at all. And if those already-thin harvests were to be further blighted by another major volcanic eruption such as the one that caused "the Year Without a Summer", then there would be widespread starvation around the world, especially among those communities unable to afford the inevitably massive hike in food prices. This would lead to climate-induced disaster and suffering on a scale never *once* experienced during the bountiful period of global warming our civilization was lucky enough to experience between the mid-1970s and 1998.

Can anyone spot the absurdity here? Global warming is good. It has coincided with some of the most bounteous, culturally efflorescent periods in human history, including the glorious, largely peaceful recent decades now sadly past. Human beings thrive in warmth. It means we have to devote less energy to the raw business of survival and have more time to enjoy ourselves and make the great social and technological leaps, through which (unlike in cold, grim periods like the Dark Ages) each generation has grown more prosperous, longer-lived and more comfortable than the one preceding it.

In the days of our supposedly more primitive, credulous ancestors this would have gone without saying. Can you imagine a legionary, standing atop Hadrian's Wall in the middle of an English winter, in the days before fleece, Goretex and Thinsulate, grumbling to a fellow soldier: "By Jupiter, this climate is far too mild for my liking?" Can you imagine wool-merchants in the 12th Century praying anxiously for God to restore a semblance of balance to the natural order by ridding the medieval world of this satanic period of warming? This is pure speculation, I concede. But am I right or am I right? Which sane human being, at any period throughout the 10,000 or so years our kind has spent on this planet since we emerged from the horrors of the last Ice Age, has wished for the climate to grow colder rather than warmer?

None until now. Gosh what a special generation we are! How proud of ourselves we must feel! We are the first one in all history to conquer reason and logic on such a massive scale that, as far as most of our policy-makers are concerned, black is now white and white is black; warmth something to be feared, cold something to be welcomed; abundance something to be rejected, economic stagnation something actively to be sought; reason and evidence something to be shunned, frenzied emotionalism and cheap sentiment something to be stoked and encouraged. With good reason, the U.S. meteorologist Roy Spencer describes our current global warming paranoia as the "world's worst outbreak of mass hysteria."

When I'm feeling depressed and need a lift, I try telling myself how lucky I am. In many ways, Climategate and its aftermath have been the journalist's equivalent of the perfect storm.

What, after all, could be more satisfying than a story in which: you get to play the plucky little David against the ugly, brutish Establishment Goliath? Your side has all the best arguments while all the opposition can do is bully, bluster and bludgeon its own fast-dwindling authority. You are feted in Britain, Canada, the U.S., Australia and New Zealand—well, by some people, anyway—as a crusading hero. You can write an amusing, discursive book based on your experiences which, with any luck, will sell in such vast quantities that you won't have to do a single day's work for at least the next fortnight…

Still I'd much rather live in a more rational world where Climategate never happened and writing this book was entirely unnecessary.

They say it's a pretty terrifying experience when you wake up one morning to find your teenage friends now running the country—and I can vouch for that. But what's more terrifying still is when one of those friends declares, upon becoming your new Prime Minister, that he intends to make the wearing of tin foil hats compulsory for every citizen and that he plans to invest £18 billion a year every year, until 2050, building a series of Giant Death-Ray Lasers on every British hilltop so as to avert the potential threat of alien invasion.

All right, so Dave Cameron didn't actually phrase it quite like that when he announced his intentions to "combat climate change" and to make Britain the world's greenest economy. But the net result will be just the same: stupendous waste, outrageous governmental intrusion into free citizens' private lives, skyrocketing taxes that will be difficult to repeal, and a hefty kick into the economy's most tender regions just when it needs it least. And all of this to deal with a threat so vanishingly small, it makes about as much sense as building garlic farms to ward off vampires, or blue whale shelters in case any stray cetaceans get sucked from the oceans by freak tornadoes and dumped over the British countryside during rain showers.

This madness has been endorsed by all three of Britain's main political parties. Under the terms of the Climate Change Act 2008, Britain is currently the only country in the world committed by law to cut its CO_2 emissions in the next 40 years by 80 percent. Not only will this prove physically impossible without shutting down the economy, but by the Department of Energy's own estimate it will cost the taxpayer at least £734 billion (£18 billion a year, every year for the next 40 years). It is suicidal, it is iniquitous, it is mind-bogglingly pointless. Yet when the Bill came to the vote in the House of Commons, only five MPs from any party voted against it. Such is the power of the Jonestown Cult of Climatism: once you drink the special Kool-Aid, no sacrifice is too great, no act of self-debasement too demeaning, no grand gesture too suicidal.

There's a temptation, to which even I succumb occasionally, where you say to yourself: "Oh come on! No liberal democracy is *that* stupid. Especially not during a major global recession. You're never going to get a government that wipes out its economy, shackles and fleeces its citizenry, and destroys its countryside in order to deal with a problem that doesn't actually exist. Calm down. Be realistic. It just *ain't going to happen.*"

Then you look around the world, pinch yourself to be sure you're not dreaming, and realize that it *is happening already.* Britain's Climate Change Act 2008. It's there. On the statute books. Enshrined in law. British ministers are now legally obliged to destroy their economy—a.k.a. drastically reduce their carbon dioxide emissions, which amounts to the same thing because CO_2 is a natural by-product of almost all industrial processes. All of this to achieve an entirely arbitrary target. (Why 80 percent? Why not 64 percent? Or 92.3 percent?) which will make not the slightest difference to global warming (even if it were happening, which it currently isn't) but which will most certainly lead to severe energy shortages, massively rising costs, industrial disruption, unemployment, declining standards of living, fuel poverty—and increase the death rate among the infirm and elderly. And should you require further convincing, consider this statement:

> I suspect the public doesn't realise how radical this legislation is… These cuts are going to have to be very deep and they go long-term. And we are now going to see changes occurring over time which do impact very significantly on people and I'm not sure the public fully understands that yet.

These words did not originate with some rabid climate change denier. In fact, they came from a BBC Radio 4 interview in May 2010 with one of the people who helped shaped the Act—Michael Jacobs, formerly Prime Minister Gordon Brown's special adviser on Climate Change in the Environment.

Rather appropriately for this apocalyptic final chapter—and entirely typically of the BBC—the documentary was called "Doomed By Democracy?" If you hadn't already guessed, the program suggested that climate change was now such a serious threat that the only effective way to deal with it might be to suspend the democratic process. Jacobs seemed to think that this had more or less happened already. Justin Rowlatt, the presenter, asked Jacobs whether it wasn't a bit "anti-democratic" having all three main political parties railroading through legislation based on a "consensus" that the public hadn't actually approved.

Jacobs replied pertly: "I don't think it's right to call something anti-democratic if it has the consent of the public, even if you couldn't say that they were actively in favor of it."

Hmm. So the public didn't vote for it. And they're not in favor of it. But legislation that they don't understand and will ruin their lives is still OK because, hey, it's not actually "anti-democratic."

But the problem is not confined to Britain. In his excellent book *Climatism!*, Steve Goreham offers many more depressing examples of the kind of ruin, both economic and physical, that is being inflicted around the world by eco-zealot officials convinced that something must be done to "combat Climate Change"—even if that something ends up doing more harm than good.

Consider the disastrous example of Spain, hailed in March 2009 by President Obama as an example the US should follow: "Spain generates almost 30 percent of its power by harnessing the wind". Then the inconvenient truth emerged that pursuit of green jobs and a low carbon economy have been that hapless country's ruination, not its salvation. As I mentioned earlier, research by a Spanish economics professor, Dr. Gabriel Calzada Alvarez of Madrid's University of Rey Juan Carlos, states that each of the 50,000 jobs created by massive government subsidy ("feed-in tariffs") in the renewable energy sector cost the taxpayer $716,000. Furthermore, Dr. Alvarez calculated, the combination of investment opportunity cost, paying for renewable subsidies, and more expensive electricity, meant that for every "green job" created by the Spanish government, another 2.2 jobs were destroyed in the real economy.

Or: Surrey School District in British Columbia, Canada, where already cash-strapped education authorities are being forced to squander $500,000 of their limited budget on—go on, guess what.... Did you guess books? Nope. Interactive whiteboards? Nope. Extra teaching staff? Nope. Sports equipment? Nope. Thanks to a province-wide decree requiring all public sector organizations to be "carbon neutral", the school was required to buy half a million dollars' worth of carbon offsets from a crown corporation called Pacific Carbon Trust, which will invest in "green projects" across the province. And what might these projects include? Why, things like a new "hybrid heating system" at a ski-resort, a deal at a cement plant whereby, it replaces a portion of the coal it uses with bio-mass, and the erection of "energy curtains" to conserve heat at some greenhouses. All these marvels were funded by the $25 million paid out by the province's 130 public service organizations, for no other reason than that some bright spark, somewhere believed the myth that CO_2 is not just plant food, but something dangerous, and that carbon offset companies aren't the biggest con trick since the South Sea Bubble.

Or maybe you've heard about the thousands of farmers in Australia whose land was rendered all but worthless by a government-imposed ban on tree clearance. The ban was, essentially, a scam designed to help John Howard's Liberal/National Coalition Australian government fulfill its "obligations" under the Kyoto Protocol without actually having to go through the awkward, economy-hampering process of imposing limits on carbon emissions by its heavily-fossil-fuel-dependent industries. By designating the trees as "carbon sinks", the federal government was able to "save"—at the stroke of a pen—83.7 million tons of carbon dioxide. Yet it has conspicuously neglected to compensate the affected landowners and land-users for this blight on their property values. That's because Australia's federal government created a loophole by persuading its state governments simultaneously to pass new Vegetation Management laws, which technically absolved the federal government of responsibility for the farmers' losses. The land grab caused massive hardship among farmers. Some committed suicide, and others resorted to desperate measures. Peter Spencer, a New South Wales farmer, went on a hunger strike for 51 days to raise awareness of his government's ruthless and cynical power grab.

Denmark is another victim of Climatism. Thanks to its government's fanatical commitment to sustainability and green values, it has the world's highest density of wind towers—5,200, one for every 1,000 people. In return for this monstrous blight on their once beautiful landscape, the Danes enjoy the privilege of paying the highest energy prices in Europe and about four times the U.S. average. Their wind power is so inefficient that it's only viable with a massive taxpayer subsidy at the behest of the government: about 50 percent of the 2008 Danish household electricity rate of 28 eurocents per kilowatt hour is tax.

Between 1996 and 2004, the Danish taxpayer spent an average of of €257 million per year subsidizing wind farms. Half of this subsidy ended up benefiting the citizens of Sweden and Norway, to whom Denmark exports 50 percent of its wind power. Why? Because unlike hydrocarbon-derived energy, wind power cannot be turned on and off according to need. It is entirely dependent on—duh!—the power of the wind which, in Denmark, can go from zero to 13 meters per second in a short space of time.

Denmark has placed itself in the invidious position of having either too much power at any given moment, or not enough. Luckily, its neighbors Sweden and Norway are able to absorb these power surges. That's because these countries are blessed with large quantities of hydroelectric power, which, unlike wind, can easily be turned on and off. When the wind is blowing, they import Denmark's taxpayer-funded wind energy; when it's not they charge the Danes for their hydroelectric power.

This precarious situation indicates yet another problem with wind farms: no matter how many are built, they always require a conventional power source as back up. So in fact the amount of CO_2 wind farms "save" is virtually zero. Even with all its wind farms, Denmark only managed to reduce its carbon emissions between 1990 and 2007 by 0.3 percent. It doesn't seem likely that the country will meet its ambitious target of a 20 percent reduction in CO_2 emissions by 2020.

Oh, one final fact puts Denmark's green program into perspective: the total average output of its 5,200 wind turbines is 817 megawatts. You could produce the same amount of power from just one 1,000 MW coal-fired or nuclear plant. And without ruining every view, and without fleecing every taxpayer, and without chopping up every passing sea bird in the process.

Or...Well, I'm sure wherever you are reading this in the world you'll be able to furnish your own local examples of the miseries, inconveniences, expenses and thoroughgoing outrages being imposed on you and your neighborhood by well-meaning bureaucrats in their eager desperation to "combat Climate Change."

Perhaps it's something small and niggling, like the cloying eco-propaganda song your child was taught to sing at school or the $2 million bridge your state built with your tax money so that wildlife can cross over a new road development. Or maybe it takes the form of those ever-increasing energy bills, which are being artificially inflated by your government to offset its subsidies to owners of useless, pointless solar panels. Maybe it's the headaches induced by the flickering eco-friendly light bulbs, since your government decided to outlaw the incandescent bulb. Or it could be something truly life-ruining: the erection of a wind farm which blights your favorite view and wipes out the value of your family home, the closure of the steel mill where you work because the owner finds it more cost effective to shift production to the Indian Subcontinent where he can better exploit the "carbon credits" system. Possibly, it will be all of the above and more.

This, you may have noticed, is the problem with the all-enveloping, all-encompassing new world religion of Climatism. Whether you subscribe to the faith or not, it doesn't much matter: you're still going to end up being billed for full membership, anyway.

But wait just a moment. Before you top yourself, as I'm sure must be very tempting after reading this catalogue of doom, misery, idiocy, corruption, rent-seeking, mendacity, hypocrisy, power grabbing and eco-fascist world domination, I want to conclude on a positive note.

Right at the beginning of this book, I said it's up to you whether our livelihoods, our economies, our entire civilization go down the pan, or whether we continue to blossom and flourish as our rivers grow cleaner, our seas and skies less polluted, with as much wide-open-space as ever for future generations to enjoy. I meant it. *Without* you—and people like you—we are screwed. *With* you—and people like you—the possibilities for improvement are almost limitless.

What makes you so special? Well you've read this book, for a start. Not only are you now better informed than almost anyone you know about the science surrounding Catastrophic Anthropogenic

WATERMELONS: THE GREEN MOVEMENT'S TRUE COLORS

Global Warming (CAGW) theory but—and here you're really ahead of the game—you understand why that science is almost a sublime irrelevance.

Almost. Obviously, the CAGW debate matters inasmuch as vast swathes of government policy, taxation, and regulation have been attached to it, affecting every detail of our lives. Obviously it matters too since it will indeed be a useful advance for mankind when climate scientists are able genuinely to understand the real causes of "climate change"—as opposed to engaging in idle (and extremely expensive) speculation via tenuous computer models.

But as regards the *real* ideological struggle taking place in the world right now, CAGW is little more than a red herring. Or, if you prefer, just one more damn head on the Hydra. Lop off the head spewing messages of doom about CAGW, and instead of killing the beast you'll find that two more heads are snapping at you in its place. Perhaps one of them will be hissing something about "Ocean Acidification" and the other growling about "Biodiversity," though the precise details won't much matter. All you need to know is that—like Rachel Carson's DDT-induced cancer epidemic and Paul Ehrlich's global food crisis, like the Seventies "ice-age scare" and the Eighties acid rain "threat"—"climate change" is just another of those here-today-gone-tomorrow eco scares exaggerated by the environmental movement to advance a particular agenda.

And having read this book you know what that agenda is. Ultimately, it's about control.

As I said earlier, you are perfectly entitled to align yourself with that agenda. You may feel, as do many in the green movement, that the human species is a cancer on the face of the earth. You may believe that capitalism is evil and that economic growth is something we should strive to curtail, because hey, there's so much more to life than greed and consumption. You may have decided that, when left to their own devices, people generally do the wrong thing and the only possible way to make our planet fair and just and good is for everyone to have some of their freedoms removed, so that they can be coerced into correct behavior by "experts" from the government who know better.

Lots of people think these things, among them some really nice, well-meaning, caring people so, don't worry: you're definitely not alone if you think this way too. But all I ask, before you make up your mind, is that you consider the logical consequences of your position.

You'd be amazed at how many people don't, how many have simply drifted into a certain set of opinions because they happen to be fashionable, promulgated by the media, by their chattering class friends, by government propaganda, by what Doctor Johnson called "the Clamour of the Times".

"Overpopulation", for example. OK. So you may think it's a major worry. Perhaps you've even referred to it as the "elephant in the room". Fine. Maybe it is. But if so, what are you going to do about it? Are you going to stop people from reproducing– and if so, which people and how? Mass sterilization? A ruthlessly enforced one-child per family, policy, as has wrought such misery in China? A sly, below-the-line extermination campaign, such as was successfully effected by the ban on DDT? Free condoms for every African? Or what?

Economic growth—there's another thing I sometimes hear nice, decent, sane middle-class people yearning to abolish. "The perpetual growth model, it just can't work," they declare. Perhaps they're just echoing something they heard the Dalai Lama say, or read in the *New York Times*. Or maybe they decided for themselves after being struck on their summer vacation by how much nicer it would be if we spent the rest of our lives chasing butterflies and dipping our toes in cool, clear streams and travelling by horse and cart, and escaped the "want want want" of the modern rat race.

Yes, I quite agree. It would indeed be absolutely marvelous if we could spend the rest of our lives swanning around in some carefree pastoral idyll. But unfortunately, that wouldn't actually happen if you stopped—or, worse still, reversed—economic growth. Instead, you'd get stagnation, increased poverty, ill-health and crime, decaying infrastructures, and greater global tension and competition as the growing world population competed for fewer resources. You certainly wouldn't have much time for paddling in streams or chasing butterflies: leisure is the product of economic abundance and specialization of labor, not of pre-industrial age "self-sufficiency". Nor would you bequeath a better world for your children and grandchildren. They'd be the first in generations to enjoy a lower standard of living than their parents.

Scarce resources, then. You're worried about the thing they call "Peak Oil". You think there's only a limited amount of *stuff* on our planet to exploit, and that we have a moral duty to safeguard as much of it as possible for future generations, even if this means state-enforced rationing.

Yep, well I understand your concerns. Of course your gut feeling that resources are bound to run out eventually makes some sense. But it fails to take into account the power of human ingenuity and market processes. "The stone age didn't end because man suddenly ran out of rocks," the saying goes. And while glib, it's also true. Maybe if ships were still made of wood, we'd now be suffering a grave shortage of forests. Maybe if our transport was still drawn by horses, our cities would now be buried in manure. Neither crisis came to pass, however, because of technological innovation. Steel-built ships and the internal combustion engine saved the day, in much the same way that future technological advances will overcome our dependence on dwindling quantities of oil.

That impending "peak oil" crisis exists only in the imagination of green doom-mongers and watermelons. How can I be so confident? Because that is how markets work. Long before the oil runs out, its rarity value will have driven the price so high that it ceases to be economically useful. This high price will in turn send a signal to scientists and researchers and entrepreneurs to find a cheaper, more efficient energy source—which, human ingenuity being what it is, they will have done.

You may say that this is a process that our governments are merely helping to accelerate with their well-meaning green taxes and subsidies, designed to give the market a steer towards "renewable energy." But that would ignore the real world evidence that government meddling serves only to clog, corrupt and distort a natural process that would be far better—and more cheaply—effected within the private sector. Never forget that damning research from Gabriel Calzada Alvarez, the Spanish economics professor: for every single "green job" created in Spain by government subsidy, 2.2 jobs were lost in the real economy. If "renewable energy" really was any good, it wouldn't need bankrolling through government subsidy. Investors would be flocking to use it anyway.

Convinced yet? Look, I'm not pretending that I have all the answers. But what I hope at the very least I've helped you begin to understand is that the "climate change" debate is in fact about something much, much bigger and more important than man-made global warming. What it's really about is perhaps the biggest and most important questions we can ask and ever will ask:

Who are we?

Why are we here?

I'm not sure exactly what the green response would be to these questions. But to the first, it would be something like: "a species, just like any other." And to the second: "Only Gaia knows, but I wish we weren't. The planet would be far better off without us."

If you still doubt that this bitter, self-hating misanthropy lies at the very heart of the green movement, please re-read Chapter 9. It is a battle between two world views—one where humans are an asset, the other where humans are a liability. It's not as though I've had to work very hard to pin this vile philosophy on the many leading watermelons I've quoted: they're quite capable of condemning themselves in every speech they make and every book they write.

This is why I myself am not a "green". And why I hope I've managed to persuade you that you're not one either.

It's not because I'm selfish. It's not because I'm greedy. It's not because I don't love plants and animals and beautiful countryside and fresh water and clean air. It's not because I'm too lazy to change my ways. It's not because I've been lavishly funded by Big Oil or Big Carbon or (one more time) Big Koch.

It's because I believe we're better than that.

I believe that we humans are here for a purpose and that this purpose is to flourish.

Sure we've made mistakes and continue to make mistakes. But just think of the wonders we've achieved on the way:

We've painted the Sistine Chapel and sculpted "The Thinker" and choreographed Swan Lake and designed the Taj Mahal. We've written the U.S. Constitution and the complete works of Shakespeare and the Goldberg Variations and the Battle of Evermore and The Chronic 2001. We've climbed Mount Everest with and without oxygen. (And the north face of the Eiger, and K2). We've invented football and baseball and cricket and ice hockey and bridge and tiddlywinks and curling and liar dice and Monopoly and Settlers of Catan. We've discovered fire and the wheel and longitude and the neutron and double entry book keeping and how to fly. We've invented the internet, the microscope, the clock, the pepper grinder and the concept of zero. We can do yoga and t'ai chi and Swedish massage and Pilates and calisthenics and judo and ballet and acupuncture.

We've shaped our planet to suit our special needs and whims, from the Panama and Suez Canals to the faces carved on Mount Rushmore to the drained swamps of New Orleans to the reclaimed polderland of the Netherlands. Our population has swollen from a few million to nearly seven billion and—despite the gloom-and-doom predictions made by each generation—we've achieved this without mass starvation and while living in ever-increasing comfort.

And still we've managed to preserve vast swathes of wilderness and unspoiled countryside, teeming with animal and plant life.

And this list I've just described barely scratches the surface of our species' myriad achievements. Truly we are amazing, and blessed. The longer we stay on the planet, it seems, the more amazing we grow. With each new generation, our technological advances are accelerating, while simultaneously that proportion of our planet's inhabitants living in absolute poverty grows smaller and smaller.

How can we reconcile all this with the widespread view—as taught to our children in schools and repeated to us every day by progressive churchmen and bleeding heart enviro-campaigners and MSM editorials– that we humans are a blot on the landscape, a crime against nature, something the world would be much better without?

We cannot. It's impossible. Either you believe, as I do, that we humans are essentially a beneficent presence on earth. Within certain legal and social constraints—such as property rights and the rule of law—we are all best left to our own devices, free from government interference, and we can generally be trusted to do the right thing and enjoy all those benefits that, history tells us, accrue from free markets and free trade and personal liberty.

Or you take the pessimistic view that we're a menace to be contained and constrained with ever-greater regulation and control from experts over whom we have no democratic control—and over whom we have no need of democratic control because, after all, they're the experts and they have our best interests at heart. Rest assured, this kind of collectivism—in all of its ugly forms—will always end in tears.

There is no middle way. Even if you think there is a middle way, the people who would wish to steal your freedoms and your democratic rights in the name of "environmentalism" have seen to it that there is not.

It really is that simple: optimism or pessimism; freedom or tyranny; joy or misery. You choose.

REFERENCES

Chapter 1: Imagine

Page 1 *"In searching for a new enemy to unite us..."*—King, Alexander and Schneider, Bertrand (1991) *The First Global Revolution: A Report by the Council of the Club of Rome,* Pantheon Books, New York, 1991.

Page 3 "the case of Lee Bidgood Jr"—See Lee Bidgood Jr.'s letter at: http://www.newsweek.com/2009/11/06/letters-november-9-2009.html [Accessed January 15, 2011].

Page 4 "the Hockey Stick was – and to some extent still is – the central pillar"—See Figure 1B at: http://www.grida.no/publications/other/ipcc_tar/?src=/climate/ipcc_tar/wg1/figspm-1.htm [Accessed January 14, 2011].

Page 4 "That, at least, is how the IPCC's Third Assessment Report (TAR) chose to interpret it"—For the IPCC's Third Assessment Report (TAR) see: http://www.ipcc.ch/ipccreports/tar/ [Accessed January 14, 2011]. For the Summary for Policymakers see: http://www.grida.no/publications/other/ipcc_tar/?src=/climate/ipcc_tar/wg1/005.htm [Accessed January 14, 2011].

Page 4 "Every household in Canada received a leaflet"—McIntyre, Steve (2005). (climateaudit.org), "Revisiting the 'stick'", *Financial Post,* June 17.

Page 5 "As Andrew Montford, author of *The Hockey Stick Illusion,* explains"—Montford, A. (2010). "Climate science after the 'hockey stick' affair". Spiked Online, June 22. http://www.spiked-online.com/index.php/debates/copenhagen_article/9056

Page 5 "Mann's witheringly contemptuous posting at RealClimate"— Quoted in Montford, A. (2010), *The Hockey Stick Illusion: Climategate and the Corruption of Science*, (Turkey: Stacey International), p. 180.

Pages 5–6 "a letter to a Dutch science journalist, Marcel Crok"—Quoted in *Ibid.*, p. 183.

Page 8 "It's been anatomized in books like Allan Bloom's"—Bloom, A. (1988), *The Closing of the American Mind*, (USA: Touchstone/Simon & Schuster).

Page 10 "Britain was groovy again. No less an authority than Vanity Fair told us so in its Cool Britannia edition"—For instance see Kamp, D. (1997), "London Swings! Again!", *Vanity Fair*, March. Available at: http://www.vanityfair.com/magazine/archive/1997/03/london199703 [Accessed January 14, 2011].

Page 11 "In its thirteen years in power, the New Labour government managed to create over 3,000 new offences"—See Jenkins, S. (2009), "In its mania for jailing people, Britain has declared trivial offences crimes", *The Guardian: Comment is Free*, 10 December. Available at: http://www.guardian.co.uk/commentisfree/2009/dec/10/conrad-black-labour-law-crime [Accessed January 14, 2011].

Page 12 "an Italian Marxist named Antonio Gramsci"—For discussion of "culture war" see "Why There is a Culture War", http://www.hoover.org/publications/policy-review/article/7809

Page 12 "In his appendix to *1984*"—See Orwell, G. (2008), *Nineteen Eighty-Four*, (England: Penguin Group). For an excerpt see: http://www.newspeakdictionary.com/ns-prin.html [Accessed January 15, 2011].

Page 13 "As observed by Dan Hannan"—Hannan, D. (2001). "New Word Order." *The Spectator*, October 27. http://www.spectator.co.uk/politics/all/9430/part_3/new-word-order.thtml

Page 13 "As Christopher Booker and Richard North note in their excellent book *Scared to Death*"—Booker, C. & North, R. (2007), *Scared to Death, From BSE to Global Warming: Why Scares Are Costing Us The Earth* (Wiltshire: Continuum).

Chapter 2: Climategate: How It Happened

Page 16: "By the late tenth to twelfth centuries most of the world"—
Lamb, H.H. (1982), *Climate, History and the Modern World* (London:
Routledge). p.162.

Page 16: "If you own any shares in alternative energy companies"—
Delingpole, J. (2009), "Climategate: the final nail in the coffin
of 'Anthropogenic Global Warming'?", *Telegraph Online Blogs*,
November 20. Available at: http://blogs.telegraph.co.uk/news/
jamesdelingpole/100017393/climategate-the-final-nail-in-the-coffin-of-
anthropogenic-global-warming/ [Accessed January 14, 2011]

References from original blog:

Page 16 "(Hat tip: Watts Up With That?)."—Watts, A. (2009), "Breaking
News Story: CRU has apparently been hacked – hundreds of files
released", *Watts Up With That*, November 19. Available at: http://
wattsupwiththat.com/2009/11/19/breaking-news-story-hadley-cru-has-
apparently-been-hacked-hundreds-of-files-released/#more-12937 [Accessed
January 14, 2011].

Page 17 "As Andrew Bolt puts it"—Bolt, A. (2009), "Climate Gate:
Warmist Conspiracy Exposed?", *Herald Sun,* November 20. Available
at: http://blogs.news.com.au/heraldsun/andrewbolt/index.php/heraldsun/
comments/hadley_hacked/ [Accessed January 14, 2011].

Page 17 "One of the alleged emails has a gentle gloat over the death in
2004 of John L. Daly"—See Overington, C. (2009), "British Climate
Expert 'Cheered' by Aussie's Death", *News.com*. Available at: http://www.
news.com.au/features/environment/british-climate-expert-cheered-by-aussies-
death/story-e6frflpo-1225801905609 [Accessed January 14, 2011].

Page 17 "Manipulation of evidence"—See: http://www.eastangliaemails.com/
emails.php?eid=154&filename=942777075.txt [Accessed January 14, 2011].

Note: Eastangliaemails.com is a comprehensive database of all the alleged
emails from the University of East Anglia's 'Climate Research Unit',
covering the period March 1996 to November 2009.

"Private doubts about whether the world really is heating up"—See:
http://www.eastangliaemails.com/emails.php?eid=1048 [Accessed January 14,
2011].

Page 18 "Suppression of evidence"—See: http://www.eastangliaemails.com/ emails.php?eid=891 [Accessed January 14, 2011].

Page 18 "Fantasies of violence against prominent Climate Skeptic scientists"—See: http://www.eastangliaemails.com/emails.php?eid=1045 [Accessed January 14, 2011].

Page 18 "Attempts to disguise the inconvenient truth of the Medieval Warm Period (MWP)"—See: http://www.eastangliaemails.com/emails. php?eid=319 [Accessed January 14, 2011].

Page 18 "And, perhaps most reprehensibly, a long series of communications discussing how best to squeeze dissenting scientists out of the peer review process."—See: http://www.eastangliaemails.com/ emails.php?eid=295 [Accessed January 14, 2011].

Page 19 "In September – I wrote the story up here"—Delingpole, J. (2009), "How the global warming industry is based on one MASSIVE lie", Telegraph Online Blogs, September 29. Available at: http://blogs. telegraph.co.uk/news/jamesdelingpole/100011716/how-the-global-warming-industry-is-based-on-one-massive-lie/ [Accessed January 14, 2011].

Page 19 "This matters because CRU, established in 1990 by the Met Office [sic]"—This statement, written in original blog, was incorrect. The CRU was established in 1971 as part of the University of East Anglia School of Environmental Sciences. The Met Office's Hadley Centre was established in 1990, and is based in Exeter.

Page 20 "I first read the story at Watts' website"—"Breaking news story: CRU has apparently been hacked – hundreds of files released" Watts, A. (2009), November 19. Available at: http://wattsupwiththat. com/2009/11/19/breaking-news-story-hadley-cru-has-apparently-been-hacked-hundreds-of-files-released/#more-12937 [Accessed January 14, 2011].

Page 21 "I've seen it happen to Daniel Hannan"—Hannan, D. (2009) "Daniel Hannan MEP: The devalued Prime Minister of a devalued Government", YouTube, March 24. Available at: http://www.youtube. com/watch?v=941W6Y4tBXs [Accessed January 14, 2011].

Page 22 "Here's Elizabeth May, head of Canada's Green Party."—See Pearce, F. (2010), "How the 'Climategate' scandal is bogus and based on climate sceptics' lies", Guardian Online, February 1. Available at:

http://www.guardian.co.uk/environment/2010/feb/01/climate-emails-sceptics [Accessed January 19, 2011].

Page 22 "Here's Professor Myles Allen of Oxford University."—Allen, M. (2009), "Science forgotten in climate emails fuss", *Guardian Online*, 11 December. Available at: http://www.guardian.co.uk/commentisfree/2009/dec/11/science-climate-change-phil-jones [Accessed January 19, 2011].

Page 22 "Here's Professor Kerry Emanuel of MIT."—See Bishop Hill blog, March 22, 2010. Available at: http://bishophill.squarespace.com/blog/2010/3/22/emmanuel-on-the-climategate-emails.html [Accessed January 19, 2011].

Page 22 "Here's a RealClimate regular, Steve Easterbrook"—Easterbrook, S. (2010), "Academic Culture from the Inside", Hosted at: *ClimateSight*, March 25. Available at: http://climatesight.org/2010/03/25/academic-culture-from-the-inside-a-guest-post-by-steve-easterbrook/ [Accessed January 19, 2011].

Page 23 "Here is Fred Pearce, a British environmental journalist, writing in the *Guardian*"—Pearce, F. (2010) "Climate emails cannot destroy proof that humans are warming the planet", February 5. Available at: http://www.guardian.co.uk/environment/2010/feb/05/climate-change-hacked-emails

Page 23 "And Pearce continues"—Pearce, F. (2010), "How the 'climategate' scandal is bogus and based on climate sceptics' lies", *Guardian Online*, February 1. Available at: http://www.guardian.co.uk/environment/2010/feb/01/climate-emails-sceptics [Accessed January 19, 2011].

Page 25 "This 'you scratch my back, I'll scratch yours' approach is most deliciously exemplified in an email exchange"—*See* "13 years of Climategate emails show tawdry manipulation of science by a powerful cabal at the heart of the global warming campaign", *Poneke's Weblog*, January 15, 2010. Available at: http://poneke.wordpress.com/2010/01/15/gate/ [Accessed January 19, 2011]

Page 26 "Four months later, Mann decides that a sufficiently decent interval has elapsed for him to be able to ask Jones on-so-parenthetically"—*See:* http://www.eastangliaemails.com/emails.php?eid=975 [Accessed January 19, 2011].

Page 27 "For this same reason, there's no point dwelling on emails"—
See Overington, C. (2009), "British Climate Expert 'Cheered' by
Aussie's Death", *News.com*. Available at: http://www.news.com.au/
features/environment/british-climate-expert-cheered-by-aussies-death/story-
e6frflpo-1225801905609 [Accessed January 14, 2011].

Page 27 "Or the one from October 9, 2009, where Ben Santer writes"—
See: http://assassinationscience.com/climategate/1/FOIA/mail/1255100876.txt
[Accessed January 19, 2011].

Page 28 "As Phil Jones himself puts it in one of his emails"—*See:* http://
assassinationscience.com/climategate/1/FOIA/mail/1256765544.txt [Accessed
January 19, 2011].

Page 29 "The Medieval Warm Period (given very short shrift at
Wikipedia, incidentally, for reasons not unconnected with
Wikipedia's extreme Warmist bias)"—See: http://blogs.telegraph.co.uk/
news/jamesdelingpole/100020515/climategate-the-corruption-of-wikipedia/
[Accessed January 19, 2011].

Page 30 "Costella believes that what is essentially going on here is
a breach of trust."—Costella, J.P. (2010), "Why Climategate is so
Distressing to Scientists", *The Citizen Scientist. Available* at: http://
www.sas.org/tcs/weeklyIssues_2010/2010-03-05/feature3/index.html [Accessed
January 19, 2011].

Page 30 "The one everyone has heard of, not least because it was
turned into a catchy viral hit on YouTube by Minnesotans for Global
Warming"—*See* "Minnesotans for Global Warming Song (If We Had
Some Global Warming)", *YouTube.* Available at: http://www.youtube.
com/watch?v=qJUFTm6cJXM [Accessed January 19, 2011].

Page 31 "Here's the relevant passage – in an email from Phil Jones to
Ray Bradley, Mike Mann, Malcolm Hughes, Keith Briffa and Tim
Osborn"—*See:* http://www.eastangliaemails.com/emails.php?eid=154
[Accessed January 19, 2011].

Page 31 "Just so it's not taken out of context, here is Briffa outlining
the problem"—*See:* http://www.eastangliaemails.com/emails.php?eid=136
[Accessed January 19, 2011].

Page 33 "Here he outlines his scheme."—*See:* http://assassinationscience.com/
climategate/1/FOIA/mail/0938018124.txt [Accessed January 19, 2011].

Page 35 "read what the U.S. National Academy of Sciences has to say'"—
"On Being a Scientist: A Guide to Responsible Conduct in Research:
Third Edition" (2009), Committee on Science, Engineering, and
Public Policy (COSEPUP). Available at: http://www.nap.edu/openbook.
php?record_id=12192&page=8 [Accessed January 19, 2011].

Page 37 "Here, for example, is Tom Wigley's suggestion of how to deal
with them."—*See:* http://assassinationscience.com/climategate/1/FOIA/
mail/1061300885.txt [Accessed January 19, 2011].

Page 37 "discussing how best to blacken the name of the peer-review
journal *Climate Research*"—*See:* http://assassinationscience.com/
climategate/1/FOIA/mail/1051190249.txt [Accessed January 19, 2011].

Page 38 "Michael Mann has another idea."—*See:* http://assassinationscience.
com/climategate/1/FOIA/mail/1051202354.txt [Accessed January 19, 2011].

Page 38 "he dismisses another peer-reviewed journal *Energy and
Environment*."—*See:* http://assassinationscience.com/climategate/1/FOIA/
mail/1196872660.txt [Accessed January 19, 2011].

Chapter 3: It's Not About "The Science"

Page 40 *"For generations, we have assumed that the efforts of mankind
would leave the fundamental equilibrium of the world's systems and
atmosphere stable"*—The full transcript of Baroness Thatcher's speech
can be found at: http://www.margaretthatcher.org/document/107346
[Accessed January 15, 2011].

Page 40 *"Recently three changes in atmospheric chemistry have become
familiar subjects of concern. The first is the increase in the greenhouse
gases"*—*Ibid.*

Page 41 "Indeed it has been suggested"—Courtney, R. "Global Warming:
How It All Began". Available at: http://www.john-daly.com/history.htm
[Accessed January 15, 2011].

Page 41 "The Hadley Centre, in turn, helped to produce the primary
data set"—Met Office website [accessed March 13, 2011]. http://www.
metoffice.gov.uk/climate-change/resources/hadley

Page 42 "Certainly it was at Tickell's suggestion that she made"—*See*
Booker, C. (2009) *The Real Global Warming Disaster* (Cornwall:
Continuum), p. 43.

Pages 42 "inspired him in 1977 to publish a book on the imminent doom facing mankind"—Tickell, C. (1978), *Climate Change and World Affairs* (Oxford: Pergamon).

Page 43 "Eleven years later, in the revised 1988 edition"—*Ibid.* See also: http://www.crispintickell.com/page79.html [Accessed January 15, 2011].

Page 43 "Perhaps unsurprisingly given his job, Tickell's proposed solution to this apparently urgent crisis (the precise nature of which he did not yet understand) was the creation of a new supranational environmental body"—See: http://www.crispintickell.com/page77.html [Accessed January 15, 2011].

Page 44 "The Times incisively analyzed this process"—*Quoted in* Booker, C. & North, R. (2005), *The Great Deception: Can the EU Survive?*, (Continuum).

Page 46 "Professor Bert Bolin, the mild-mannered, self-effacing Swedish meteorologist"—*See* Science News (May 9, 1959) at: http://www. sciencenews.org/view/generic/id/43155/title/Science_Past_from_the_issue_of_ May_9,_1959 [Accessed January 15, 2011].

Page 46 "He was also author of the 500-page, keynote paper which set the alarmist tone for an influential UN-sponsored conference"—Bolin, B. (1987), *Our Common Future,* World Commission on Environment and Development, (Oxford, New York: Oxford University Press).

Page 46 "As Al Gore said on collecting his Nobel Peace Prize"—*Quoted in* Brown, P. (2008), "Obituary: Bert Bolin", *Guardian Online,* January 9. Available at: http://www.guardian.co.uk/environment/2008/jan/09/ climatechange.mainsection [Accessed January 15, 2011].

Page 48 "according to science historian Spencer Weart"—Weart, S. (2004), *The Discovery of Global Warming* (USA: Harvard University Press).

Page 50 "Revelle's skepticism proved most inconvenient for Al Gore."— Gore, A. (2000), *Earth in Balance: Forging a New Common Purpose* (London: Earthscan).

Page 50 "In July 1988, he had written to Senator Tim Wirth of Colorado"—As quoted in: Singer, S.F. (2000), "Gore's 'global warming mentor' in his own words", The Heartland Institute. Available at: http://www.heartland.org/policybot/results/9858/

Gores_global_warming_mentor_in_his_own_words.html [Accessed January 15, 2011].

Page 50 "Later, Revelle made his skepticism even more explicit in a paper"—Singer, S.F., Revelle, R. & C. Starr (1992), "What to Do About Greenhouse Warming: Look Before You Leap", *Cosmos* Vol.2, No.5. Available at: http://www.his.com/~sepp/key%20issues/glwarm/cosmos.html [Accessed January 15, 2011].

Pages 50–51 "Koppel noted that there was 'some irony in the fact that Vice President Gore'"—Koppel, T. (1994) "Is Environmental Science for Sale?" ABC News Nightline Transcript, February 24.

Page 52 "Unless his name rings a bell as the guy from the Climategate emails who wanted to 'beat the crap out of' climate skeptic Pat Michaels"—See: http://www.eastangliaemails.com/emails.php?eid=1045 [Accessed January 15, 2011].

Page 52 "He achieved this in his role as 'lead author' of Chapter 8"—The "IPCC Second Assessment Report" is available at: http://www.ipcc. ch/pdf/climate-changes-1995/ipcc-2nd-assessment/2nd-assessment-en.pdf [Accessed January 15, 2011].

Pages 52–53 "It included these passages"—Singer, S.F. & Avery D.T. (2006), *Unstoppable Global Warming: Every 1500 Years*, (Rowman & Littlefield), pp. 63–4.

Page 53 "In a *Wall Street Journal* article titled 'A Major Deception on Global Warming"—Seitz, F. (1996), "A Major Deception on 'Global Warming'", *Wall Street Journal,* June 12. Available at: http:// stephenschneider.stanford.edu/Publications/PDF_Papers/WSJ_June12.pdf [Accessed January 15, 2011].

Page 54 "A letter issued by the U.S. State Department to Sir John Houghton, then head of the IPCC"—as discussed in Singer, S.F. & Avery D.T. (2006), *Unstoppable Global Warming: Every 1500 Years* (Rowman & Littlefield), p. 64.

Page 54 "The reason for this change in attitude, Senator Wirth admitted"—Remarks by Timothy Wirth before the Second Conference of Parties to the UN Framework Convention on Climate Change, July 17, 1996. Available at: http://dosfan.lib.uic.edu/ERC/briefing/dispatch/1996/ html/Dispatchv7no30.html [Accessed April 13, 2011].

Page 54 "Dr. James Hansen...testified that 'the earth is warmer in 1988 than at any time in the history of instrumental measurements.'" — Testimony of James Hansen before U.S. Senate Environment and Public Works Committee, June 23, 1988.

Page 55 "No wonder *Time* magazine was inspired to write a big story" — Brand, D. & Dorfman, A. (1988), "Is The Earth Warming Up?", *Time Magazine*, July 4. Available at: http://www.time.com/time/magazine/article/0,9171,967822,00.html [Accessed January 15, 2011].

Page 55 "and the *New York Times* to report" — Shabecoff, P. (1988), "Global Warming Has Begun, Expert Tells Senate", *New York Times*, June 24. Available at: http://query.nytimes.com/gst/fullpage.html?res=940DE7DF133AF937A15755C0A96E948260 [Accessed January 15, 2011].

Page 55 "No wonder a senior *New York Times* journalist subsequently described the moment as a major breakthrough" — Philip Shabecoff, *New York Times*, as quoted in 2007 PBS documentary "Hot Politics", http://www.pbs.org/wgbh/pages/frontline/hotpolitics/etc/script.html [accessed March 4, 2011]

Page 55 "Then, as Wirth proudly confessed to a US PBS documentary in 2007, they rigged the hearing room temperature" — PBS interview, January 17, 2007, http://www.pbs.org/wgbh/pages/frontline/hotpolitics/interviews/wirth.html [accessed March 4, 2011]

Page 56 "I'm thinking, for example, of the British government's 2009 'Bedtime Stories' advertising campaign" — Webster, B (2009), "Ministers target climate change doubters in prime-time TV advert", *Times Online*, October 9. Available at: http://www.timesonline.co.uk/tol/news/environment/article6867046.ece [Accessed January 18, 2011].

Page 56 "After nearly a thousand complaints from members of the public..." — See: "Climate change 'exaggerated' in government ads", *BBC News*, March 17, 2010. Available at: http://news.bbc.co.uk/1/hi/uk_politics/8571353.stm [Accessed January 18, 2011].

Pages 56–57 "One poster said: "Jack and Jill went up the hill to fetch a pail of water. There was none as extreme weather due to climate change had caused a drought." *See* Revoir, P (2010), "Jack and Jill hyped up the risks of global warming in government adverts for children", *Daily Mail Online*, March 18, 2010. Available at: http://www.dailymail.co.uk/

news/article-1258712/Jack-Jill-hyped-risks-global-warming-government-adverts-children.html [Accessed January 18, 2011].

Page 57 "The other said: 'Rub a dub dub, three men in a tub — a necessary course of action due to flash flooding caused by climate change.'" *Ibid.*

Page 57 "If the ASA had been better informed and more robust, it would surely also have censured the most offensive advert of the lot…"—See: "ACTONC02 'Bedtime Stories' TV Advertisement, October 2009", *YouTube. Available* at: http://www.youtube.com/watch?v=w62gsctP2gc [Accessed January 18, 2011].

Page 58 "Consider, for example, this statement made in Britain's House of Lords in July 2010 by Lord Marland…"—Lords Hansard, July 5, 2010 Main Chamber Debates. Available at: http://services.parliament.uk/hansard/Lords/bydate/20100705/mainchamberdebates/part004.html [Accessed January 18, 2011].

Page 58 "the disastrous experience in Spain"—Calzada, G.A. et al (2009), "Study of the effects on employment of public aid to renewable energy sources", Universidad Rey Juan Carlos. Available at: http://www.juandemariana.org/pdf/090327-employment-public-aid-renewable.pdf [Accessed January 18, 2011].

Page 59 "Among the many wise individuals who have seen through…"—Thatcher, M (2003), *Statecraft,* (Harper Collins).

Chapter 4: In the Pay of Big Koch

Page 60 "Carter Roberts, President and CEO, World Wildlife Fund Inc., Total Compensation (2009): $455,147"—IRS Form 990 for 2009, page 77. Available at: http://www.worldwildlife.org/who/financialinfo/WWFBinaryitem20499.PDF

Page 60 "Frances Beinecke, President, Natural Resources Defense Council, Total Compensation (2009): $432,742"—IRS Form 990 for 2009, page 38. Available at: http://www.nrdc.org/about/NRDC_990_2009.pdf

Page 60 "Fred Krupp, President, Environmental Defense Fund, Total Compensation (2009): $423,359"—IRS Form 990 for 2009, page 45. Available at: http://www.edf.org/documents/11602_2010-09_EDF_990_FINAL_PUBLIC_VERSION_SECURED.pdf

Page 62 "according to environmental activist George Monbiot…"—
Monbiot, G. (2009), "The denial industry case notes", *Guardian
Online*, 07 December. Available at: http://www.guardian.co.uk/
environment/georgemonbiot/2009/dec/07/george-monbiot-blog-climate-
denial-industry [Accessed January 18, 2011].
Page 64 *"An insight into how skeptics work – follow the funding."*—See
Campaign Against Climate Change's website at: http://www.campaigncc.
org/sceptics#sceptic_insight [Accessed January 18, 2011].
Page 65 "what philosopher Jamie Whyte calls the 'Motive Fallacy'"—
Whyte, J. (2003), *Bad Thoughts: A Guide to Clear Thinking*. (Corvo
Books).
Page 66 "a Guardian article he'd written in 2006…"—Monbiot, G.
(2006), "The threat is from those who accept climate change, not
those who deny it", *Guardian Online*, September 21. Available at: http://
www.guardian.co.uk/commentisfree/2006/sep/21/comment.georgemonbiot
[Accessed January 19, 2011].
Page 66 "Al Gore pushing this line"—Gore, A. (2006) *An Inconvenient
Truth: The Planetary Emergency of Global Warming and What We Can
Do About It,* (New York: Rodale Press), p. 263.
Page 67 "Here is one (October 2003) from our friend Michael Mann to
Robert Matthews…"—*See:* http://assassinationscience.com/climategate/1/
FOIA/mail/1065125462.txt [Accessed January 19, 2011].
Page 67 "Or, as Michael Mann hilariously put it in February 2010…"—
See: http://hw.libsyn.com/p/8/7/e/87e0736aa2decb69/POI_2010_02_26_
Michael_Mann.mp3?sid=461ae31a711c74222f40fc1d2920cf6d&1_sid=18988&1
_eid=&1_mid=1770538 [Accessed January 19, 2011]
Page 69 "£1.1 million spent by British Council on 'Challenge Europe'…"—
EU Referendum Blog, February 4, 2010. Available at: http://eureferendum.
blogspot.com/2010/02/british-council-spends-35-million-on.html [Accessed
January 19, 2011].
Page 69 "£2.5 million spent by British Council on International Climate
Champions programme"—*See* "British Council spends £3.5 million on
climate change propaganda", *EU Referendum Blog,* February 4, 2010.
Available at: http://eureferendum.blogspot.com/2010/02/british-council-
spends-35-million-on.html [Accessed January 19, 2011].

Page 69 "£6 million spent by British government on 'hard-hitting' Bedtime Stories ad targeting climate skeptics..."—Webster, B (2009), "Ministers target climate change doubters in prime-time TV advert", *Times Online,* October 9. Available at: http://www.timesonline.co.uk/tol/ news/environment/article6867046.ece [Accessed January 18, 2011].

Page 69 "£13.7 million received in grants since 1990 by Phil Jones, director of the Climatic Research Unit at University of East Anglia."— Mendick, R. (2009), "'Climategate' professor Phil Jones awarded £13 million in research grants'", *Telegraph Online,* December 5. Available at: http://www.telegraph.co.uk/earth/copenhagen-climate-change-confe/6735846/ Climategate-professor-Phil-Jones-awarded-13-million-in-research-grants.html [Accessed January 19, 2011].

Page 69 "A$ 13.9 million – spent by Australian government on its 2009 Think Climate Think Change ad campaign."—*See* Maiden, S. (2009), "Rudd advertising campaign on climate change costs $13.9 million", *The Australian Online,* January 7. Available at: http://www.theaustralian. com.au/news/think-climate-think-rudds-14m-ads/story-e6frg6n6-1111118501252 [Accessed January 19, 2011].

Page 69 "$70 million pledged by Rockefeller Foundation..."—*See:* http:// philanthropy.com/article/Rockefeller-Commits/62676/ [Accessed January 19, 2011].

Page 69 "$100 million donated by ExxonMobil ...to Stanford University's Global Climate and Energy Project."—*See* Stanford University's Global Climate and Energy Project at: http://gcep.stanford.edu/about/sponsors. html [Accessed January 19, 2011].

Page 69 "£243 million – paid by UK government since 1990 to fund Met Office's 'climate prediction' programme"—*See* "Money Talking", *EU Referendum Blog.* Available at: http://eureferendum.blogspot.com/2010/02/ money-talking.html [Accessed January 19, 2011].

Page 69 "£650 million – paid by European Union for..."—*See* "Money Talking", *EU Referendum Blog,* February 19, 2010. Available at: http:// eureferendum.blogspot.com/2010/02/money-talking.html [Accessed January 19, 2011].

Page 69 "$4 billion allocated in the 2011 US Federal budget for climate research."—*See* Horn, A. (2011), "How Much of Your Money Wasted on 'Climate Change'? Try $10.6 Million a Day", *Pajamas Media Blog*, 15 January. Available at: http://pajamasmedia.com/blog/how-much-of-your-money-wasted-on-climate-change-try-10-6-million-a-day/ [Accessed January 19, 2011].

Page 70 "$126 billion World Bank estimate of carbon trading industry turnover in 2008."—*See* Capoor, K. & Ambrosi, P. (2009) "State and Trends of Carbon Market 2009", *World Bank. Available* at: http://siteresources.worldbank.org/INTCARBONFINANCE/Resources/State___Trends_of_the_Carbon_Market_2009-FINAL_26_May09.pdf [Accessed January 19, 2011], p. 1.

Page 70 "The best estimate so far comes from Australian blogger Jo Nova…"—Nova, J. (2010), "The Money Trail", *ABC Online*, March 4. Available at: http://www.abc.net.au/unleashed/stories/s2835581.htm [Accessed January 19, 2011].

Page 70 "Dr. Richard North did some calculations of his own."—North, R. (2010), "Five times the cost of the Manhattan Project", *EU Referendum Blog*, 05 March. Available at: http://eureferendum.blogspot.com/2010/03/five-times-cost-of-manhattan-project.html [Accessed January 19, 2011].

Page 74 "As the UK's Natural Environment Research Council subsequently confirmed"—NERC (1996) "First Report of the Scientific Group on Decommissioning Offshore Structures." Bourne Press: Bournemouth.

Page 75 "*At first, many of the causes were championed, such as opposition to nuclear testing and protection of whales…*"—Moore, P. (2008), "Why I Left Greenpeace", *Wall Street Journal*, April 22. Available at: http://online.wsj.com/article/SB120882720657033391.html?mod=opinion_main_commentaries [Accessed January 19, 2011].

Page 76 "campaign leaflets like this one…from Friends of the Earth"—See: http://dev.foe.co.uk/campaigns/economy/press_for_change/profet_before_planet_23627.html [Accessed April 13, 2011]

Page 77 "Probably the most ambitious is the WWF…"—Booker, C. (2010), "WWF hopes to find $60 billion growing on trees", *Telegraph Online*, March 20. Available at: http://www.telegraph.co.uk/comment/columnists/christopherbooker/7488629/

WWF-hopes-to-find-60-billion-growing-on-trees.html [Accessed January 19, 2011].

Page 79 "You see this cropping up in the Climategate files, in a July 1999 email from the WWF's Adam Markham..."—*See:* http:// assassinationscience.com/climategate/1/FOIA/mail/0933255789.txt [Accessed January 19, 2011].

Page 79 "Most egregious still is the influence green NGOs have been allowed over the supposedly authoritative, neutral IPCC."— Laframboise, D. (2010), "Greenpeace and the Nobel Winning Climate Report", *No Frakking Consensus Blog. Available* at: http:// nofrakkingconsensus.blogspot.com/2010/01/greenpeace-and-nobel-winning-climate_28.html [Accessed January 19, 2011].

Page 80 "Gustave Le Bon"—Le Bon, G. (2005), *The Crowd: A Study of the Popular Mind,* (United States: Filiquarian Pub.). Available at: http:// books.google.co.uk/books?id=5kOgI_Oz4H8C [Accessed April 13, 2011]

Page 81 *"When an affirmation has been sufficiently repeated and there is unanimity in this repetition"—Ibid.* page 121.

Page 82 "the work of a man from Phoenix, Arizona named Russell Cook..."—Cook, R. (2010), "Has the Mainstream Media Trusted Enviro-activists for Advice on Listening to Skeptic Scientists?", *Climate Realists,* August 23. Available at: http://climaterealists.com/index. php?id=6175 [Accessed January 19, 2011].

Chapter 5: The Science is Unsettled

Page 85 *"Let's be clear: the work of science has nothing whatever to do with consensus."*—Crichton, M. (2003), "Aliens Cause Global Warming", January 17. Event info: http://media.caltech.edu/events/35247 Text available at: http://brinnonprosperity.org/crichton2.html [Accessed January 23, 2011].

Page 87 "an unusually rapid dramatic version of what Thomas Kuhn... called a 'paradigm shift.'"—Kuhn, T. (1996), *The Structure of Scientific Revolutions,* Third Edition (Chicago; London: University of Chicago Press).

Page 88 "As the philosopher Karl Popper first argued in the 1930s..."— Popper, K. (1992), *The Logic of Scientific Discovery,* (London: Routledge).

Page 91 "the Royal Society issued an important and definitive statement"—Royal Society, December 16, 2009. Available at: http://royalsociety.org/Preventing-dangerous-climate-change/ [Accessed January 23, 2011].

Page 91 "There is no such thing as 'safe' climate change."—*Ibid.*

Page 92 "several prominent members of the Royal Society effectively forced the organization to issue a retraction"—"Climate change: A summary of the science", September 2010. Available at http://royalsociety.org/WorkArea/DownloadAsset.aspx?id=4294972963 [Accessed 13 April 2011]

Pages 93–94 "Post Normal Science: a concept you won't have heard of, invented by two men you've never heard of either…"—Ravetz, J.K. & Funtowicz, S. (2003), "Post Normal Science", *International Society for Ecological Economics. Available* at: http://www.ecoeco.org/pdf/pstnormsc.pdf [Accessed January 23, 2011].

Page 94 "…as Thomas Spratt pointed out as early as 1667"—Spratt, T. (1667), *History of the Royal Society of London: for the improving of natural knowledge,* (London : printed by T[homas]. R[oycroft]. for J. Martyn at the Bell without Temple-bar, and J. Allestry at the Rose and Crown in Duck-lane, printers to the Royal Society)

Pages 94–95 "This was what President Eisenhower was warning about"—"Farewell Address to the Nation", January 17, 1961. Available at: http://mcadams.posc.mu.edu/ike.htm [Accessed January 23, 2011].

Page 95 "As David Michaels noted in the Washington Post…"—Michaels, D. (2008), "It's not the answers that are biased, it's the questions", *Washington Post,* July 15. Available at: http://www.washingtonpost.com/wp-dyn/content/article/2008/07/14/AR2008071402145.html [Accessed January 23, 2011].

Page 95 "Recently, my 'climate skepticism' was challenged on a BBC documentary"—*See* "Science Under Attack", *BBC Horizon,* Description Available at: http://www.bbc.co.uk/programmes/b00y4yql [Accessed January 23, 2011]. Preview available on YouTube: http://www.youtube.com/watch?v=4SmPjVCfTgM

Page 96 "Enstrom and Kabat analyzed thirty years of American Cancer Society data"—Kabat, Geoffrey C. (2008). *Hyping Health Risks:*

Environmental Hazards in Daily Life and the Science of Epidemiology.
New York: Columbia Press. pp.147–182.

Page 97 "...the BBC made an uncharacteristically fair and balanced attempt at examining some of these issues..."—*See* "Can science ever be truly morally neutral?", *BBC Radio 4 "The Moral Maze"*, Description available at: http://www.bbc.co.uk/programmes/b00p2z8m [Accessed January 23, 2011].

Page 98 "At first Schneider appears to be in full agreement with Professor Wolpert..."—*Schneider, S.* "'Mediarology': The Roles of Citizens, Journalists, and Scientists in Debunking Climate Change Myths". Available at: http://stephenschneider.stanford.edu/Mediarology/Mediarology. html [Accessed April 13, 2011].

Page 99 "*Time* magazine...'The Heat Is On' cover story"—Lemonick, M.D. (1987), "The Heat Is On", *Time Magazine*, October 19. Available: http://www.time.com/time/magazine/article/0,9171,965776,00.html [Accessed January 23, 2011].

Page 100 "I got this sensation again when reading one of the guest posts on Watts Up With That?"—Watts, A. (2010) "Climategate: Plausibility and the blogosphere in the post-normal age", *Watts Up With That?*, February 9. Available at: http://wattsupwiththat.com/2010/02/09/climategate-plausibility-and-the-blogosphere-in-the-post-normal-age/ [Accessed January 23, 2011].

Page 101 "A few weeks earlier, I remembered reading his essay on Post Normal Science..."—*See* "Climate Change and the Death of Science", *Buy The Truth Blog*, October 31, 2009. Available at: http://buythetruth. wordpress.com/2009/10/31/climate-change-and-the-death-of-science/ [Accessed January 23, 2011].

Page 103 "In the abstract for their 1993 treatise 'Science for the Post Normal Age'..."—Ravetz, J.R. & Funtowicz, O.E. (1993), "Science for the Post Normal Age", Futures, September, 25(7): 739–55.

Page 104 "Among those who certainly understood this early on was Mike Hulme of the Tyndall Centre..."—Hulme, M. (2007), "The Appliance of Science", *Guardian Online*, March 14. Available at: http://www. guardian.co.uk/society/2007/mar/14/scienceofclimatechange.climatechange [Accessed January 23, 2011].

Page 105 "At least Joseph Bast...was wise to his game..."—Bast, J. (2009) "What Climate Change Can Do for the Left", *American Thinker*, July 17. Available at: http://www.americanthinker.com/2009/07/what_climate_change_can_do_for.html [Accessed January 23, 2011].

Pages 105–106 "Hulme employs the beguiling technique of hiding his views in plain sight, as when he declares"—Hulme, M. (2009), *Why We Disagree about Climate Change: Understanding Controversy, Inaction and Opportunity*, (UK: Cambridge University Press).

Chapter 6: A Few Things You Should Know About "Global Warming"

Page 107 "DIANE : This generation are disaster junkies...."—from "The Heretic" (2011), a play by Richard Bean performed at the Royal Court Theatre, London, February 4 – March 19, 2011.

Pages 109–110 "Pachaurigate has exposed the shady dealings of Dr. Rajendra Pachauri..."—North, R. (2009) "A busy man", EU Referendum, December 14. Available at: http://eureferendum.blogspot.com/2009/12/busy-man.html [accessed March 5, 2011].

Page 110 "Why does [TERI] run a golf course in a parched district of India, using up to 300,000 gallons of water a day?"—Watts, A. (2010), "Pachauri's TERI institute golf course – water hog in a city desperate for fresh water", *Watts Up With That*, February 20. Available at: http://wattsupwiththat.com/2010/02/20/pachauris-teri-institute-golf-course-water-hog-in-a-city-desparate-for-fresh-water/ [Accessed January 23, 2011].

Page 111 "Africagate, for example, has exposed its dubious claim that climate change could by 2020 cause yields from rain-fed agriculture in some African countries to fall by as much as 50 per cent."—North, R. (2010). "And now for Africagate", February 7. http://eureferendum.blogspot.com/2010/02/and-now-for-africagate.html [Accessed March 5, 2011]

Page 111 "Amazongate concerned another dodgy claim made in the [Fourth Assessment Report]"—North, R. (2010), "And now for Amazongate", January 25. http://eureferendum.blogspot.com/2010/01/and-now-for-amazongate.html [accessed March 5, 2011]. See also "Amazongate: The Missing Evidence", *Telegraph Online*, June

26. Available at: http://www.telegraph.co.uk/comment/columnists/
christopherbooker/7856474/Amazongate-the-missing-evidence.html

Page 111 "Most damaging, though, was Glaciergate."—Booker, C. (2010),
"Pachauri: the real story behind the Glaciergate scandal", *Telegraph
Online*, January 23. Available at: http://www.telegraph.co.uk/comment/
columnists/christopherbooker/7062667/Pachauri-the-real-story-behind-the-
Glaciergate-scandal.html [Accessed January 23, 2011].

Page 113 "Pachauri began back-tracking. First he claimed it was a slip-
up..."—Dunlop, W.G. (2010), "IPCC chief defends panel in Himalaya
glacier flap", *AFP*, January 19. Available at: http://www.google.com/
hostednews/afp/article/ALeqM5iYbUYSAqzBzVfNdFTN9EeP5gXbNg [Accessed
January 23, 2011].

Page 113 "According to another IPCC author, however, it was no such
thing."—*North, R.* (2010), "Glaciergate – Still a Long Way From
The Truth", *EU Referendum Blog*, January 31. Available at: http://
eureferendum.blogspot.com/2010/01/glaciergate-still-long-way-from-truth.html
[Accessed January 23, 2011].

Page 113 "Obviously it was hard on occasion to resist the temptation to
gloat..."—Delingpole, J. (2009), "Climategate goes uber-viral, Gore
flees leaving evil henchmen to defend crumbling citadel", *Telegraph
Online*, December 4. Available at: http://blogs.telegraph.co.uk/news/
jamesdelingpole/100018847/climategate-goes-uber-viral-gore-flees-leaving-evil-
henchmen-to-defend-crumbling-citadel/ [Accessed January 23, 2011].

Page 114 "The first, a cursory parliamentary investigation by the
House of Commons Science committee..."—House of Commons
Science and Technology Committee, "The disclosure of climate data
from the Climatic Research Unit at the University of East Anglia".
Available at: http://www.publications.parliament.uk/pa/cm200910/cmselect/
cmsctech/387/387i.pdf [Accessed January 23, 2011].

Page 114 "The second inquiry, though, made the first one look tougher
than the Spanish Inquisition."—Booker, C. (2010), "Can We Trust
the Climategate Inquiry", March 27. Available at: http://www.telegraph.
co.uk/comment/7530961/Can-we-trust-the-Climategate-inquiry.html [Accessed
January 23, 2011].

Page 115 "The third inquiry, headed by Sir Muir Russell, was also a whitewash."—See Montford, A. (2010), "Slanted inquiries", September 17. Available at: http://opinion.financialpost.com/2010/09/17/slanted-inquiries/ [Accessed April 13, 2011]

Page 117 "As Professor Bob Carter notes and summarises…"—Carter, R.M. (2010), *Climate: The Counter Consensus*, (Turkey: Stacey International).

Page 119 "This open letter sent by 141 scientists to UN Secretary General Ban Ki-moon…"—*See:* "Open Letter to UN Secretary-General", December 8, 2009. Available at: http://www.copenhagenclimatechallenge. org/index.php?option=com_content&view=frontpage&Itemid=1 [Accessed January 23, 2011].

Pages 120–121 "In 1670, the French philosopher Pascal argued that even if there is no proof for the existence of God…"—Pascal, B. (1996), *Pensees*, (England: Penguin Books).

Page 124 "Rising sea levels"—Mörner, Nils-Axel (2010). "Some problems in the reconstruction of mean sea level and its changes with time" *Quaternary International*, Volume 221, Issues 1–2, 1 July, pp. 3–8/

Page 125 Maldives—Mörner, Nils-Axel; Tooley, Michael; Possnert, Göran (2004). "New perspectives for the future of the Maldives". *Global and Planetary Change* 40 (1–2): 177–182. Available at: http://www. sciencedirect.com/science/article/pii/S0921818103001085.

Page 125 Flooding in Bangladesh—"River sediment may counter Bangladesh sea level rise" (2010), SciDev.net, citing research by the Center for Environmental and Geographic Information Services, Dhaka. Available at: http://www.scidev.org/en/news/river-sediment-may-counter-bangladesh-sea-level-rise.html

Page 126 Polar bears—IUCN (2009), Proceedings of the 15th Working Meeting of the IUCN/SSC Polar Bear Specialist Group, 29 June-3 July. Available at: http://data.iucn.org/dbtw-wpd/edocs/SSC-OP-043.pdf. See also: http://www.animalinfo.org/species/carnivor/ursumari.htm

Page 127 Opening of the Northwest Passage—McKie, R. (2007), "Arctic thaw opens fabled trade route", *Guardian Online*, September 16. Available at: http://www.guardian.co.uk/environment/2007/sep/16/ climatechange [Accessed January 23, 2011].

Page 127 "Al Gore's hero Bill McKibben grew similarly excited"—
McKibben, B. (2009) "Think Again: Climate Change", *Foreign Policy*,
January 1. http://www.foreignpolicy.com/articles/2009/01/05/think_again_
climate_change [Accessed April 13, 2011]

Page 127 "As Ian Wishart records"—Wishart, I. (2009), *Air Con: The
Seriously Inconvenient Truth About Global Warming*, (HATM
Publishing).

Page 127 "According to the World Bank…"—World Bank, (2007),
"Development Actions and the Rising Incidence of Disasters",
Independent Evaluation Group. Available at: http://siteresources.
worldbank.org/INTOED/Resources/developing_actions.pdf [Accessed
January 23, 2011]. See also: van der Vink, G., et al. (1998) "Why the
United States is becoming more vulnerable to natural disasters"
*EOS, Transactions, American Geophysical Union, vol .79, pp.533–537
November 3.* Available at: http://seismo.berkeley.edu/~rallen/pub/1998ushaz/
index.php
See also Goklany, I. (2005). "Evidence to the House of Lords Select
Committee on Economic Affairs On Aspects of the Economics of
Climate Change", Energy and Environment, Vo1.16, No.3&4. Available
at: http://goklany.org/library/EEv16–3+4_GoklanyHoL_Evidence.pdf

Page 127 "And according to the IPCC's Fourth Assessment report"—
IPCC Fourth Assessment Report. Available at: http://www.ipcc.ch/
publications_and_data/publications_and_data_reports.shtml#1 [Accessed
January 23, 2011].

Page 128 "A press release from IPCC author Kevin Trenberth"—
See "Chris Landsea Leaves IPCC", Prometheus Blog,
January 17, 2005. http://cstpr.colorado.edu/prometheus/archives/
science_policy_general/000318chris_landsea_1

Page 128 "Reuters reported"—Fox, M. (2004). "Global warming effects
faster than feared", *Reuters*, October 24. http://www.planetark.com/
dailynewsstory.cfm/newsid/27825/story.htm

Page 128 "Landsea wrote to Dr. Pachauri"—For Landsea's correspondence
see: http://cstpr.colorado.edu/prometheus/archives/ipcc-correspondence.pdf
[Accessed January 23, 2011].

Page 129 "The IPCC, wrote Landsea"—Ferguson, R. (2010), "Dr Chris Landsea leaves the IPCC", *Science and Public Policy Institute Blog,* January 20. Available at: http://sppiblog.org/news/dr-chris-landsea-leaves-the-ipcc [Accessed January 23, 2011].

Page 129 "The handy one they have settled on is "Ocean Acidification", first popularised by a 2005 report by the (fanatically alarmist) Royal Society..."—*See* "Ocean acidification due to increasing atmospheric carbon dioxide", *Royal Society,* June 2005. Available at: http://dge.stanford.edu/labs/caldeiralab/Caldeira%20downloads/RoyalSociety_OceanAcidification.pdf [Accessed January 23, 2011]. *See also* **I.E. Hendriks, C.M. Duarte, and M. Álvarez (2010),** "Vulnerability of marine biodiversity to ocean acidification: A meta-analysis" Estuarine, Coastal and Shelf Science, Volume 86, Issue 2, 20 January, Pages 157–164. From summary: "Active biological processes and small-scale temporal and spatial variability in ocean pH may render marine biota far more resistant to ocean acidification than hitherto believed." Available at: http://www.sciencedirect.com/science/article/pii/S027277140900537X

Chapter 7: Watermelons
Page 131 *"Global Warming is the mother of all environmental scares..."*— Wildavsky, A. (1992) Foreword to *The Heated Debate* by Robert Balling (San Francisco: Pacific Research Institute).

Page 132 "the green movement as it chooses to represent itself in books such as *Time's Up..."*—Farnish, K. (2009), *Time's Up: An Uncivilized Solution To A Global Crisis,* (Cornwall: Green Books).

Page 133 "One of these people is a guy named James Hansen..."— Editorial Reviews, *Time's Up* [ibid.] http://www.amazon.com/Times-Up-Uncivilized-Solution-Global/dp/190032248X/ref=ntt_at_ep_dpt_1 [Accessed April 13, 2011]

Page 134 Hansen, J. (2009) *"Coal fired power stations are death factories. Close them."* The Observer, February 15.

Page 136 "But then again, when asked by the Radio Times which animal he wouldn't mind seeing extinct..."—Gallagher, W. (2009), "Autumnwatch's Chris Packham: 'Let Pandas Die", *Radio Times,* 22

September. Available at: http://www.radiotimes.com/blogs/745-news-autumnwatchs-chris-packham-let-pandas-die/ [Accessed January 23, 2011].

Page 137 "Consider this statement from the late professional 60s gambler-turned-zookeeper John Aspinall…"—Quoted in Gray, J. (1993), *Beyond the New Right: Markets, Government and the Common Environment*, (GB: Routledge), p. 178.

Page 138 "the Optimum Population Trust"—"Assuming the global biocapacity and average footprint remain stable at the 2003 level, then, to become sustainable, the world population needs to contract to a maximum of 5.1 billion". See: http://www.optimumpopulation.org/opt.optimum.html [Accessed April 13, 2011]

Page 138 "I was first alerted to this green movement's curious psychopathology"—See: "Any Questions", *BBC Radio 4. Available* at: http://www.bbc.co.uk/iplayer/episode/boom45do/Any_Questions_21_08_2009/ [Accessed January 23, 2011], from 35:00 onwards.

Page 140 "Without this book, the environmental movement might have been long delayed…"—Gore, A. (1994), *Introduction to Silent Spring. Available* at: http://www.uneco.org/ssalgoreintro.html [Accessed January 23, 2011].

Page 141 "the Environmental Protection Agency's seven-month hearing (and more than 9,000 pages of testimony) prior to the ban being enacted"—Sweeney, Edmund (1972). "EPA hearing examiner's recommendations and findings concerning DDT hearings" 40 CFR 164.32. As cited in *The Excellent Powder: DDT's Political and Scientific History* (2010) Donald Roberts, Richard Tren. (Indianapolis: Dog Ear Publishing).

Page 141 "On Earth Day in 2007, thirteen prominent environmentalists (among them Al Gore) paid tribute to her legacy in an essay collection called *Courage to the Earth*."—Matthiessen, P. eds. (2007), *Courage for the Earth: Writers, Scientists, and Activists Celebrate the Life and Writing of Rachel Carson*, (USA: Houghton Mifflin Company).

Pages 142 "Ehrlich is best known for *The Population Bomb*, the 1968 bestseller which terrified hippies…"—Ehrlich, P.R. (1971), *The Population Bomb*, (Cutchogue, N.Y.: Buccaneer Books).

Page 143 "Commoner propounded his theory in his 1971 bestseller *The Closing Circle*"—Commoner, B. (1971), *The Closing Circle: Nature, Man and Technology*, (New York: Alfred Knopf).

Page 143 "At about the same time, the British research scientist James Lovelock was formulating his 'earth feedback hypothesis'…"— Lovelock, J. (1979) *Gaia: A New Look at Life on Earth*. (Oxford University Press)

Page 144 "Lovelock spells it out in a recent book"—Lovelock, J. (2007), *The Revenge of Gaia: Why the earth is fighting back—and how we can still save humanity*, (London: Penguin).

Page 144 "In an interview about the book, he crows"—James Lovelock interviewed in *Daily Mail*, March 22, 2008, "We're all doomed". Available at: http://www.dailymail.co.uk/news/article-541748/Were-doomed-40-years-global-catastrophe-theres-NOTHING-says-climate-change-expert.html [Accessed April 13, 2011]

Page 144 "And *The Ecologist* was with him all the way"—See: *The Ecologist*, 1(1): 3–5. Available at: http://exacteditions.theecologist.org/exact/browsePages.do?issue=5337&size=3&pageLabel=3 [Accessed January 23, 2011].

Page 145 "In his December 1942 decree 'On the Treatment of the Land in the Eastern Territories', "—Bruggemeier, F.J., Cioc, M. & T. Zeller eds. (2005), *How Green Were the Nazis?: Nature, Environment, and Nation in the Third Reich* (Athens, OH: Ohio University Press).

Page 146 "the essay collection *How Green Were the Nazis?*"—Ibid.

Page 147 "its instincts remained little changed – just look at books like Harrison Brown's"—Brown, H. (1954), *The Challenge of Man's Future*, (Secker & Warburg), p. 260.

Page 147 "Thus we could sterilize or in other ways discourage the mating of the feeble-minded."—*Ibid*, pp. 104–5.

Page 145 "At this point the reader is probably saying to himself…"—*Ibid*, p. 221.

Page 148 "…Holdren was arguing for similar policies in a book he wrote in 1977…"—Holdren, J., Ehrlich, A. & Ehrlich, P. (1977), *Ecoscience: Population, Resources, Environment*. *Available* at: http://zombietime.com/john_holdren/#white_house_statement [Accessed January 23, 2011].

Page 149 "This Planetary Regime – perhaps run under the auspice of 'UNEP and the United Nations population agencies'"—*Ibid.*, pp. 942–3.

Page 149 "an armed international organization"—*Ibid.*, p. 917.

Chapter 8: Welcome to the New World Order

Page 151 "*It may be better to live under robber barons than under omnipotent moral busybodies...*"—Lewis, C.S. (1998), *God in the Dock* (Fount)

Page 151 "*Evil men don't get up in the morning saying*"—(personal communication with Christopher Booker)

Page 152 "Or, as Aurelio Peccei once put it..." Peccei, A.—(1969) *The Chasm Ahead* (New York: MacMillan Press).

Page 154 "The catalyst was the Club of Rome's first publication, a seminal 1972 book called *Limits to Growth.*"—Meadows, D.H. et al. (1972), *Limits to Growth: A Report on the Club of Rome's Project on the Predicament of Mankind,* (London: Earth Island).

Page 154 "Among these was John Maddox, editor of *Nature,* who in the same year, 1972, published a counterblast..."—Maddox, J. (1972), *The Doomsday Syndrome,* (London: Macmillan).

Page 155 "Here is the most infamous Club of Rome statement"— Schneider, B. & King, A. (1993), *The First Global Revolution,* (Orient Longman). Available at: http://www.archive.org/details/ TheFirstGlobalRevolution [Accessed January 24, 2011].

Page 157 "That evening the group was invited to Gvishiani's suite in the Imperial Hotel in Vienna. He served his favourite fruit vodka"— Whitehead, J.R. (1999), *Memoirs of a Boffin,* (Sutton Publishing). Available at: http://www3.sympatico.ca/drrennie/chap13.html [Accessed January 24, 2011].

Page 158 "*[The Club of Rome] provided the climate in which new ideas were generated...*"—*Ibid.*

Page 158 "Probably the best analysis of the Club of Rome's tangible effects on global environmental policy come courtesy of a website called The Green Agenda."—See: http://www.green-agenda.com/globalrevolution.html [Accessed January 24, 2011].

Page 158 "Here, for example, is the Club of Rome's Master Plan…"—
Mesarovic, M. & Pestel, E. (1975), *Mankind at the Turning Point: The
Second Report to the Club of Rome* (London: Hutchinson).

Page 160 "As Green Agenda puts it…"—See: http://www.green-agenda.com/
sustainabledevelopment.html [Accessed January 24, 2011].

Page 160 "This was certainly the context in which Maurice Strong
used the 's' word"—Strong, M. (1991), "The relationship between
demographic trends, economic growth, unsustainable consumption
patterns and environmental degradation," UNCED PrepCom report,
August 1991. Quoted by GreenTrack International, Report 26, August
15, 1991, Libertytown, MD, p. 3.

Page 162 "As he once put it: 'Our concept of ballot-box democracy may
need'…"—*Quoted in* Foster, P. (2009), "Chairman Mo's Little Red
Website", *National Post,* November 12. Available at: http://network.
nationalpost.com/NP/blogs/fpcomment/archive/2009/11/12/peter-foster-
chairman-mo-s-little-red-website.aspx#ixzzopolCkooJ [Accessed January 24,
2011].

Page 162 *"Sustainable global development requires that those who are
more affluent…"*—*See* "Our Common Future: From One Earth to One
World", *UN Documents.* Available at: http://www.un-documents.net/ocf-ov.
htm [Accessed January 24, 2011].

Page 163 *"We do not pretend that the process is easy or
straightforward…"*—*Ibid.*

Page 163 *"1.1 Humanity stands at a defining moment in history…"*—*See*
"Agenda 21, *UN Department of Economic and Social Affairs (Division
for Sustainable Development). Available* at: http://www.un.org/esa/dsd/
agenda21/res_agenda21_00.shtml [Accessed January 24, 2011].

Page 164 "The concept of national sovereignty has been an immutable,
indeed sacred, principle of international relations."—as quoted by
Raeburn, Paul (1992). "Ecology Remedy Costly", Associated Press,
March 12.

Page 166 "To give you a rough idea of the UN's spread…" UNEP
Evaluation and Oversight Unit (2004), "Study of the Environmental
Management Group." *See also:* Russell, G. (2009), "UN Says its Own
Eco-Management Out of Control", *Fox News,* February 24. Available

at: http://www.foxnews.com/story/0,2933,499244,00.html. **See also:** http://www.foxnews.com/projects/pdf/022409_JIU_Environment_Report.pdf [Accessed April 13, 2011].

Page 167 "This becomes clear in a 1998 UN discussion document"— Lawrence, G. (1998) "The Future of Local Agenda 21 in the New Millennium", available at: http://www.unedforum.org/publications/millennium/mill%20paper2.pdf

Page 168 *"As noted in a recent study"—Melia, S., Parkhurst, G. and Barton, H. (forthcoming 2012), "The paradox of intensification." Journal of Transport Policy, 18(1).*

Page 170 "the fact that Portland's eight percent increase in population density between 1990 and 2000 contribute to a 65 percent increase in traffic congestion"—Schrank, D. and Lomax, T., (2009) *2009 Urban Mobility Report.* Texas Transportation Institute, The Texas A&M University System.

Page 171 "In an article for the website 'Big Government'"— James Simpson (2011), Available at: http://biggovernment.com/jmsimpson/2011/01/23/agenda-21-part-ii-globalist-totalitarian-dictatorship-invading-a-town-near-you-with-your-permission/ [Accessed April 13, 2011].

Page 172 " ...which enabled Maurice Strong to describe in his autobiography the prospect of billions of environmental deaths as *"a glimmer of hope."—Quoted in* Foster, P. (2009), "Chairman Mo's Little Red Website", *National Post,* November 12. Available at: http://network.nationalpost.com/NP/blogs/fpcomment/archive/2009/11/12/peter-foster-chairman-mo-s-little-red-website.aspx#ixzzopolCkooJ [Accessed January 24, 2011].

Page 173 "In 1991, he established the Gorbachev Foundation"—*See* "The Green Web", *The Green Agenda. Available* at: http://green-agenda.com/greenweb.html [Accessed January 24, 2011].

Page 173 "Gorby was also responsible, in collaboration with Maurice Strong, for the Earth Charter (2000)."—*See* "The Earth Charter", *The Earth Charter Initiative.* Available at: http://www.earthcharterinaction.org/content/pages/Read-the-Charter.html [Accessed January 24, 2011].

Page 173 "This is a collection of principles"—*See* "Earth Council Alliance", *MauriceStrong.net*. Available at: http://www.mauricestrong. net/2009013070/earth-charter.html [Accessed January 24, 2011].

Page 173 "Principle 10, for example, asks that we *Ensure that economic activities and institutions…*"—*See* "The Earth Charter", *The Earth Charter Initiative*. Available at: http://www.earthcharterinaction.org/ content/pages/Read-the-Charter.html [Accessed January 24, 2011].

Page 174 *"One of the worst of the new dangers is ecological"*—Quotation from 46th John Findley Greed Foundation Lecture; Westminster College, Fulton, Missouri; May 6, 1992.

Page 174 *"Please stand up, delegates of the world, hold each other's hand and let us swear together…"*—Muller, R., "The Absolute, Urgent Need for Proper Earth Government", *Good Morning World. Available* at: http://www.goodmorningworld.org/earthgov/ [Accessed January 24, 2011].

Page 175 "Besides the Earth Charter, the Ark contains over 1000 *'Temenos Books'…"*—*Ark of Hope. Available* at: http://www.arkofhope.org/index.html [Accessed January 24, 2011].

Page 175 "MAINTAIN HUMANITY UNDER 500,000,000"—*See* "Let These Be Guidestones to an Age of Reason". Available at: http://www. thegeorgiaguidestones.com/Message.htm [Accessed January 24, 2011].

Page 176 *"BE NOT A CANCER ON THE EARTH"* says one."—*Ibid*.

Page 176 *"A total world population of 250–300 million people, a 95 per cent decline from present levels, would be ideal."*—Ted Turner interview, *Audubon* Magazine, 1996. As quoted by AIM: http://www.aim.org/wls/ five-percent-of-the-present-population-would-be-ideal/ [Accessed April 13, 2011]

Page 176 "…the Duke of Edinburgh, who – in a foreword to a book called *If I Were an Animal* – once wrote…"—Prince Philip (1986). Foreword, *If I Were an Animal*, (UK: Robin Clark Ltd.).

Page 176 "In his memoirs, King confided somewhat chillingly: '*My chief quarrel with DDT'"*—*The Discipline of Curiosity* (1990) Elsevier: Burlington, MA. P.43. as cited in Bethell, T. (2008) *The Politically Correct Guide to Science* (Regnery), p.76.

Page 177 "I quite like the definition offered by (green MSM opinion former) David Aaronovitch"—Aaronovitch, D. (2010) *Voodoo*

Histories: How Conspiracy Theory Has Shaped Modern History (Vintage).

Page 179 "…John Holdren calling for 'de-development'…"—Ballasy, N. (2010), "White House Science Czar Says He Would Use 'Free Market' to 'De-Develop the United States", *CNS News*, 16 September. Available at: http://www.cnsnews.com/news/article/75388 [Accessed January 24, 2011].

Page 179 "… 'We have only 100 months left to save the world from Climate Change'"—See Alderson, A. (2009), "Prince Charles: 100 months to save the world", *Telegraph Online*, March 7. Available at: http://www.telegraph.co.uk/news/newstopics/theroyalfamily/4952918/Prince-Charles-we-have-100-months-to-save-the-world.html [Accessed January 24, 2011].

Page 179 "his biofuel-powered royal train to tour Britain"—See Booth, R. (2010), "Prince Charles embarks on lavish train trip to spread green message", *Guardian Online*, September 6. Available at: http://www.guardian.co.uk/uk/2010/sep/06/prince-charles-green-train-campaign [Accessed January 24, 2011].

Chapter 9: Malthus & Co.

Page 181 "*The enormous amount of coal required…*"—Lord Kelvin (1902) "Windmills Must Be the Future Source of Power", *Philadelphia North American*, May 18. Available at: http://zapatopi.net/kelvin/papers/windmills_future_power.html

Page 182 "And we all know about what happened at Easter Island"—Diamond, J. (2006), *Collapse: How Societies Choose to Fail or Survive*, (London: Penguin Books).

Page 182 "Malthus observed the 'constant tendency in all animated life to increase beyond the nourishment prepared for it'"—Malthus, T. (1826), *An Essay on the Principle of Population*. Sixth Edition, Book 1, Chapter 1, page 3. (London: Ward, Lock & Co. Ltd.).

Page 183 "Britain's population swelled more than four-fold – while between 1780 and 1914, her economy grew thirteen times larger."—Population figures: Between 1781–90 and 1905–13, Great Britain's population grew around 4.3 times in size, from 9,369,000 to 40,062,000. Economic growth measured as "commodity output"

– between 1781–90 and 1905–13, Great Britain's commodity output grew around 13.3 times in size. O'Brien, P. & Keyder, C., *Economic Growth in Britain and France, 1780–1914: Two Paths to the Twentieth Century,* (1978, London: Allen & Unwin), p. 58.

Page 183 "Among the first to take up his noble cause of cussed pessimism against all objective evidence was one Harrison Brown"—Brown, H. (1954), *The Challenge of Man's Future,* (Secker & Warburg).

Page 184 "the average human being now earns nearly three times as much money…"—Ridley, M. (2010), *The Rational Optimist: How Prosperity Evolves,* (GB: Fourth Estate), p. 14.

Page 184 *"Our teeming population is the strongest evidence our numbers are burdensome to the world"*—Tertullian (2010), *Treatise of the Soul,* (Kessinger Publishing).

Page 185 "Matt Ridley offers a delicious example in *The Rational Optimist"*—Ridley, M. (2010), *The Rational Optimist: How Prosperity Evolves,* (GB: Fourth Estate). pp.12–13.

Page 186 "Simon challenged Ehrlich to choose any five commodities he liked"—Regis, E. (1997), "The Doomslayer", *Wired 5.02. Available* at: http://www.wired.com/wired/archive/5.02/ffsimon_pr.html

Page 187 "This certainly was the experience of one of Simon's acolytes"— Lomborg, B. (2001), *The Skeptical Environmentalist: Measuring the Real State of the World,* (UK: University of Cambridge Press).

Page 189 "the criticisms of the Danish Committee on Scientific Dishonesty"—*See* "Lomborg celebrates ministry ruling", *BBC New Online,* December 22, 2003. Available at: http://news.bbc.co.uk/1/hi/sci/tech/3340305.stm [Accessed January 28, 2011].

Page 189 "Monbiot dismissed Ridley's arguments"—Monbiot, G. (2010), "This state-hating free marketeer ignores his own failed experiment", *Guardian Online,* May 31. Available at: http://www.guardian.co.uk/commentisfree/2010/may/31/state-market-nothern-rock-ridley [Accessed December 28, 2010], Monbiot, G. (2010), "Matt Ridley's Rational Optimist is telling the rich what they want to hear", *Guardian Online,* June 18. Available at: http://www.guardian.co.uk/commentisfree/cif-green/2010/jun/18/matt-ridley-rational-optimist-errors [Accessed December 28, 2010].

Page 190 "You could… fit everyone in the world into the state of Texas"—
See http://www.firetown.com/blog/2010/12/03/the-overpopulation-myth-
the-entire-world-population-could-fit-into-the-state-of-texas/. See also Sean
Corrigan's essay, "A Long Way From Reaching Our Peak", http://www.
cobdencentre.org/2011/05/a-long-way-from-reaching-our-peak/

Page 191 "Math Lessons for Locavores"—Stephen Budiansky, *New York
Times*, August 19, 2010. Available at: http://www.nytimes.com/2010/08/20/
opinion/20budiansky.html [Accessed April 13, 2011]. See also "Yes We
Have No Bananas: A Critique of the 'Food Miles' Perspective",
Desrochers and Shimuzu (2008). Available at: http://mercatus.org/
publication/yes-we-have-no-bananas-critique-food-miles-perspective?id=24612

Page 192 "Simon admitted that he himself had begun life as a "card-
carrying anti-growth, anti-population zealot"—Regis, E. (1997), "The
Doomslayer", *Wired 5.02*. Available at: http://www.wired.com/wired/
archive/5.02/ffsimon_pr.html [Accessed January 28, 2011].

Page 193 "Simon neatly illustrated this point in a 1996 public debate with
Hazel Henderson" *Ibid*.

Page 193 *"Ecology teaches us that humankind is not the center of life…"*—
Simon, J. (1996), *The Ultimate Resource 2*, (USA: Princeton University
Press).

Page 194 "In *The Population Bomb* he airily declared"—Ehrlich, P.R.
(1971), *The Population Bomb*, (Cutchogue, N.Y. : Buccaneer Books).

Page 195 "He never much liked the term 'Cornucopian'"—Simon, J.
(1996), *The Ultimate Resource 2*, (USA: Princeton University Press).

Page 196 "the advent of shale gas"—For more on the topic, see Ridley,
M. (2011). "The Shale Gas Shock." GWPF Report 2. London: Global
Warming Policy Foundation. Available at: http://thegwpf.org/images/
stories/gwpf-reports/Shale-Gas_4_May_11.pdf

Page 197 "President Warren Harding's U.S. Coal Commission"—As
quoted in Bradley, R. (2008) *Capitalism at Work*. (Scrivener Press.) P
206.

Page 197 *"One cannot disentangle from human members the effects of
the human brain and its contents…"*—Simon, J. (1996) *The Ultimate
Resource 2. Ibid*.

Pages 197–198 "As Stephen Budiansky puts it"—"Sustainable Sentiments", September 3, 2010. Available at: http://budiansky.blogspot.com/2010/09/sustainable-sentiments.html [Accessed April 13, 2011]

Chapter 10, Propaganda and Dissent
Page 199 Lindzen, R. (1992) "Global Warming: The Origin and Nature of Alleged Scientific Consensus." *Regulation*, Vol.15, No.2, pp.87-98. Available at: http://www.cato.org/pubs/regulation/regv15n2/reg15n2g.html (Accessed April 13, 2011).
Page 205 "resignation letter written by Hal Lewis"—for discussion see Revkin, A. (2010), "A Physicist's Climate Complaints", October 15. Available at: http://dotearth.blogs.nytimes.com/2010/10/15/a-physicists-climate-complaints/ [Accessed April 13, 2011]
Page 206 "William Connolley…sought to dismiss him"—See: http://scienceblogs.com/stoat/2010/10/im_sure_dr_lewis_deserves_some.php [Accessed April 13, 2011]
Page 207 "[Australia's] state officials…cancelled or neutered flood defense programs"—See: http://eureferendum.blogspot.com/2011/01/it-was-bound-to-happen.html [Accessed April 13, 2011]
Pages 208 "the real cause of the fire: a global warming activist at a Rainbow Festival"—See: http://hauntingthelibrary.wordpress.com/2011/01/13/environmentalist-starts-israels-worst-ever-firegreenpeace-blames-global-warming/
Page 208 "Viner was quoted in a newspaper article"—Onians, C., 'Snowfalls are now just a thing of the past', *Independent Online*, March 20, 2000. Available at: http://www.independent.co.uk/environment/snowfalls-are-now-just-a-thing-of-the-past-724017.html [Accessed March 13, 2011].
Page 208 "a massive rescue operation was underway to free a Russian factory fishing ship",—North, R., "In serious trouble", *EUReferendum Blog*, January 14, 2011. Available at: http://eureferendum.blogspot.com/2011/01/in-serious-trouble.html [Accessed March 13, 2011].
Pages 208–209 "In the U.S., NASA announces that 2010 was the third hottest year since records began in 1880."—NASA (2011). "NASA Research Finds 2010 Tied for Warmest Year on Record", *Goddard*

Institute of Space Studies, January 12. Available at: http://www.giss.nasa.
gov/research/news/20110112/ [Accessed April 13, 2011]

Page 209 "The ranking 'third hottest year' is all but meaningless, as
even Hansen himself admitted"—"Despite Subtle Differences, Global
Temperature Records in Close Agreement", *NASA,* January 13, 2011.
Available at: http://www.nasa.gov/topics/earth/features/2010-climate-records.
html [Accessed March 13, 2011].

Page 210 "haranguing the American Meteorological Society for their
stubborn skepticism, using the word 'deniers' no fewer than six
times (in the online printed version), and demanding that the
'null hypothesis' on AGW theory be reversed.—Trenberth, K.E.,
"Communicating Climate Science and Thoughts On Climategate",
Joint Presidential Session on Communicating Climate Change.
Online speech (version 3), "Promoting climate information
and communication of climate change", available : http://ams.
confex.com/ams/91Annual/webprogram/Manuscript/Paper180230/
ClimategateThoughts4AMS_v3.pdf [Accessed March 13, 2011], Maue,
R.N., 'Trenberth At AMS Defends Himself Against Deniers, *Watts
Up With That,* January 26, 2011 commentary: http://wattsupwiththat.
com/2011/01/26/trenberth-at-ams-defends-himself-against-deniers/ [Accessed
March 13, 2011].

Page 211 "As Willis Eschenbach noted in a scathing essay at Watts Up
With That?"—Eschenbach, W., "Unequivocal Equivocation – An
Open Letter to Dr. Trenberth", *Watts Up With That,* January 15,
2011. Available at: http://wattsupwiththat.com/2011/01/15/unequivocal-
equivocation/ [Accessed March 13, 2011].

Page 211 "the post he particularly objected to was entitled: 'Why do I
call them Eco Nazis? Because they are Eco Nazis.'"—Delingpole, J.
(2011), 'Why do I call them Eco Nazis? Because they are Eco Nazis',
Telegraph Blogs, February 16. Available at: http://blogs.telegraph.co.uk/
news/jamesdelingpole/100076404/why-do-i-call-them-eco-nazis-because-they-
are-eco-nazis/ [Accessed March 13, 2011].

Page 211 "research by Mark Musser in *American Thinker*"—Musser, M.,
"The Nazi Origins of Apocalyptic Global Warming Theory", *American*

Thinker, February 15, 2011. Available at: http://www.americanthinker. com/2011/02/the_nazi_origins_of_apocalypti.html [Accessed March 13, 2011].

Page 212 "'Many of our most enthusiastic members were Nazis'"— personal communication with Benny Peiser.

Page 212 "a BBC Horizon documentary of January 2011"—"Science Under Attack", *BBC Horizon.* Available at: http://www.bbc.co.uk/iplayer/ episode/b00y4yql/Horizon_20102011_Science_Under_Attack/ [Accessed March 13, 2011].

Page 212–213 "an extract from a joint letter which had been published in *Science* magazine"—"Climate Change and the Integrity of Science", *Science,* May 7, 2010, 328(5979). Available at: http://www.sciencemag.org/ content/328/5979/689.full [Accessed March 13, 2011].

Chapter 11: The Perfect Storm

Page 216 "The way to crush the bourgeoisie is to grind them between the millstones of taxation and inflation." – Vladimir Lenin

Page 222 "Chris Horner in his book *Power Grab*" – Horner, C. (2010), *Power Grab: How Obama's Green Policies Will Steal Your Freedom and Bankrupt America* (New York: Regnery).

Page 222 "'We have two very powerful allies on our side', says the great Climate Realist Christopher Booker"—Personal communication.

Page 224 "With good reason, the U.S. meteorologist Roy Spencer describes our current Global Warming paranoia"—Spencer, R. (2010). *The Great Global Warming Blunder.* (Encounter Books). p. xxvii

Page 227 "I suspect the public doesn't realise how radical this legislation is"—*See* "Doomed By Democracy?", *BBC Radio 4,* May 30, 2010. Available at: http://www.bbc.co.uk/programmes/b00sfwtc [Accessed January 28, 2011].

Page 227–228 "In his excellent book *Climatism!*"—Goreham, S. (2010), *Climatism! Science, Common Sense & the 21st Century's Hottest Topic,* (RealStory Books).

Page 228 "According to research by Dr Gabriel Calzada Alvarez"— Alvarez, G.C. (2009), 'Study of the effects on employment of public aid to renewable energy sources', *Universidad Rey Juan Carlos. Available* at:

http://www.juandemariana.org/pdf/090327-employment-public-aid-renewable. pdf [Accessed January 28, 2011].

Page 228 "Or: Surrey school district in British Columbia'—*See* 'Going green strains cash-strapped B.C. schools', *CTV News*, April 14, 2010. Available at: http://www.ctvbc.ctv.ca/servlet/an/local/CTVNews/20100414/ bc_carbon_offsets_100414 [Accessed January 28, 2011].

Page 229 "the thousands of farmers in Australia whose land was rendered all but worthless by a government-imposed ban on tree clearance"— Truman, S. (2009), 'Carbongate' The Great Carbon Heist', *Crikey*, December 12. Available at: http://blogs.crikey.com.au/rooted/2009/12/12/ carbongate-the-great-carbon-heist/ [Accessed January 28, 2011].

Page 229 "Denmark…has the world's highest density of wind towers"— Goreham, S. (2010), *Climatism! Science, Common Sense & the 21st Century's Hottest Topic*, (RealStory Books), p. 323.

ABOUT JAMES DELINGPOLE

James Delingpole is a British writer, journalist, and blogger who helped expose the Climategate scandal. He is the author of numerous books including *Welcome to Obamaland: I've Seen Your Future and It Doesn't Work* (Regnery) and *365 Ways to Drive a Liberal Crazy* (Regnery). In 2005, he received the Charles Douglas-Home Memorial Trust Award and in 2010 he won the Bastiat Prize for Online Journalism.

James lives in London with his wife and children. His hobbies include: gardening, riding, surfing, wild swimming, Al-Gore-baiting and walking in hill country unspoilt by hideous wind turbines. His website is www.jamesdelingpole.com

ACKNOWLEDGMENTS

This book would simply not have been possible without the help, advice, encouragement, eagle eyes, taste, expertise, generosity, wisdom, kindness, patience, insight, passion, learning and judgement of the many friends cited below. I call them friends because that is what they have all become. Meeting them, working with them, learning from them and generally hanging out with them: this has been the greatest pleasure and privilege of writing this book. If you're not mentioned below and feel you ought to have been, consider yourself added—and I beg your forgiveness.

Special, special, uber thanks go to my team of expert advisers/encouragers/phone confidantes/fact-checkers/ego boosters. They are: Christopher Booker, Bob Carter, AN Ditchfield, Andrew Montford, Julian Morris, Richard North, Ian Plimer, Matt Ridley.

Thanks to my editorial team: Kendra Okonski, Stuart Bramwell, Teri Moore, Michael Nolan, Diana LeCore and Jonathan Harley.

Thanks to all the wonderful scientists/bloggers/polemicists/politicians/cartoonists/illustrators/economists/think-tankers/fellow travellers I have befriended on the way—and to the friends who were already friends but whom I now love still more. They include, in no particular order: Josh, Fenbeagle, Christopher Monckton, Marc Morano, Benny Peiser, Donna Laframboise, Andrew Bolt, Jo Nova, Douglas Murray, Steve McIntyre, Ross McKitrick, Nigel Lawson, Anthony Watts, Willis Eschenbach (and the WUWT gang), Chris Horner, Roddy Campbell, Josie Jackson, Pat Michaels,

Victoria Michaels, Robert Michaels, Roger Helmer MEP, Godfrey Bloom MEP, Anthony Howard, Myron Ebell (and all at CEI), Steve Goreham, Avril Terri Jackson, Fred Goldberg, Fred Singer, Hans Labohm, Cory Bernardi, Ian Wishart, Indur Goklany, John Fund, the Fox & Friends team, John Stossel, Kim Strassel, David S. Taylor, Douglas Murray, Henrik Svensmark, David Archibald, Brendan O'Neill, Max Borders, Bridgett Wagner, Brittany Balmer (and all at the Heritage Foundation), Melanie Philips, Joe Bast, James Taylor, Nikki Comerford (and all at Heartland), Joe D'Aleo, Eric Worrall, Malcolm Delingpole, Richard Delingpole, Charlie Delingpole, Tiffany Daneff, Stephen Daneff, Mark Musser, Philip Foster, Alain de Botton, Alan Oxley, John O'Sullivan, Phelim McAleer, Ann McElhinney, Steven Milloy, C3 Headlines, Donna Edmunds, Redmond Weissenberger, Ken Shock, Fay Kelly-Tuncay, Hillsdale College, Cami, Casey, Rob, Mo, Betty and the rest of the Facebook gang, Martin Helme, Fraser Nelson, Mary Wakefield, Freddy Gray, Liz Anderson, Harry Crocker, Philip Hensher, John Barnes (Washington Policy Center), John Pollock, Paul Chesser (American Tradition Institute), Barbara "Babe In The Bunker" Simpson, Arlene Bynon, Rush Limbaugh, Glenn Beck, Michael Savage, G. Gordon Liddy, Dennis Miller, Haunting The Library blog, Biased BBC blog, Susan Hill, Paul Feine, Michael Kelly, Lubos Motl, Rajan Alexander, Tim Worstall, Ecotretas, P Gosselin, Aaron Levisay, Terence Corcoran, Fill In Your Name Here...

Thanks to the Telegraph blogs team: Milo Yiannopoulos, Marcus Warren, Toby Young, Ed West, Dan Hannan, Will Heaven, Lucy Jones, Daniel Knowles, Toby Harnden, Katharine Birbalsingh, Nile Gardiner, Ben Brogan, Ed Roussel and above all, Damian Thompson, without whom there would have been no blog, and consequently no *Watermelons*.

And finally, thanks to the blog commentators listed below, for all their support and tips.

1 acepilot101	34 c777
2 adextra	35 caridnor
3 adrianpeirson	36 cat_in_the_hat
4 agricola	37 catweazle
5 alb_einstein	38 cd
6 alfredo	39 cerberus
7 alhamilton	40 chairmanofselectors
8 alibarbs	41 cherokeekid
9 alistairharrison	42 cheshirered
10 Amanda	43 chillwind
11 amerloque	44 ClemenceDR
12 anzon	45 Clothilde S
13 Apdavidson	46 cloudman
14 archie	47 coldfinger
15 aurelian	48 colliemore
16 avataruk	49 colliemum
17 Barry Laughton	50 colrouge
18 benfrommo	51 coltek
19 bersher	52 CommonSenseMajority
20 bickers	53 corton
21 Bill Sticker	54 creativities
22 Blackswan	55 Crownarmourer
23 bluebell	56 Daed Parrot
24 bob1972	57 danoconnor
25 bob3 (pike)	58 davebr
26 Bomber the Cat	59 Davedinburgh
27 Bravo	60 delboy36
28 brooksyfxx	61 dickgreendoxon
29 Brown Bess	62 dirlada
30 brownsoup	63 docholliday
31 bswallocks	64 doesntplaywellwithothers
32 bufo75	65 dogboy
33 burgess	66 doomdelayed

67 doppelganger
68 dozzer
69 drdave
70 dropstone
71 drover
72 emmiem
73 englishgrit
74 ephraingadsby
75 Eric_The_Half_A_Bee
76 ericworral
77 esotericist
78 EU brainwashing
79 extricate
80 fangface
81 farmerbrown
82 fedupeffedoff
83 Fenbeagle
84 FergalR
85 ferret
86 Finbar Saunders
87 flyinthesky
88 Fortnum
89 fox1fox2
90 foxy
91 FrankMcB
92 frankv
93 Franky
94 frenchliz
95 g11gam3sh
96 geoffyank
97 ghost_dance
98 Gilliebc
99 golfcharlie

100 grandsmalls
101 Greensand
102 Gypsey
103 Hagar
104 hamish Redux
105 heathcliffe
106 henrietta
107 herkinderkin
108 hessepee
109 hondaboy2001
110 hospitaller
111 hostile logic
112 incensed
113 IRISHBOY
114 irridium
115 itchybeard
116 Itzman
117 jackfrost
118 Jacob_UK
119 jayson
120 jimimac
121 johannesritter
122 johnmcevoy
123 Johnny
124 JohnnyRottenborough
125 jondenver
126 julier
127 Juniper_Sprinkles
128 knight
129 LadyMoneypenny
130 laurean
131 lilenglander
132 Lizzyrose

WATERMELONS: THE GREEN MOVEMENT'S TRUE COLORS

133 locustsandwildhoney
134 loganberry1
135 logz
136 lonewolf
137 love_my_dobb
138 Mack (Mack's Ghost)
139 magicturtle
140 manonthemoor
141 Mary M
142 marys
143 maturecheese
144 mayday
145 megawati
146 meltemian
147 memoryvault
148 MichaelSuba
149 MJHopeC
150 Morningstar
151 motorwaydrifter
152 mountaingorilla
153 msher1
154 naomimuse
155 napiersabre
156 neibes
157 nellie
158 Nige Cook
159 Nigel Rogers
160 noidea
161 Old Goat
162 oldmanmow
163 oppugner
164 oriphus
165 orkneylad

166 owda180
167 ozboy
168 paulo anonymous
169 peartree
170 peteh
171 Peter Crawford
172 peterhirsch
173 peterooo
174 phantomsby
175 philantony
176 philip
177 phinniethewoo
178 phyics graduate
179 Piers Corbyn
180 plantsman
181 pointer
182 pointman
183 poptech
184 pragmatist
185 publicspirit
186 Q46
187 ramonelove
188 rapscallion
189 rarebreed
190 rastech
191 ravenscar
192 rbw152
193 realityreturns
194 renewabilly
195 Richard Courtney
196 Richard North
197 RichardBruce
198 RichardDrake

199 rifleman
200 Robbydot
201 Robert Eve
202 rogercuul
203 roman_column
204 roman68
205 ruralidiot
206 same_old_dog
207 scambuster
208 scientificanomoly
209 Scott of East Anglia
210 scousebilly
211 Scud1
212 sevendobbs
213 shakassoc
214 sherlockcaptain
215 sheumais,
216 shub
217 sickofsocialism
218 Simxn.
219 Skeptik
220 skicarver
221 Snowmaneasy
222 Sparks
223 spartacusisfree
    staceey (formerly
224 coldplay)
225 Stan J
226 Stephen Jenner
227 Steve Tierney
228 stevedobbs
229 stoater

230 suffolkboy
231 sumdood
232 tanker21
233 Tayles
234 termite
235 TerribleTurk
236 texaslady1
237 thammond65
238 theguvnor
239 therealmoptop
240 theunbrainwashed
241 tooboot
242 travis
243 tyndale
244 unimpressedone
245 upik
246 vitriolla
247 wallhousewart
248 Walter James O'Brien
249 wearedoomed
250 webferret
251 webmaster
252 whereisthehope
253 Wilbur
254 wi118ace
255 willh
256 wolfiesmiff
257 woolfie
258 xrayco2
259 yaosxx
260 zeusgoose

INDEX

Polar bear numbers, 1965–2009

This graph shows estimates of the total number of polar bears, from the mid-1960s to 2009. While the estimates are imprecise, the trend is clear: polar bear numbers increased substantially until the 1990s and have remained relatively stable. (Also, it is worth noting that the main cause of premature deaths of adult polar bears is hunting.)

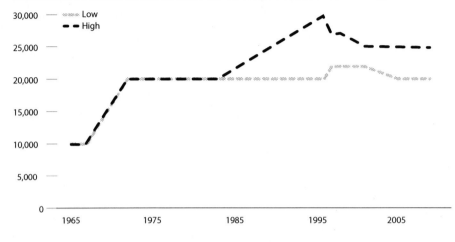

The data for 1965 to 2006 are from http://www.animalinfo.org/species/carnivor/ursumari.htm, which summarises various studies (we have assumed a figure of 25,000 for the "high" estimate in 2001 because no estimate is given in the study; the "low" figure for the study conducted in that year is 22,000 and the "high" figure for the study conducted in 2005 is 25,000). The data for 2009 come from the IUCN's most recent report, available here: http://data.iucn.org/dbtw-wpd/edocs/SSC-OP-043.pdf

Ehrlich was wrong

In his fictional account of the future, "Eco-Catastrophe" (Ramparts, September 1969), Paul Ehrlich offered the following prognosis for humanity: "Hundreds of millions of people will soon perish in smog disasters in New York and Los Angeles…the oceans will die of DDT poisoning by 1979…the U.S. life expectancy will drop to 42 years by 1980 due to cancer epidemics." The graph shows U.S. life expectancy at birth from 1900 to 2007.

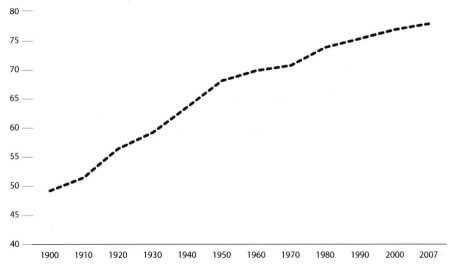

Source: National Vital Statistics Reports (2010), Vol.58, No.21, June 28. Available at: http://www.cdc.gov/nchs/data/nvsr/nvsr58/nvsr58_21.pdf

Resurgent malaria: a consequence of environmentalism?

"Over the last five decades, the careful, limited use of DDT house spraying has saved tens of millions of lives from malaria, which kills one in twenty children in Africa. Yet DDT is under pressure to be eliminated as never before. Where environmentalists have pushed successfully to eliminate DDT in many countries, the relationship between falling DDT use and increasing malaria cases is worryingly clear," says Amir Attaran.

Attaran and co-authors explain this figure: "Data from the Pan-American Health Organization show a strong inverse correlation between malaria cases and rates of spraying houses (1959–1992) in South America, even after DDT resistance became widespread in the 1960s. Here, 'cumulative cases' represent the population-adjusted, 'running' total of cases that exceed or fall short of the average annual number of cases from 1959 to 1979 (years in which World Health Organization strategy emphasized house spraying). Cumulative cases increase considerably in later years, coincident with a sharp decrease in rates of spraying houses."

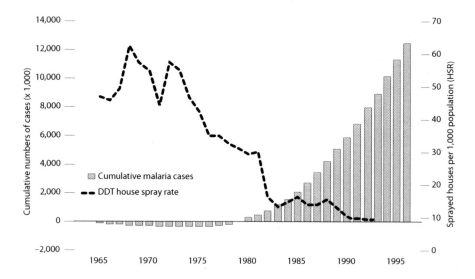

Original graph title: House Spray Rates, 1965–92, and Cumulative Malaria Cases, pre- vs. post-1979, (Brazil, Colombia, Ecuador, Peru, Venezuela)
Sources: Amir Attaran (2001), "International Donor Support for Phasing out POPs", Harvard CID Working Paper No. 67, May. Available at:
http://www.hks.harvard.edu/var/ezp_site/storage/fckeditor/file/pdfs/centers-programs/centers/cid/publications/faculty/wp/067.pdf
Amir Attaran, Donald R. Roberts, Chris F. Curtis & Wenceslaus L. Kilama (2000). "Balancing risks on the backs of the poor," **Nature Medicine**
Volume 6, Number 7, pp 729–731. Available at: http://www.nature.com/nm/journal/v6/n7/fig_tab/nm0700_729_F1.html

Hurricanes and sea surface temperature: no relationship

Graph shows the average number of hurricanes making landfall in the US by decade from 1880 to 2006, and the average temperature of the sea in the Northern tropics (between the equator and 30 degrees North), which is where hurricanes form. As can be seen, there is no relationship between average sea surface temperature and average number of hurricanes.

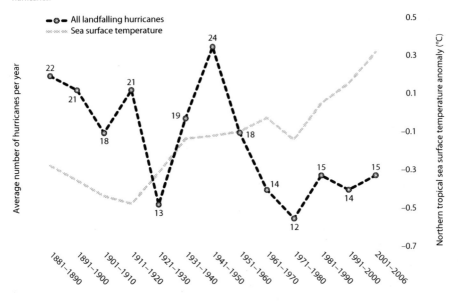

Source: Eric S. Blake, Edward N. Rappaport and Christopher W. Landsea (2007). The Deadliest, Costliest and Most Intense United States Tropical Cyclones from 1851 to 2006 (and Other Frequently Requested Hurricane Facts). Updated 15 April 2007 for return period information, NOAA: NOAA Technical Memorandum NWS TPC-5 Available at: http://www.nhc.noaa.gov/pdf/NWS-TPC-5.pdf
Sea surface temperature from ftp://eclipse.ncdc.noaa.gov/pub/ersstv3b/pdo/aravg.ann.ocean.00N.30N.asc
The temperature data is described here; http://www.ncdc.noaa.gov/ersst/#grid

It was warmer in the time of the Pharaohs

The graph, taken from page 118 of Professor H. H. Lamb's classic study, *Climate, History and the Modern World* (1982), shows the average height of the upper tree line on the mountains in temperate latitudes. As Professor Lamb explains, "The limit is essentially controlled by the prevailing summer temperature." On the right side of the graph, Prof. Lamb has indicated the average July temperature at the same altitudes today. We can infer that summer temperatures in temperate latitudes have fallen by about 2 degrees Celsius in the past 5,000 years.

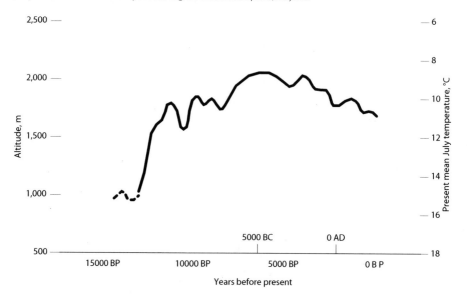

Source: Lamb, H.H. (1982), *Climate, History and the Modern World*. p.118